Er

The following errata list is for Chapter [...]
Age of New Literacies, "Moving Audien[...]
Difference" by Sharon McKenzie Stevens, pp. 229–243.

The page number is incorrect in note 1. The footnote refers to Lunsford and Ede's questions on pages 43–44 of this collection.

A number of references were inadvertently cut from the works cited list:

Anzaldúa, Gloria. *Borderlands/La Frontera: The New Mestiza.* 2nd ed. San Francisco: Aunt Lute, 1999.

Bakhtin, Mikhail M., "The Problem of Speech Genres." *Speech Genres and Other Late Essays.* Trans. Vern W. McGee. Ed. Caryl Emerson and Michael Holquist. Austin: U of Texas P, 1986. 60–102.

Behar, Ruth. *Translated Woman: Crossing the Border with Esperanza's Story.* 10th anniversary ed. Boston: Beacon, 2003.

Biesecker, Barbara A. "Rethinking the Rhetorical Situation from within the Thematic of *Différance.*" *Philosophy and Rhetoric* 22 (1989): 110–30.

Bitzer, Lloyd F. "The Rhetorical Situation." *Philosophy and Rhetoric* 1 (1968): 1–14.

Ede, Lisa, and Andrea Lunsford. "Audience Addressed/Audience Invoked: The Role of Audience in Composition Theory and Pedagogy." *College Composition and Communication* 35 (1984): 155–71.

Fenton, Sabine, and Paul Moon. "The Translation of the Treaty of Waitangi: A Case of Disempowerment." *Translation and Power.* Ed. Maria Tymoczko and Edwin Gentzler. Amherst: U of Massachusetts P, 2002. 25–44.

The Last of the Mohicans. Dir. Michael Mann. Perf. Daniel Day-Lewis. 20th Century Fox, 1992.

LeCourt, Donna. "WAC as Critical Pedagogy: The Third Stage?" *JAC* 16 (1996): 389–405.

Rabassa, Gregory. *If This Be Treason: Translation and Its Dyscontents: A Memoir.* New York: New Directions, 2005.

Sakai, Naoki. "Translation." *Theory, Culture and Society* 23.2–3 (2006): 71–78.

Sanchez, Raul. Review of *Bootstraps: From an American Academic of Color*, Victor Villanueva Jr. *JAC* 15.1 (1995): 163–68.

Simon, Sherry. "The Language of Cultural Difference: Figures of Alterity in Canadian Translation." *Rethinking Translation: Discourse, Subjectivity, Ideology.* Ed. Lawrence Venuti. London: Routledge, 1992. 159–76.

Venn, Couze. "Translation: Politics and Ethics." *Theory, Culture and Society* 23.2–3 (2006): 82–84.

Venuti, Lawrence. "Translation, Community, Utopia." *The Translation Studies Reader.* 2nd ed. Ed. Lawrence Venuti. London: Routledge, 2004. 482–502.

Villanueva, Victor. "The Politics of Literacy Across the Curriculum." *WAC for the New Millennium: Strategies for Continuing Writing-Across-the-Curriculum Programs.* Ed. Susan H. McLeod et al. Urbana, IL: NCTE, 2001. 165–78.

ENGAGING AUDIENCE

Engaging Audience
Writing in an Age of New Literacies

M. Elizabeth Weiser
The Ohio State University

Brian M. Fehler
Tarleton State University

Angela M. González
Whitworth University

National Council of Teachers of English
1111 W. Kenyon Road, Urbana, Illinois 61801-1096

Staff Editor: Carol Roehm
Interior Design: Jenny Jensen Greenleaf
Cover Design: Pat Mayer

NCTE Stock Number: 02299

It is the policy of NCTE in its journals and other publications to provide a
forum for the open discussion of ideas concerning the content and the teaching of English and the language arts. Publicity accorded to any particular
point of view does not imply endorsement by the Executive Committee, the
Board of Directors, or the membership at large, except in announcements
of policy, where such endorsement is clearly specified.

Every effort has been made to provide current URLs and email addresses,
but because of the rapidly changing nature of the Web, some sites and
addresses may no longer be accessible.

Library of Congress Cataloging-in-Publication Data

Weiser, M. Elizabeth.
    Engaging audience : writing in an age of new literacies / M. Elizabeth
Weiser, Brian M. Fehler, Angela M. González.
       p. cm.
    Includes bibliographical references and index.
    ISBN 978-0-8141-0229-9 ((pbk.))
    1. Literacy. 2. Technological literacy. 3. Written communication.
4. Language and education. I. Title.
    LC149.W35 2010
    808'.0420711—dc22

                              2009031742

We would like to dedicate this book to our former professors in the Texas Christian University Rhetoric and Composition Program, who guided each of us into our professional careers. Ann George, Rich Enos, Carrie Leverenz, Brad Lucas, Charlotte Hogg, and Ronald Pitcock—our mentors, colleagues, and friends; surely you embody all that we could have wished for in a graduate faculty.

CONTENTS

I The Audience Stream: Following the Current of Audience Theory

Twenty-Five Years of Composition Work with Andrea A. Lunsford and Lisa Ede

II Theory Streams: Ebbs and Flows of Audience through Composition and Communication

Placing Ede and Lunsford's Work into Contemporary Conversation

III Praxis Streams: Audience Wending through Classrooms and Communities

Scholars Respond to Audiences Addressed and Invoked, Diverse, and Interactive

CONTENTS

PREFACE

Engaging Audience: Writing in an Age of New Literacies brings together theorists and practitioners—compositionists from departments of English, communications, public relations, and writing—to examine the rhetorical concept of audience from multiple perspectives in multiple settings. We begin with Lisa Ede and Andrea Lunsford's germinal essay, "Audience Addressed/ Audience Invoked: The Role of Audience in Composition Theory and Pedagogy" (affectionately shorted to AA/AI by our authors), and then follow up with their own later critique, "Representing Audience: Successful Discourse and Disciplinary Critique," followed by their reenvisioned exploration of audience in the twenty-first century, "Among the Audience: On Audience in an Age of New Literacies," written especially for this collection. From there our contributors approach audience from divergent perspectives—history, composition pedagogy, new media studies, service learning and professional writing, and rhetorical and literary theory—while uniting in their engagement with Ede and Lunsford's work. Collectively, the book adds a third category to the addressed/invoked binary, an "audience updated," that takes various professional and cultural forms but is most evidently "audience interacting." The authors argue not only that audience as a concept in the twenty-first century needs to be readdressed, but also that the varieties of writing opportunities available to today's students make this discussion newly exciting for writing scholars and teachers. Their combined perspectives provide a helpful guide to incorporating audience awareness much more richly into the contemporary classroom.

Because it can seem so deceptively obvious and yet carry so many meanings, audience is brought up in every composition and communications course in the nation and then, usually, left behind. While Walter Ong's "The Writer's Audience Is Always a Fiction" first addressed the shift in audience constructs from oral to written communication in 1975, most of the work on audience took place in the decade between 1982 and 1992. After Russell Long and then Douglas Park raised the question of the meanings of "audience" (Park), CCC published a special issue on the complexity of identifying audience which included not only AA/AI but also another article by Ede, "Audience: An Introduction to Research." By 1990, Gesa Kirsch and Duane Roen had compiled the variety of theoretical approaches to audience identification into their collection *A Sense of Audience in Written Communication*, and then in 1992 James Porter's *Audience and Rhetoric* suggested that writers think of audience not as the end recipient of the composing process but as a "discourse community" actively engaged in the writer's process of identifying with them to build a common text. This more Burkean approach allowed concepts of audience to align with a social constructivist approach to composition.

Since 1992, however, few articles and books, with the notable exception of Rosa Eberly's *Citizen Critics* (2000), have explored audience in any depth. As David Beard notes in his chapter for our collection, audience continued to be debated in interpersonal and mass communications, but almost none of that research entered the purview of writing instruction. And as Traci Zimmerman writes in her chapter, literary theorists have debated the intersections of audiences and texts for some time, but again, those insights have not consistently made their way into conversations about textual production. Composition textbooks still encourage writers to "consider their audience" and make generalizations about audience expectations, just as Aristotle recommended to his students 2,500 years ago.

This collection, then, brings together for the first time the breadth of field-knowledge focusing on audience. It also unites theoretical inquiries about audience with practical discussion about using those theories to teach audience to new writers. Finally, in an era when composing pedagogy has expanded beyond the composition class into advanced writing, professional writing, writing for publication, and other courses, and when composing processes have equally expanded into not only word processing but the interactive conversations of online writing, this collection marks the first time that a discussion of why and how audience is addressed and invoked takes place within these new, twenty-first-century contexts. We hope the collection enriches and enlivens discussions of audience in many fields, including composition and rhetoric, communications, and media studies. It is for you, the teacher and student of audience theory, that this book exists.

No one could be more central to the past twenty-five years of audience theory in composition than Ede, in the Center for Writing and Learning at Oregon State University, and Lunsford, in the Program in Writing and Rhetoric at Stanford University. As Lee Nickoson-Massey notes in her chapter in this collection, "the influence of AA/AI is present in nearly all work on composing on a sort of subterranean level—it has become so deeply ingrained that it is simply a part of an implicitly shared knowledge of how we conceive of audience" (305). Ede and Lunsford's follow-up pieces in 1996 and in 2009 (introduced in this volume) add the dynamics of audience diversity and new media interactions to the rhetorical communication triangle between author, text, and audience.

Following the Lunsford and Ede introductory texts are two chapters that place their work into theoretical dialogue with the two fields most often associated with composition studies, literary studies and communication. In "Authors, Audiences, and the Gaps Between," Traci Zimmerman frames her response to the work on audience by Michel Foucault and Roland Barthes and suggests that the audience is the place where writing is made to have meaning, not merely the point at which a message is delivered. In "Communicating with the Audience," David Beard argues that the rich empirical tradition of communication studies research gives composition scholars multiple ways to discuss audience response to a text and so enriches student conceptions of audience in their own reading and writing processes. The two chapters together signal the diversity of the composition/rhetoric field in which audience plays a role.

The remainder of the book shows these mingling and diverging streams of audience awareness instantiated in thought and practice throughout writing classrooms. The diversity of classes that focus on composing texts is notable. Not just in first-year composition, not just in English classes, not just with words on the page but infused across multiple disciplines at multiple levels for multiple genres, writing instruction is ongoing throughout the university and, increasingly, in the links between university and community, or home and school. Rather than try to separate this diverse array into subject-specific subheads, we have instead chosen a more organic arrangement. The attentive reader can follow roughly the path of interests from Lunsford and Ede's "Audience Addressed" to "Representing Audience" to "Among the Audience"—not with clear breaks in between, but more in the manner of a leaf following a current, swirling into side currents, turning in eddies, then flowing on. In this case, the chapters flow from questions of invoked audience toward issues of audience makeup on into discussions of audience interface.

Thus, there are two chapters examining the addressing of invoked audiences (or the invocation of addressed audiences). The first is "New Media's Personas and Scenarios" by David Dayton, who argues that procedures created by researchers in information architecture and user experience design are useful for the teaching of audience in the classroom, in particular the creation of a persona—an in-depth psychographic profile of the typical "user," or audience member—and the scenario, or detailed setting. Similarly, in "Tactician and Strategist," Robert (Bob) Batchelor advocates writing courses with a more decidedly public relations perspective, focusing on the audience-user of any text and thus turning students into future tacticians and long-term strategic counselors.

Next, in three essays that consider specific instances of "public" writing, Tom Pace describes a semester-long introductory composition course in which student writers collaborate in small groups to develop, write for, and produce their own academic journal. "I Can Take a Stance" draws from interviews with student writers and from a variety of academic journals to show how students gain audience awareness in writing across the curriculum when their audience is the real student-faculty readership of the "journals." In "When the Teacher Is the Audience," Marie C. Paretti considers the problems involved in classroom/community partnership, recognizing that students taking part in client projects must shift from performing knowledge to providing information—a shift that can be initially handled by assigning projects that do not rely on external audiences but on the classroom itself. Finally, Alexandria Peary argues in "The Self-Addressed Stamped Envelope" that an especially effective way of teaching college composition students about audience is to encourage undergraduate publication beyond the university. Grounding her project in activity theory, Peary outlines a first-year course in which students are required to write for publication in external journals.

The shift toward a concern for the diversity of audiences accelerates with the next three chapters. Phyllis Mentzel Ryder, in her chapter "The Stranger Question of Audience," urges academics, deeply involved as we are in our own often highly specialized discourse communities, to challenge our own notions of audience when teaching. Ryder identifies the rhetorical moves used by writers to sustain publics and shows how these strategies are specifically applied in a service-learning pedagogy with diverse institutions that highlights the very question of audience. In "Moving Audience, Translating Writers, and Negotiating Difference," Sharon McKenzie Stevens expands upon the multivariate nature of audience theory to argue that the idea of translation has applicability to theorizing audience within unequal but potentially dynamic relationships, especially in the context of cultural difference. Recognizing the power of translation to both increase and alienate audiences, Stevens believes, is particularly important because students, especially culturally marked students, are often urged to shift subjectivities in order to enter into relationships with their audiences. One such culturally marked group is conservative religious students, and Traci Freeman discusses the common problem of working with students who want to support arguments with examples and evidence from their own religious faith. In "Can I Get a Witness: Faith-Based Reasoning and the Academic Audience," she argues that in order for discussions of audience to be authentic, composition instructors need to do more than ask students to examine their biases; we as compositionists need to examine our own values as part of the larger institutional structure.

Two authors focus particularly on the consequences of the interactive nature of the twenty-first-century audience. Erin Karper expands the notion of audience beyond addressed and invoked to include the hybrid audience of Internet communication. "Theorizing Audience in Web-Based Self-Presentation" recognizes that inside and outside the classroom people grapple with issues of audience and appropriateness in Web writing situations both personal and professional. Dan Keller uses a longitudinal study to demonstrate in "Reading Audiences" that the multiple, often conflicting, audience roles caused by students' multigenre, multimedia reading experiences suggest new challenges in the classroom. Media convergence, blurring the lines between author and audience, provides new opportunities to revisit readers' agency and help students respond to their multiple roles.

Finally, Lee Nickoson-Massey's chapter "Writing Assessment as New Literacy" continues the attention on the interactive reading audience while also bringing the whole collection to closure. Nickoson-Massey draws on an ethnographic study of a first-year writing classroom to argue that writing assessment actually forms the basic language, or conduit, students use to read, produce, and respond to written texts. In the context of the class, peer response and, by extension, assessment are forwarded as dynamic and complex rhetorical acts that demonstrate experientially the role of audiences invoked, addressed, and interactive.

The writers in the collection, therefore, approach audience from different perspectives—ones dependent on their own backgrounds, interests, and teaching contingencies. Yet each difference is transcended by the enduring power of Ede and Lunsford's article from a quarter century ago to evoke agreement, disagreement, and expansion—in short, to invoke an audience in each new generation of compositionists that enters into dialogue with itself across boundaries to forge new understandings of this ancient topic. As Lunsford and Ede put it in their own look back at their work, "Does this mean that we wish to reject the term *audience*? No, it does not. . . . We continue to believe, then, that the concept of audience provides a helpful theoretical and practical grounding for efforts to understand how texts (and writers and readers) work in today's world" (Among the Audience 47). As we look over the diversity of ideas and practices in conversation with AA/AI and its tributaries, we cannot but agree.

Works Cited

Eberly, Rosa A. *Citizen Critics: Literary Public Spheres.* History of Communication. Urbana, IL: University of Illinois P, 2000.

Ede, Lisa. "Audience: An Introduction to Research." *CCC* 35.2 (1984): 140–54.

Kirsch, Gesa, and Duane H. Roen, eds. *A Sense of Audience in Written Communication.* Sage Focus Editions, Vol. 121. Newbury Park, CA: Sage, 1990.

Long, Russell C. "Writer-Audience Relationships: Analysis or Invention?" *CCC* 31.2 (1980): 221–226.

Ong, Walter J. "The Writer's Audience Is Always a Fiction." *PMLA* 90.1 (1975): 9–21.

Park, Douglas B. "The Meanings of 'Audience.'" *College English* 44.3 (1982): 247–257.

Porter, James E. *Audience and Rhetoric: An Archaeological Composition of the Discourse Community.* Prentice Hall Studies in Writing and Culture. Englewood Cliffs, NJ: Prentice Hall, 1992.

ACKNOWLEDGMENTS

We would like to thank the deans of our respective colleges at The Ohio State University, Tarleton State University, and Whitworth University for providing the time to complete this project, and particularly The Ohio State University at Newark for providing funding for a student research and editorial assistant. To that assistant, Jonathan Holmes, we owe a great debt of gratitude for all his help in bringing the collection to fruition, and we welcome this excellent undergraduate into the English profession.

Of course we owe profound thanks to each of our contributors: to Lisa and Andrea, whom we approached for a possible short preface and were rewarded instead with the generous collaboration of a new, groundbreaking essay and both its original antecedents; and to the thirteen chapter authors, who so cheerfully gave so many hours of their time to writing and revising—and revising and revising—the pages of this book. How can we say enough thanks? There would be no book without you.

Finally, in the spirit of this work, we thank you, our audience, for reading and, we hope, interacting with, modifying, and incorporating these words into your teaching and theorizing about that ancient rhetorical member of the twenty-first-century communication triangle.

THE AUDIENCE STREAM: FOLLOWING THE CURRENT OF AUDIENCE THEORY

Twenty-Five Years of Composition Work with Andrea A. Lunsford and Lisa Ede

Audience Addressed/Audience Invoked: The Role of Audience in Composition Theory and Pedagogy

LISA EDE AND ANDREA A. LUNSFORD

One important controversy currently engaging scholars and teachers of writing involves the role of audience in composition theory and pedagogy. How can we best define the audience of a written discourse? What does it mean to address an audience? To what degree should teachers stress audience in their assignments and discussions? What *is* the best way to help students recognize the significance of this critical element in any rhetorical situation?

Teachers of writing may find recent efforts to answer these questions more confusing than illuminating. Should they agree with Ruth Mitchell and Mary Taylor,[1] who so emphasize the significance of the audience that they argue for abandoning conventional composition courses and instituting a "cooperative effort by writing and subject instructors in adjunct courses. The cooperation and courses take two main forms. Either writing instructors can be attached to subject courses where writing is required, an organization which disperses the instructors throughout the departments participating; or the composition courses can teach students how to write the papers assigned in other concurrent courses, thus centralizing instruction but diversifying topics." Or should teachers side with Russell Long, who asserts that those advocating greater attention to audience overemphasize the role of "observable physical or occupational characteristics" while ignoring the fact that most writers actually create their audiences.

Reprinted from *College Composition and Communication* 35 (1984): 155–171. Reprinted with permission.

Long argues against the usefulness of such methods as developing hypothetical rhetorical situations as writing assignments, urging instead a more traditional emphasis on "the analysis of texts in the classroom with a very detailed examination given to the signals provided by the writer for his audience."[2]

To many teachers, the choice seems limited to a single option—to be for or against an emphasis on audience in composition courses. In the following essay, we wish to expand our understanding of the role audience plays in composition theory and pedagogy by demonstrating that the arguments advocated by each side of the current debate oversimplify the act of making meaning through written discourse. Each side, we will argue, has failed adequately to recognize (1) the fluid, dynamic character of rhetorical situations; and (2) the integrated, interdependent nature of reading and writing. After discussing the strengths and weaknesses of the two central perspectives on audience in composition—which we group under the rubrics of *audience addressed* and *audience invoked*[3]—we will propose an alternative formulation, one which we believe more accurately reflects the richness of "audience" as a concept.*

Audience Addressed

Those who envision audience as addressed emphasize the concrete reality of the writer's audience; they also share the assumption that knowledge of this audience's attitudes, beliefs, and expectations is not only possible (via observation and analysis) but essential. Questions concerning the degree to which this audience is "real" or imagined, and the ways it differs from the speaker's audience,

---

*A number of terms might be used to characterize the two approaches to audience which dominate current theory and practice. Such pairs as identified/ envisaged, "real"/fictional, or analyzed/created all point to the same general distinction as do our terms. We chose "addressed/ invoked" because these terms most precisely represent our intended meaning. Our discussion will, we hope, clarify their significance; for the present, the following definitions must serve. The "addressed" audience refers to those actual or real-life people who read a discourse, while the "invoked" audience refers to the audience called up or imagined by the writer.

are generally either ignored or subordinated to a sense of the audience's powerfulness. In their discussion of "A Heuristic Model for Creating a Writer's Audience," for example, Fred Pfister and Joanne Petrik attempt to recognize the ontological complexity of the writer-audience relationship by noting that "students, like all writers, must fictionalize their audience."[4] Even so, by encouraging students to "construct in their imagination an audience that is as nearly a replica as is possible of *those many readers who actually exist in the world of reality*," Pfister and Petrik implicitly privilege the concept of audience as addressed.[5]

Many of those who envision audience as addressed have been influenced by the strong tradition of audience analysis in speech communication and by current research in cognitive psychology on the composing process.[6] They often see themselves as reacting against the current-traditional paradigm of composition, with its a-rhetorical, product-oriented emphasis.[7] And they also frequently encourage what is called "real-world" writing.[8]

Our purpose here is not to draw up a list of those who share this view of audience but to suggest the general outline of what most readers will recognize as a central tendency in the teaching of writing today. We would, however, like to focus on one particularly ambitious attempt to formulate a theory and pedagogy for composition based on the concept of audience as addressed: Ruth Mitchell and Mary Taylor's "The Integrating Perspective: An Audience-Response Model for Writing." We choose Mitchell and Taylor's work because of its theoretical richness and practical specificity. Despite these strengths, we wish to note several potentially significant limitations in their approach, limitations which can be observed to varying degrees in much of the current work of those who envision audience as addressed.

In their article, Mitchell and Taylor analyze what they consider to be the two major existing composition models: one focusing on the writer and the other on the written product. Their evaluation of these two models seems essentially accurate. The "writer" model is limited because it defines writing as either self-expression or "fidelity to fact" (255)—epistemologically naïve assumptions which result in troubling pedagogical inconsistencies. And the "written product" model, which is characterized by an emphasis on "certain intrinsic features [such as a] lack of comma splices and fragments" (258), is challenged by the continued inability of teachers of writing (not to mention those in other professions) to agree upon the precise intrinsic features which characterize "good" writing.

Most interesting, however, is what Mitchell and Taylor *omit* in their criticism of these models. Neither the writer model nor the written product model pays serious attention to invention, the term used to describe those "methods designed to aid in retrieving information, forming concepts, analyzing complex events, and solving certain kinds of problems."[9] Mitchell and Taylor's lapse in not noting this omission is understandable, however, for the same can be said of their own model. When these authors discuss the writing process, they stress that "our first priority for writing instruction at every level ought to be certain major tactics for structuring material because these structures are the most important in guiding the reader's comprehension and memory" (271). They do not concern themselves with where "the material" comes from—its sophistication, complexity, accuracy, or rigor.

Mitchell and Taylor also fail to note another omission, one which might be best described in reference to their own model (Figure 1.1).

This model has four components. Mitchell and Taylor use two of these, "writer" and "written product," as labels for the models they condemn. The third and fourth components, "audience" and "response," provide the title for their own "audience-response model for writing" (249).

Mitchell and Taylor stress that the components in their model interact. Yet despite their emphasis on interaction, it never seems to occur to them to note that the two other models may fail in large part because they overemphasize and isolate one of the four elements—wrenching it too greatly from its context and thus inevitably distorting the composing process. Mitchell and Taylor do not consider this possibility, we suggest, because their own model has the same weakness.

Mitchell and Taylor argue that a major limitation of the "writer" model is its emphasis on the self, the person writing, as the only potential judge of effective discourse. Ironically, however, their own emphasis on audience leads to a similar distortion.

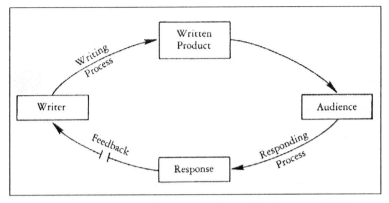

FIGURE 1.1. *Mitchell and Taylor's "general model of writing" (250).*

In their model, the audience has the sole power of evaluating writing, the success of which "will be judged by the audience's reaction: 'good' translates into 'effective,' 'bad' into 'ineffective.'" Mitchell and Taylor go on to note that "the audience not only judges writing; it also motivates it" (250),[10] thus suggesting that the writer has less control than the audience over both evaluation and motivation.

Despite the fact that Mitchell and Taylor describe writing as "an interaction, a dynamic relationship" (250), their model puts far more emphasis on the role of the audience than on that of the writer. One way to pinpoint the source of imbalance in Mitchell and Taylor's formulation is to note that they are right in emphasizing the creative role of readers who, they observe, "actively contribute to the meaning of what they read and will respond according to a complex set of expectations, preconceptions, and provocations" (251), but wrong in failing to recognize the equally essential role writers play throughout the composing process not only as creators but also as *readers* of their own writing.

As Susan Wall observes in "In the Writer's Eye: Learning to Teach the Rereading/Revising Process," when writers read their own writing, as they do continuously while they compose, "there are really not one but two contexts for rereading: there is the writer-as-reader's sense of what the established text is actually saying, as of this reading; and there is the reader-as-writer's judgment of what the text might say or should say...."[11] What is missing from Mitchell and Taylor's model, and from much work done from the perspective of audience as addressed, is a recognition of the crucial importance of this internal dialogue, through which writers analyze inventional problems and conceptualize patterns of discourse. Also missing is an adequate awareness that, no matter how much feedback writers may receive after they have written something (or in breaks while they write), as they compose writers must rely in large part upon their own vision of the reader, which they create, as readers do their vision of writers, according to their own experiences and expectations.

Another major problem with Mitchell and Taylor's analysis is their apparent lack of concern for the ethics of language use. At one point, the authors ask the following important question: "Have we painted ourselves into a corner, so that the audience-response model must defend sociologese and its related styles?" (265). Note first the ambiguity of their answer, which seems to us to say no and yes at the same time, and the way they try to deflect its impact:

> No. We defend only the right of audiences to set their own standards and we repudiate the ambitions of English departments to monopolize that standard-setting. If bureaucrats and scientists are happy with the way they write, then no one should interfere.
> But evidence is accumulating that they are not happy. (265)

Here Mitchell and Taylor surely underestimate the relationship between style and substance. As those concerned with Doublespeak can attest, for example, the problem with sociologese is not simply its (to our ears) awkward, convoluted, highly nominalized style, but the way writers have in certain instances used this style to make statements otherwise unacceptable to laypersons, to "gloss over" potentially controversial facts about programs and their consequences, and thus violate the ethics of language use. Hence, although we support Mitchell and Taylor when they insist that we must better understand and respect the linguistic traditions of other disciplines and professions, we object to their assumption that style is somehow value-free.

As we noted earlier, an analysis of Mitchell and Taylor's discussion clarifies weaknesses inherent in much of the theoretical and pedagogical research based on the concept of audience as addressed. One major weakness of this research lies in its narrow focus on helping students learn how to "continually modify their work with reference to their audience" (251). Such a focus, which in its extreme form becomes pandering to the crowd, tends to undervalue the responsibility a writer has to a subject and to what Wayne Booth in *Modern Dogma and the Rhetoric of Assent* calls "the art of discovering good reasons."[12] The resulting imbalance has clear ethical consequences, for rhetoric has traditionally been concerned not only with the effectiveness of a discourse, but with truthfulness as well. Much of our difficulty with the language of advertising, for example, arises out of the ad writer's powerful concept of audience as addressed divorced from a corollary ethical concept. The toothpaste ad that promises improved personality, for instance, knows too well how to address the audience. But such ads ignore ethical questions completely.

Another weakness in research done by those who envision audience as addressed suggests an oversimplified view of language. As Paul Kameen observes in "Rewording the Rhetoric of Composition," "discourse is not grounded in forms or experience or audience; it engages all of these elements simultaneously."[13] Ann Berthoff has persistently criticized our obsession with one or another of the elements of discourse, insisting that meaning arises out of their synthesis. Writing is more, then, than "a means of acting upon a receiver" (Mitchell and Taylor, 250); it is a means of making meaning for writer and reader.[14] Without such a unifying, balanced understanding of language use, it is easy to overemphasize one aspect of discourse, such as audience. It is also easy to forget, as Anthony Petrosky cautions, that "reading, responding, and composing are aspects of understanding, and theories that attempt to account for them outside of their interaction with each other run the serious risk of building reductive models of human understanding."[15]

Audience Invoked

Those who envision audience as invoked stress that the audience of a written discourse is a construction of the writer, a "created fiction" (Long, 225). They do not, of course, deny the physical reality of readers, but they argue that writers simply cannot know this reality in the way that speakers can. The central task of the writer, then, is not to analyze an audience and adapt discourse to meet its needs. Rather, the writer uses the semantic and syntactic resources of language to provide cues for the reader—cues which help to define the role or roles the writer wishes the reader to adopt in responding to the text. Little scholarship in composition takes this perspective; only Russell Long's article and Walter Ong's "The Writer's Audience Is Always a Fiction" focus centrally on this issue.[16] If recent conferences are any indication, however, a growing number of teachers and scholars are becoming concerned with what they see as the possible distortions and oversimplifications of the approach typified by Mitchell and Taylor's model.[17]

Russell Long's response to current efforts to teach students analysis of audience and adaptation of text to audience is typical: "I have become increasingly disturbed not only about the superficiality of the advice itself, but about the philosophy which seems to lie beneath it" (221). Rather than detailing Long's argument, we wish to turn to Walter Ong's well-known study. Published in *PMLA* in 1975, "The Writer's Audience Is Always a Fiction" has had a significant impact on composition studies, despite the fact that its major emphasis is on fictional narrative rather than expository writing. An analysis of Ong's argument suggests that teachers of writing may err if they uncritically accept Ong's statement that "what has been said about fictional narrative applies ceteris paribus to all writing" (17).

Ong's thesis includes two central assertions: "What do we mean by saying the audience is a fiction? Two things at least. First, that the writer must construct in his imagination, clearly or vaguely, an audience cast in some sort of role. . . . Second, we mean that the audience must correspondingly fictionalize itself (12). Ong emphasizes the creative power of the adept writer, who can both project and alter audiences, as well as the complexity of the reader's role. Readers, Ong observes, must learn or "know how to play the game of being a member of an audience that 'really' does not exist" (12).

On the most abstract and general level, Ong is accurate. For a writer, the audience is not *there* in the sense that the speaker's audience, whether a single person or a large group, is present. But Ong's representative situations—the orator addressing a mass audience versus a writer alone in a room—oversimplify the potential range and diversity of both oral and written communication situations.

Ong's model of the paradigmatic act of speech communication derives from traditional rhetoric. In distinguishing the terms audience and reader, he notes that "the orator has before him an audience which is a true audience, a collectivity. . . . Readers do not form a collectivity, acting here and now on one another and on the speaker as members of an audience do" (11). As this quotation indicates, Ong also stresses the potential for interaction among members of an audience, and between an audience and a speaker.

But how many audiences are actually collectives, with ample opportunity for interaction? In *Persuasion: Understanding, Practice, and Analysis,* Herbert Simons establishes a continuum of audiences based on opportunities for interaction.[18] Simons contrasts commercial mass media publics, which "have little or no contact with each other and certainly have no reciprocal awareness of each other as members of the same audience" with "face-to-face work groups that meet and interact continuously over an extended period of time." He goes on to note that: "Between these two extremes are such groups as the following: (1) the *pedestrian audience,* persons who happen to pass a soapbox orator. . . ; (2) the *passive, occasional audience,* persons who come to hear a noted lecturer in a large auditorium . . . ; (3) the *active, occasional audience,* persons who meet only on specific occasions but actively interact when they do meet" (97–98).

Simons's discussion, in effect, questions the rigidity of Ong's distinctions between a speaker's and a writer's audience. Indeed, when one surveys a broad range of situations inviting oral communication, Ong's paradigmatic situation, in which the speaker's audience constitutes a "collectivity, acting here and now on one another and on the speaker" (11), seems somewhat atypical. It is certainly possible, at any rate, to think of a number of instances where speakers confront a problem very similar to that of writers: lacking intimate knowledge of their audience, which comprises not a collectivity but a disparate, and possibly even divided, group of individuals, speakers, like writers, must construct in their imaginations "an audience cast in some sort of role."[19] When President Carter announced to Americans during a speech broadcast on television, for instance, that his program against inflation was "the moral equivalent of warfare," he was doing more than merely characterizing his economic policies. He was providing an important cue to his audience concerning the role he wished them to adopt as listeners—that of a people braced for a painful but necessary and justifiable battle. Were we to examine his speech in detail, we would find other more subtle, but equally important, semantic and syntactic signals to the audience.

We do not wish here to collapse all distinctions between oral and written communication, but rather to emphasize that speaking and writing are, after all, both rhetorical acts. There are important differences between speech and writing. And the broad distinction between speech and writing that Ong makes is both commonsensical and particularly relevant to his subject, fictional narrative. As our illustration demonstrates, however, when one turns to precise, concrete situations, the relationship between speech and writing can become far more complex than even Ong represents.

Just as Ong's distinction between speech and writing is accurate on a highly general level but breaks down (or at least becomes less clear-cut) when examined closely, so too does his dictum about writers and their audiences. Every writer must indeed create a role for the reader, but the constraints on the writer and the potential sources of and possibilities for the reader's role are both more complex and diverse than Ong suggests. Ong stresses the importance of literary tradition in the creation of audience: "If the writer succeeds in writing, it is generally because he can fictionalize in his imagination an audience he has learned to know not from daily life but from earlier writers who were fictionalizing in their imagination audiences they had learned to know in still earlier writers, and so on back to the dawn of written narrative" (p. 11). And he cites a particularly (for us) germane example, a student "asked to write on the subject to which schoolteachers, jaded by summer, return compulsively every autumn: 'How I Spent My Summer Vacation'" (11). In order to negotiate such an assignment successfully, the student must turn his real audience, the teacher, into someone else. He or she must, for instance, "make like Samuel Clemens and write for whomever Samuel Clemens was writing for" (11).

Ong's example is, for his purposes, well-chosen. For such an assignment does indeed require the successful student to "fictionalize" his or her audience. But why is the student's decision to turn to a literary model in this instance particularly appropriate? Could one reason be that the student knows (consciously or unconsciously) that his English teacher, who is still the literal audience of his essay, appreciates literature and hence would be entertained (and here the student may intuit the assignment's actual aim as well) by such a strategy? In Ong's example the audience—the "jaded" schoolteacher—is not only willing to accept another role but, perhaps, actually yearns for it. How else to escape the tedium of reading twenty-five, fifty, seventy-five student papers on the same topic? As Walter Minot notes, however, not all readers are so malleable:

> In reading a work of fiction or poetry, a reader is far more willing to suspend his beliefs and values than in a rhetorical work dealing with some current social, moral, or economic issue. The effectiveness of the created audience in a rhetorical situation is likely to depend on such constraints as the actual identity of the reader, the subject of the discourse, the identity and purpose of the writer, and many other factors in the real world.[20]

An example might help make Minot's point concrete.

Imagine another composition student faced, like Ong's, with an assignment. This student, who has been given considerably more latitude in her choice of a topic, has decided to write on an issue of concern to her at the moment, the possibility that a home for mentally retarded adults will be built in her neighborhood. She is alarmed by the strongly negative, highly emotional reaction of most of her neighbors and wishes in her essay to persuade them that such a residence might not be the disaster they anticipate.

This student faces a different task from that described by Ong. If she is to succeed, she must think seriously about her actual readers, the neighbors to whom she wishes to send her letter. She knows the obvious demographic factors—age, race, class—so well that she probably hardly needs to consider them consciously. But other issues are more complex. How much do her neighbors know about mental retardation, intellectually or experientially? What is their image of a retarded adult? What fears does this project raise in them? What civic and religious values do they most respect? Based on this analysis—and the process may be much less sequential than we describe here—she must, of course, define a role for her audience, one congruent with her persona, arguments, the facts as she knows them, etc. She must, as Minot argues, *both* analyze and invent an audience.[21] In this instance, after detailed analysis of her audience and her arguments, the student decided to begin her essay by emphasizing what she felt to be the genuinely admirable qualities of her neighbors, particularly their kindness, understanding, and concern for others. In so doing, she invited her audience to see themselves as she saw them: as thoughtful, intelligent people who, if they were adequately informed, would certainly not act in a harsh manner to those less fortunate than they. In accepting this role, her readers did not have to "play the game of being a member of an audience that 'really' does not exist" (Ong, "The Writer's Audience," 12). But they did have to recognize in themselves the strengths the student described and to accept her implicit linking of these strengths to what she hoped would be their response to the proposed "home."

When this student enters her history class to write an examination, she faces a different set of constraints. Unlike the historian who does indeed have a broad range of options in establishing the reader's role, our student has much less freedom. This is because her reader's role has already been established and formalized in a series of related academic conventions. If she is a successful student, she has so effectively internalized these conventions that she can subordinate a concern for her complex and multiple audiences to focus on the material on which she is being tested and on the single audience, the teacher, who will respond to her performance on the test.[22]

We could multiply examples. In each instance the student writing—to friend, employer, neighbor, teacher, fellow readers of her daily newspaper—would need, as one of the many conscious and unconscious decisions required in composing, to envision and define a role for the reader. But how she defines that role— whether she relies mainly upon academic or technical writing conventions, literary models, intimate knowledge of friends or neighbors, analysis of a particular group, or some combination thereof—will vary tremendously. At times the reader may establish a role for the reader which indeed does not "coincide[s] with his role in the rest of actual life" (Ong, 12). At other times, however, one of the writer's primary tasks may be that of analyzing the "real life" audience and adapting the discourse to it. One of the factors that makes writing so difficult, as we know, is that we have no recipes: each rhetorical situation is unique and thus requires the writer, catalyzed and guided by a strong sense of purpose, to reanalyze and reinvent solutions.

Despite their helpful corrective approach, then, theories which assert that the audience of a written discourse is a construction of the writer present their own dangers.[23] One of these is the tendency to overemphasize the distinction between speech and writing while undervaluing the insights of discourse theorists, such as James Moffett and James Britton, who remind us of the importance of such additional factors as distance between speaker or writer and audience and levels of abstraction in the subject. In *Teaching the Universe of Discourse*, Moffett establishes the following spectrum of discourse: recording ("the drama of what is happening"), reporting ("the narrative of what happened"), generalizing ("the exposition of what happens"), and theorizing ("the argumentation of what will, may happen").[24] In an extended example, Moffett demonstrates the important points of connection between communication acts at any one level of the spectrum, whether oral or written:

> Suppose next that I tell the cafeteria experience to a friend some time later in conversation. . . . Of course, instead of recounting the cafeteria scene to my friend in person I could write it in a letter to an audience more removed in time and space. Informal writing is usually still rather spontaneous, directed at an audience known to the writer, and reflects the transient mood and circumstances in which the writing occurs. Feedback and audience influence, however, are delayed and weakened. . . . *Compare in turn now the changes that must occur all down the line when I write about this cafeteria experience in a discourse destined for publication and distribution to a mass, anonymous audience of present and perhaps unborn people.* I cannot allude to things and ideas that only my friends know about. I must

use a vocabulary, style, logic, and rhetoric that anybody in that mass audience can understand and respond to. I must name and organize what happened during those moments in the cafeteria that day in such a way that this mythical average reader can relate what I say to some primary moments of experience of his own. (37–38; our emphasis)

Though Moffett does not say so, many of these same constraints would obtain if he decided to describe his experience in a speech to a mass audience—the viewers of a television show, for example, or the members of a graduating class. As Moffett's example illustrates, the distinction between speech and writing is important; it is, however, only one of several constraints influencing any particular discourse.

Another weakness of research based on the concept of audience as invoked is that it distorts the processes of writing and reading by overemphasizing the power of the writer and undervaluing that of the reader. Unlike Mitchell and Taylor, Ong recognizes the creative role the writer plays as reader of his or her own writing, the way the writer uses language to provide cues for the reader and tests the effectiveness of these cues during his or her own rereading of the text. But Ong fails adequately to recognize the constraints placed on the writer, in certain situations, by the audience. He fails, in other words, to acknowledge that readers' own experiences, expectations, and beliefs do play a central role in their reading of a text, and that the writer who does not consider the needs and interests of his audience risks losing that audience. To argue that the audience is a "created fiction" (Long, 225), to stress that the reader's role "seldom coincides with his role in the rest of actual life" (Ong, 12), is just as much an oversimplification, then, as to insist, as Mitchell and Taylor do, that "the audience not only judges writing, it also motivates it" (250). The former view overemphasizes the writer's independence and power; the latter, that of the reader.

Rhetoric and Its Situations[25]

If the perspectives we have described as audience addressed and audience invoked represent incomplete conceptions of the role of audience in written discourse, do we have an alternative? How can we most accurately conceive of this essential rhetorical element? In what follows we will sketch a tentative model and present several defining or constraining statements about this apparently slippery concept, "audience." The result will, we hope, move us closer to a full understanding of the role audience plays in written discourse.

Figure 1.2 represents our attempt to indicate the complex series of obligations, resources, needs, and constraints embodied in the writer's concept of audience. (We emphasize that our goal here is *not* to depict the writing process as a whole—a much more complex task—but to focus on the writer's relation to audience.) As our model indicates, we do not see the two perspectives on audience described earlier as necessarily dichotomous or contradictory. Except for past and anomalous audiences, special cases which we describe paragraphs hence, all of the audience roles we specify—self, friend, colleague, critic, mass audience, and future audience—may be invoked or addressed.[26] It is the writer who, as writer and reader of his or her own text, one guided by a sense of purpose and by the particularities of a specific rhetorical situation, establishes the range of potential roles an audience may play. (Readers may, of course, accept or reject the role or roles the writer wishes them to adopt in responding to a text.)

Writers who wish to be read must often adapt their discourse to meet the needs and expectations of an addressed audience. They may rely on past experience in addressing audiences to guide their writing, or they may engage a representative of that audience in the writing process. The latter occurs, for instance, when we ask a colleague to read an article intended for scholarly publication. Writers may also be required to respond to the intervention of others—a teacher's comments on an essay, a supervisor's suggestions for improving a report, or the insistent, catalyzing questions of an editor. Such intervention may in certain cases represent a powerful stimulus to the writer, but it is the writer who interprets the suggestions—or even commands—of others, choosing what to accept or reject. Even the conscious decision to accede to the expectations of a particular addressed audience may not always be carried out; unconscious psychological resistance, incomplete understanding, or inadequately developed ability may prevent

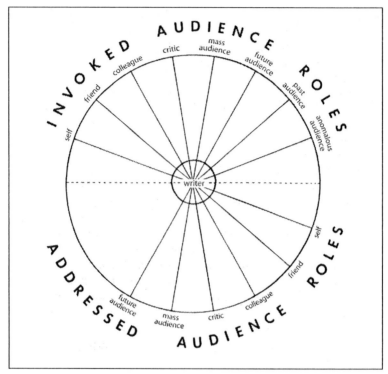

FIGURE 1.2. *The concept of audience.*

the writer from following through with the decision—a reality confirmed by composition teachers with each new set of essays.

The addressed audience, the actual or intended readers of a discourse, exists outside of the text. Writers may analyze these readers' needs, anticipate their biases, even defer to their wishes. But it is only through the text, through language, that writers embody or give life to their conception of the reader. In so doing, they do not so much create a role for the reader—a phrase which implies that the writer somehow creates a mold to which the reader adapts—as invoke it. Rather than relying on incantations, however, writers conjure their vision—a vision which they hope readers will actively come to share as they read the text—by using all the resources of language available to them to establish a broad, and ideally coherent, range of cues for the reader. Technical writing conventions, for instance, quickly formalize any of several writer-reader relationships, such as colleague to colleague or expert to lay reader. But even comparatively local semantic decisions may play an equally essential role. In "The Writer's Audience Is Always a Fiction," Ong demonstrates how Hemingway's use of definite articles in *A Farewell to Arms* subtly cues readers that their role is to be that of a "companion in arms . . . a confidant" (13).

Any of the roles of the addressed audience cited in our model may be invoked via the text. Writers may also invoke a past audience, as did, for instance, Ong's student writing to those Mark Twain would have been writing for. And writers can also invoke anomalous audiences, such as a fictional character—Hercule Poirot, perhaps. Our model, then, confirms Douglas Park's observation that the meanings of audience, though multiple and complex, "tend to diverge in two general directions: one toward actual people external to a text, the audience whom the writer must accommodate; the other toward the text itself and the audience implied there: a set of suggested or evoked attitudes, interests, reactions, conditions of knowledge which may or may not fit with the qualities of actual readers or listeners."[27] The most complete understanding of audience thus involves a synthesis of the perspectives we have termed audience addressed, with its focus on the reader, and audience invoked, with its focus on the writer.

One illustration of this constantly shifting complex of meanings for "audience" lies in our own experiences writing this essay. One of us became interested in the concept of audience during an NEH Seminar, and her first audience was a small, close-knit seminar group to whom she addressed her work. The other came to contemplate a multiplicity of audiences while working on a textbook; the first audience in this case was herself, as she debated the ideas she was struggling to present to a group of invoked students. Following a lengthy series of conversations, our interests began to merge: we shared notes and discussed articles written by others on audience, and eventually one of us began a draft. Our long-distance telephone bills and the miles we traveled up and down I-5 from Oregon to British Columbia attest most concretely to the power of a coauthor's expectations and criticisms and also illustrate that one person can take on the role of several different audiences: friend, colleague, and critic.

As we began to write and re-write the essay, now for a particular scholarly journal, the change in purpose and medium (no longer a seminar paper or a textbook) led us to new audiences. For us, the major "invoked audience" during this period was Richard Larson, editor of this journal, whose questions and criticisms we imagined and tried to anticipate. (Once this essay was accepted by *CCC*, Richard Larson became for us an addressed audience: he responded in writing with questions, criticisms, and suggestions, some of which we had, of course, failed to anticipate.) We also thought of the readers of *CCC* and those who attend the annual CCCC, most often picturing you as members of our own departments, a diverse group of individuals with widely varying degrees of interest in and knowledge of composition. Because of the generic constraints of academic writing, which limit the range of roles we may define for our readers, the audience represented by the readers of *CCC* seemed most vivid to us in two situations: (1) when we were concerned about the degree to which we needed to explain concepts or terms; and (2) when we considered central organizational decisions, such as the most effective way to introduce a discussion. Another, and for us extremely potent, audience was the authors—Mitchell and Taylor, Long, Ong, Park, and others—with whom we have seen ourselves in silent dialogue. As we read and reread their analyses and developed our responses to them, we felt a responsibility to try to understand their formulations as fully as possible, to play fair with their ideas, to make our own efforts continue to meet their high standards.

Our experience provides just one example, and even it is far from complete. (Once we finished a rough draft, one particular colleague became a potent but demanding addressed audience, listening to revision upon revision and challenging us with harder and harder questions. And after this essay is published, we may revise our understanding of audiences we thought we knew or recognize the existence of an entirely new audience. The latter would happen, for instance, if teachers of speech communication for some reason found our discussion useful.) But even this single case demonstrates that the term *audience* refers not just to the intended, actual, or eventual readers of a discourse, but to *all* those whose image, ideas, or actions influence a writer during the process of composition. One way to conceive of "audience,"

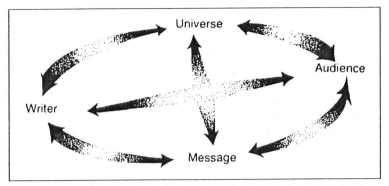

FIGURE 1.3. *Corbett's model of "The Rhetorical Interrelationships" (5).*

then, is as an overdetermined or unusually rich concept, one which may perhaps be best specified through the analysis of precise, concrete situations.

We hope that this partial example of our own experience will illustrate how the elements represented in Figure 1.3 will shift and merge, depending on the particular rhetorical situation, the writer's aim, and the genre chosen. Such an understanding is critical: because of the complex reality to which the term audience refers and because of its fluid, shifting role in the composing process, any discussion of audience which isolates it from the rest of the rhetorical situation or which radically overemphasizes or underemphasizes its function in relation to other rhetorical constraints is likely to oversimplify. Note the unilateral direction of Mitchell and Taylor's model (7), which is unable to represent the diverse and complex role(s) audience(s) can play in the actual writing process—in the creation of meaning. In contrast, consider the model used by Edward P. J. Corbett in his *Little Rhetoric and Handbook*.[28]

This representation, which allows for interaction among all the elements of rhetoric, may at first appear less elegant and predictive than Mitchell and Taylor's. But it is finally more useful since it accurately represents the diverse range of potential interrelationships in any written discourse.

We hope that our model also suggests the integrated, interdependent nature of reading and writing. Two assertions emerge from this relationship. One involves the writer as reader of his or her own work. As Donald Murray notes in "Teaching the Other Self: The Writer's First Reader," this role is critical, for "the reading writer—the map-maker and map-reader—reads the word, the line, the sentence, the paragraph, the page, the entire text. This constant back-and-forth reading monitors the multiple complex relationships between all the elements in writing."[29] To ignore or devalue such a central function is to risk distorting the writing process as a whole. But unless the writer is composing a diary or journal entry, intended only for the writer's own eyes, the writing process is not complete unless another person, someone other than the writer, reads the text also. The second assertion thus emphasizes the creative, dynamic duality of the process of reading and writing, whereby writers create readers and readers create writers. In the meeting of these two lies meaning, lies communication.

A fully elaborated view of audience, then, must balance the creativity of the writer with the different, but equally important, creativity of the reader. It must account for a wide and shifting range of roles for both addressed and invoked audiences. And, finally, it must relate the matrix created by the intricate relationship of writer and audience to all elements in the rhetorical situation. Such an enriched conception of audience can help us better understand the complex act we call composing.

Notes

1. Ruth Mitchell and Mary Taylor, "The Integrating Perspective: An Audience-Response Model for Writing," *CE* 41 (November, 1979): 267. Subsequent references to this article will be cited in the text.

2. Russell C. Long, "Writer-Audience Relationships: Analysis or Invention," *CCC* 31 (May, 1980): 223 and 225. Subsequent references to this article will be cited in the text.

3. For these terms we are indebted to Henry W. Johnstone, Jr., who refers to them in his analysis of Chaim Perelman's universal audience in *Validity and Rhetoric in Philosophical Argument: An Outlook in Transition* (University Park, PA: The Dialogue Press of Man & World, 1978), 105.

4. Fred R. Pfister and Joanne F. Petrik, "A Heuristic Model for Creating a Writer's Audience," *CCC* 31 (May, 1980): 213.

5. Pfister and Petrik, 214; our emphasis.

6. See, for example, Lisa S. Ede, "On Audience and Composition," *CCC* 30 (October, 1979): 291–295.

7. See, for example, David Tedlock, "The Case Approach to Composition," *CCC* 32 (October, 1981): 253–261.

8. See, for example, Linda Flower's *Problem-Solving Strategies for Writers* (New York: Harcourt Brace Jovanovich, 1981) and John P. Field and Robert H. Weiss's *Cases for Composition* (Boston: Little Brown, 1979).

9. Richard E. Young, "Paradigms and Problems: Needed Research in Rhetorical Invention," in *Research on Composing: Points of Departure*, ed. Charles R. Cooper and Lee Odell (Urbana, IL: National Council of Teachers of English, 1978), 32 (footnote #3).

10. Mitchell and Taylor do recognize that internal psychological needs ("unconscious challenges") may play a role in the writing process, but they cite such instances as an "extreme case (often that of the creative writer)" (p. 251). For a discussion of the importance of self-evaluation in the composing process, see Susan Miller, "How Writers Evaluate Their Own Writing," *CCC* 33 (May, 1982): 176–183.

11. Susan Wall, "In the Writer's Eye: Learning to Teach the Rereading/ Revising Process," *English Education* 14 (February, 1982): 12.

12. Wayne Booth, *Modern Dogma and the Rhetoric of Assent* (Chicago: The University of Chicago Press, 1974), xiv.

13. Paul Kameen, "Rewording the Rhetoric of Composition," *Pre/Text* 1 (Spring-Fall, 1980): 82.

14. Mitchell and Taylor's arguments in favor of adjunct classes seem to indicate that they see writing instruction, wherever it occurs, as a skills course, one instructing students in the proper use of a tool.

15. Anthony R. Petrosky, "From Story to Essay: Reading and Writing," *CCC* 33 (February, 1982): 20.

16. Walter J. Ong, S. J., "The Writer's Audience Is Always a Fiction," *PMLA* 90 (January, 1975): 9–21. Subsequent references to this article will be cited in the text.

17. See, for example, William Irmscher, "Sense of Audience: An Intuitive Concept," unpublished paper delivered at the CCCC in 1981; Douglas B. Park, "The Meanings of Audience: Pedagogical Implications," unpublished paper delivered at the CCCC in 1981; and Luke M. Reinsma, "Writing to an Audience: Scheme or Strategy?" unpublished paper delivered at the CCCC in 1982.

18. Herbert W. Simons, *Persuasion: Understanding, Practice, and Analysis* (Reading, MA: Addison-Wesley, 1976).

19. Ong, p. 12. Ong recognizes that oral communication also involves role-playing, but he stresses that it "has within it a momentum that works for the removal of masks" (p. 20). This may be true in certain instances, such as dialogue, but does not, we believe, obtain broadly.

20. Walter S. Minot, "Response to Russell C. Long," *CCC* 32 (October, 1981): 337.

21. We are aware that the student actually has two audiences, her neighbors and her teacher, and that this situation poses an extra constraint for the writer. Not all students can manage such a complex series of audience constraints, but it is important to note that writers in a variety of situations often write for more than a single audience.

22. In their paper on "Student and Professional Syntax in Four Disciplines" (unpublished paper delivered at the CCCC in 1981), Ian Pringle and Aviva Freedman provide a good example of what can happen when a student creates an aberrant role for an academic reader. They cite an excerpt from a third-year history assignment, the tone of which "is essentially the tone of the opening of a television travelogue commentary" and which thus asks the reader, a history professor, to assume the role of the viewer of such a show. The result is as might be expected: "Although the content of the paper does not seem significantly more abysmal than other papers in the same set, this one was awarded a disproportionately low grade" (2).

23. One danger which should be noted is a tendency to foster a questionable image of classical rhetoric. The agonistic speaker-audience relationship which Long cites as an essential characteristic of classical rhetoric is actually a central point of debate among those involved in historical and theoretical research in rhetoric. For further discussion, see: Lisa Ede and Andrea Lunsford, "On Distinctions between Classical and Modern Rhetoric," in *Classical Rhetoric and Modern Discourse: Essays in Honor of Edward P. J. Corbett*, ed. Robert Connors, Lisa Ede, and Andrea Lunsford (Carbondale, IL: Southern Illinois University Press, 1984).

24. James Moffett, *Teaching the Universe of Discourse* (Boston: Houghton Mifflin, 1968), 47. Subsequent references will be mentioned in the text.

25. We have taken the title of this section from Scott Consigny's article of the same title, *Philosophy and Rhetoric* 7 (Summer, 1974): 175–186. Consigny's effort to mediate between two opposing views of rhetoric provided a stimulating model for our own efforts.

26. Although we believe that the range of audience roles cited in our model covers the general spectrum of options, we do not claim to have specified all possibilities. This is particularly the case since, in certain instances, these roles may merge and blend—shifting subtly in character. We might also note that other terms for the same roles might be used. In a business setting, for instance, colleague might be better termed co-worker, critic, supervisor.

27. Douglas B. Park, "The Meanings of 'Audience,'" *CE* 44 (March, 1982): 249.

28. Edward P. J. Corbett, *The Little Rhetoric & Handbook*, 2nd ed. (Glenview, IL: Scott, Foresman, 1982), 5.

29. Donald M. Murray, "Teaching the Other Self: The Writer's First Reader," *CCC* 33 (May, 1982): 142.

CHAPTER TWO

Representing Audience: "Successful" Discourse and Disciplinary Critique

ANDREA A. LUNSFORD AND LISA EDE

We are wedded in language, have our being in words.
Language is also a place of struggle.

—bell hooks (*Yearning* 146)

In his February 1994 CCC editor's column, Joseph Harris provides a brief overview of the kinds of work he hopes to publish
in the journal, noting, among other things, that he is "especially
interested in pieces that take a critical or revisionary look at work
in composition studies" (7). Given the contemporary turn to self-
conscious disciplinary critique, Harris's call is hardly surprising. In
its relatively brief disciplinary history, in fact, composition studies
has engaged in a great deal of revisionary looking back, as can be
seen in the several paradigm shifts or theoretical revolutions the
field has experienced during the span of the last three decades.
This disciplinary critique has for the most part, however, been
carried out in the agonistic manner characteristic of traditional
academic discussion, with each wave of criticism, each revisionary look establishing its own efficacy by demonstrating the flaws
of prior conceptions.[1]

The notion of disciplinary progress—or success—enacted
by these discourses has in many ways served our field well. For
though composition studies could hardly be described as an
established or mainstream academic discipline, it has succeeded

Reprinted from *College Composition and Communication* 47:2 (May, 1996):
167–179. Reprinted with permission.

to a considerable extent in legitimizing and professionalizing its position in the academy. And the critical discourses of such theorists as Janet Emig, James Berlin, and Susan Miller have, we believe, contributed substantially to our understanding of how very much is at stake when scholars in composition studies profess the teaching of writing.

We are grateful for this tradition of critical discourse. Indeed we wish to respond to Harris's call to participate in a "critical or revisionary" look at work in composition studies by building on this tradition—albeit with one significant exception. We attempt here to resist traditional oppositional critique, with its tendency to focus (usually in a negative way) on the work of others. Instead, we propose here to attempt a self-critique by revisiting an essay of our own, "Audience Addressed/Audience Invoked: The Role of Audience in Composition Theory and Pedagogy" (AA/AI, hereafter), the essay that (if citations, analyses, and reprintings are any indication) of all our coauthored work might be said to have been judged most "successful" by others in our field.

We've put "successful" in quotation marks for a reason. The conventional Western understanding of success emphasizes the role that individual agency plays in achievement. In this view, particularly as played out most often in American mythologies, success comes to those individuals who work hard for it, and who thus deserve it. Business persons who work hard, who fight the good fight, are successful. Writers who write well, who use the resources of language to persuade others, similarly merit whatever recognition and achievement come their way. As conventionally understood, success in the academy is measured by "objective" and largely individualist criteria, such as publications and reprintings, citations, and the degree of response the writing engenders.

That such a view of success—and of language—has been challenged on a number of fronts goes without saying. We may write language, but language also writes us. We may desire to express our ideas, but the ideas we express may reveal more than we have intended. Rather than emphasizing individual agency, this poststructuralist view of discourse calls attention to the role that shared assumptions and ideologies play in enabling or hindering communication. It reminds us as well of the locatedness and situatedness of all texts—and of the need to inquire into what Gesa E. Kirsch and Joy S. Ritchie in a recent *CCC* essay refer to as a "politics of location" (7). Such an effort challenges researchers, Kirsch and Ritchie argue, to "theorize their locations by examining their experiences as reflections of ideology and culture, by reinterpreting their own experiences through the eyes of others, and by recognizing their own split selves, their multiple and often unknowable identities" (8). It is in the spirit of Kirsch and Ritchie's call that we turn to our earlier essay.

In attempting such a self-critique, we wish to be as clear about our goals as possible. In this essay, we intend to subject our earlier work to critical inquiry in an effort to foreground the rhetoricity of this work and to explore and learn from the cultural, disciplinary, and institutional forces at play in it. In so doing, we attempt to illuminate both the absences and presences in AA/AI, but to do so in a way that resists the lure of totalizing, oppositionalizing readings. We do not, in other words, wish to construct a bad-old-Ede-and-Lunsford, which we—in traditional agonistic fashion—will strike down in the service of representing an all-new-and-improved-Lunsford-and-Ede on audience. In revisiting our essay, then, we wish neither to reject nor defend AA/AI but rather to embrace multiple understandings of it, and to acknowledge the extent to which any discursive moment contains diverse, heterodox, and even contradictory realities—confirming (once again) the acuity of Kenneth Burke's observation that "if any given terminology is a *reflection* of reality, by its very nature as a terminology it must also be a *selection* of reality; and to this extent it must function also as a *deflection* of reality" (45). As a result of such multiple understandings, we hope to raise heuristic questions not only about our own work but also about conventional narratives (and genres) of disciplinary progress and about the relationship between "success" and traditional academic critique.

Audience and the Subject(s) of Discourse

At the time that it was written, AA/AI entered an ongoing debate on the nature and role of audience in discourse. Responding to a number of essays on the concept of audience that appeared in the late 1970s and early 1980s, AA/AI attempted to redirect current discussions of audience by arguing that previous commentators had generally taken a partial view of an unusually rich and complex concept. Some theorists, such as Ruth Mitchell and Mary Taylor, privileged what we called the *audience addressed*, "the concrete reality of the writer's audience . . . [and assumed] that knowledge of this audience's attitudes, beliefs, and expectations is not only possible (via observation and analysis) but essential" (AA/AI 156). Others, such as Walter Ong and Russell Long, emphasized the extent to which writers create or *invoke* audiences by using "the semantic and syntactic resources of language to create cues for the reader—cues which help to define the role or roles the writer wishes the reader to adopt" (160). Our own approach was to challenge the helpfulness of such dichotomous and polarizing views of audience as either wholly addressed or wholly invoked and to argue for a synthesis of these perspectives, one that acknowledges the creativity and interdependence of writers and readers, writing and reading, and that recognizes the "fluid, dynamic character of rhetorical situations" (165). Audience can perhaps best be conceptualized, we argued, as a "complex series of obligations, needs, resources, and constraints" that both enable and constrain writers and readers (165).

Ten years later, we still resist efforts to characterize audience as solely textual (invoked) or material (addressed), and we continue to affirm the importance of considering audience in the context of the rhetorical situation. Rereading our essay, we note its refusal to generate pedagogical formulas or rules for teachers and students and its attempt to argue that the most complex understanding of audience is—theoretically and pedagogically—the most useful. We also recognize, however, a number of absences in AA/AI—absences that reflect our personal and professional desire to turn away from the potential difficulties and costs entailed in successful communication.

By insisting that the concept of audience involves textual and material constraints as well as opportunities, and that it must always be considered in the context of the larger rhetorical situation, AA/AI sets the scene—but then fails to explore—the ways in which audiences can not only enable but also silence writers and readers. In addition, although AA/AI recognizes the possibility of readers rejecting "the role or roles the writer wishes them to adopt in responding to a text" (166), our essay consistently downplays the possibility of tension and contradiction, presenting the interplay of audience addressed and audience invoked as potential opportunities for the writer "catalyzed and guided by a strong sense of purpose, to reanalyze and reinvent solutions" (164). With good will and rhetorical sensitivity, AA/AI implicitly suggests, writers will be able to negotiate their ways into positions of discursive power, will achieve and maintain communicative success.

Such an understanding of writing assumes a negotiation of meaning among if not literal equals then among those with equal access to the resources of language. Such an understanding also necessitates, of course, a parallel series of assumptions about writers and readers, as well as about the genres they attempt to inhabit. We have already indicated that the subject of discourse invoked in AA/AI is a subject who feels both agency and authority—that subject is also implicitly stable, unified, and autonomous. Although we recognize in AA/AI that students have less power than teachers and thus less freedom in some rhetorical situations than in others, we do not pursue the multiple ways in which the student writer's agency and identity may be shaped and constrained not only by immediate audiences but also, and even more forcefully, by the ways in which both she and those audiences are positioned within larger institutional and discursive frameworks. Nor do we consider the powerful effects of ideology working through genres, such as those inscribed in academic essayist literacy, to call forth and thus to control and constrain writers and audiences.[2] That a student might find herself full of contradiction and conflict, might find the choices available to her as a writer confusing and even crippling—might in fact find it difficult, even undesirable, to claim the identity of "writer"—did not occur to us.[3]

That such ideas did not occur to us is a mark of the extent to which the students invoked in AA/AI were in important ways the students we had been—eager, compliant, willing to shape ourselves to rhetorical situations. Our desire to invoke such students and to (re)write experience in such a way as to highlight success not failure, consensus not conflict, progress not struggle, is, we have realized, deeply imbedded in our relationship to schooling as well as to discourse. In working on this essay, for instance, we have each recalled memories of struggle and failure, of negative educational experiences that reminded us of the degree to which, as students, we molded ourselves as willing subjects of education. Andrea found herself reflecting most often on her early grade school years, recalling, for instance, a moment when she perceived that a teacher simply did not like her—and noting the ways in which that perception led her not to challenge the teacher's views or goals but to attempt to remake herself in the image of a dutifully schooled subject less likely to invoke a hostile teacher audience. Lisa found herself drawn to memories of graduate school experiences and to the ways in which she repressed her confusion and anger as different courses required her to become not only a different audience for each professor but a different subject as well.

In reflecting on these memories, we have begun to explore the extent to which, very early in our educations, we identified with the goals and institutions of schooling. Our home communities were ones in which school was generally defined as a place for positive change and advancement. But our identification with schooling involved more than mere acceptance of these attitudes. Academic good girls, we studied, even excelled, and in so doing we came to associate both schooling and the writing we did in school with a positive sense of self, a means of validation and "success," and of hailing appreciative audiences. So powerful was this identification, in fact, that we recast those painful memories of struggle that we could not repress, reinterpreting experiences that might have led to resistance and critique as evidence of individual problems that we could remedy if only we would work harder, do (and be) better. Such an approach is congruent, of course, with the individualism inherent throughout our culture, educational institutions, and scholarly disciplines, an individualism that traditionally writes the kind of struggles we experienced as students as inevitable, even necessary and salutary, aspects of the Western narrative of individual success that AA/AI implicitly endorses.[4]

Does this critique suggest that we have now rejected our identification with schooling and its traditional individualist assumptions? It does not, or not monolithically at least, for it would be disingenuous indeed for us to ignore or devalue what we have gained both intellectually and materially as a result of our schooling. So while we recognize that schooling subjects and disciplines students, that writing is not necessarily and certainly not always a venue for power, we also recognize—and honor—the potential of both writing and schooling to enable students to enact subjectivities that they experience as positive and authorizing. Thus, like the audiences that it hails, schooling is both deeply situated and inherently paradoxical, full of contradictions and complexities—and opportunities. In this analysis of our earlier work, our goal is neither to embrace schooling unthinkingly (as we once did) nor to condemn schooling out of hand. Rather, we seek to recognize its multiple complexities and to understand as fully as possible our positioning among them as we strive not only to acknowledge but also to take responsibility for our own politics of location.

Part of this positioning, of course, involves our experiences and identities not only with schooling in general but with the field of composition in particular. When we reflect upon the disciplinary moment in which we wrote AA/AI, we find ourselves with multiple understandings and responses. From our current perspective, one informed by recent research in feminism, post-structuralism, rhetorical theory, and critical pedagogy, it is easy to look back at research in composition in the mid-1980s—with its emphasis on the writing process and cognitive models of that process—and note the field's generally uncritical identification with and appropriation of the goals of schooling. Paradoxes of institutional placement that now seem obvious—such as the tension inherent in our field's asserted desire to empower students and its curricular positioning as gatekeeper and certifier—were repressed in much of the work of the time, including our own. We want now to acknowledge and understand the implications of such repression, as well as to relinquish at least some of the dreams of disciplinary progress, of moving inexorably toward a time when we can "know" audiences, much less teach students to use such knowledge in straightforward ways to achieve "success" in writing. Yet we would not want to give up our field's commitment to teaching. Thus when we return to such efforts as Mina Shaughnessy's *Errors and Expectations*, or to early writing process studies, we find much to celebrate in their commitment to teaching, to opening up spaces in the academy for tradition-ally excluded students, and to the importance of striving for social and political change. We want now, at *this* disciplinary moment, to reaffirm these commitments, while acknowledging the importance of inquiring into the nature of both teacher and student subjectivities, and of recognizing the implications of our cultural, political, economic, and institutional embeddedness. Teachers and students are—we understand better now than in the past—not free individual agents writing their own destinies but rather constructed subjects embedded in multiple discourses, and the classroom is not a magic circle free of ideological and institutional influence. Such understandings have been and con-tinue to be chastening to us; they encourage humility and modesty in teaching and research and an increased attentiveness to the motivated and situated—that is to say deeply rhetorical—nature of our assumptions and practices.

Audience, Ideology, and the Rhetorical Tradition

As we have tried to suggest, the writers and teachers speaking through AA/AI are, in many important ways, the writers and teachers we wanted and still want to be: negotiators of rhetori-cal situations who can gain a place for ourselves, our students, and our field at the academic and social conversational table. But we can also now see repressed in our essay—metaphorically smoothed or ironed out—traces of difficulties, of pain, failure, misunderstanding, and conflict. Such repressions were both en-couraged and made possible not only by our personal identifica-tion with schooling and with the emergent field of composition studies, but also by our deep—and ongoing—commitment to the discipline of rhetoric.

In AA/AI, this commitment to traditional views of rhetoric, and particularly to the heuristic potential of the concept of the rhetorical situation, offered us a powerful framework for analyz-ing and enriching understandings of audience, a framework we still find useful. But this commitment also almost certainly insured that we would not notice the tradition's insistent impulse toward successful communication on the one hand and exclusion on the other. Indeed, the rhetorical tradition's focus on success in communicating with and persuading others is longstanding and enduring, discernible in the Western emphasis on efficiency, "getting the job done," and clarity, as well as in traditional theories and definitions of rhetoric. Think, for instance, of Aristotle's definition of rhetoric as "the faculty of discovering in the particular case what are the available means of persuasion" (7) or of Richards's view of it as "the study of misunderstanding and its remedies" (3).

This focus on successful communicative negotiation inevitably, albeit silently, casts misunderstanding, miscommunication, disagreement, resistance, and dissent as failure and, as such, as that which is to be avoided or "cured." Today it seems to us that this emphasis on "success" has exacted a high hidden price. For how better to avoid misunderstanding and failure (and to make "successful" communication more likely) than to exclude, to disenfranchise those who by their very presence in the arena of discourse raise increased possibilities for communicative failures. The student writers invoked in AA/AI, for instance, are always already within and compliant to academic discourse, and thus willing and able to "adapt their discourse to meet the needs and expectations of an addressed audience" (166). While we still hope to help students meet such needs and expectations, we would also hope to bring into relief the exclusions that will almost certainly be necessary to do so, as well as the choices students must consider in deciding to inhabit academic discourse in this way.

That the rhetorical tradition is one of persistent exclusion goes without saying. But seeing the desire for successful communication as deeply implicated in the tendency to exclude those (like women and slaves in the ancient world) who might tend to disrupt or stand in the way of that success seems to us particularly noteworthy. For the dual moves toward exclusion and successful persuasion tend to hide from view any value that misunderstanding, resistance, or similar "failures" might have in complementing and enriching our notion of "success" by opening up spaces for additional voices, ways of understanding, conversations, and avenues of communication. It's interesting to consider, in this regard, the ways in which the exclusionary tendencies of the rhetorical tradition are tied to a view of the human subject as coherent, autonomous, and unified. Such a view assumes that writers and readers have no options but to be either in—or out of—a particular rhetorical situation.

Suppressed by the double impulse toward exclusion and success are the ways in which lived experiences can cause people to create internalized audiences that can lead not only to successful communication but also to disabling silences or to attempts at manipulative control, or the ways in which the materiality of people's lives can have the same effects, can result in communicative failure, in audiences ignored, rejected, excluded, or denied. Most deeply suppressed in the persistent gesture toward success, with its accompanying silent embrace of sameness, is a concomitant inattention to issues of difference. Thus while traditional Western conceptions of rhetoric as a system do, we still wish to argue, leave a space for difference in the concepts of rhetorical situation and of audience, that space has been, in practice, more often apparent than real. But not always. For as bell hooks and many others traditionally excluded from the dominant discourse continue to demonstrate, the "place of struggle" that rhetoric encompasses *can* be broadened (albeit with difficulty) to enact differences. In terms of verbal communication, this rhetorical space is what we have to work with and in. And in order to do so in a way that makes that space as open and inclusive as possible, we must work hard to understand the complex choices, multiple responsibilities, and competing representations that communication always entails. Only thus can we open up more spaces for dialogue with others; only thus can we understand, with hooks, that:

> Spaces can be real and imagined. Spaces can tell stories and unfold histories. Spaces can be interrupted, appropriated, and transformed through artistic and literary practice. (*Yearning* 152)

Re-Presenting Audience

As we hope this discussion has suggested, situating AA/AI in a web of personal, professional, and disciplinary contexts draws attention to those multiple and sometimes conflicting desires that speak through our effort to communicate with others, to both address and invoke audiences. As we noted early on in this essay, however, this attempt at a rereading of our work has aimed not to dismiss or discredit the work we have discussed, and in this sense not to engage in the agonistic activities so characteristic of the academy and the rhetorical tradition. Rather, we have attempted to demonstrate here the value of reading one's own research with the same kind of rhetorical care often reserved for the work of others and to suggest that this kind of reading—which calls attention to absences as well as presences, to multiplicity, tension, and competing motives in discourse—can enrich our understanding in ways that oppositional or totalizing readings do not.

Reading AA/AI against the backdrop of our own commitment to and identification with schooling, for instance, helped us to understand that although we intended AA/AI both to invoke and address a broad range of audiences, it speaks most strongly to those whose identifications and experiences mirror our own, while turning away from the potential difficulties and costs often inherent in the effort to achieve the kind of academic "success" that our essay takes for granted as well as from those who would wish to subvert such "success." Similarly, reading AA/AI in the context of research in the field emphasizes the degree to which our text fails to examine common-sense understandings of the nature, purposes, and impacts of education. In addition, a single-minded focus on students' success, without an interrogation of the definitions and foundations of such success, effectively prevents us from fully recognizing the contradictions and conflicts inherent in our own (and students') positionings. Finally, seeing these desires for success and suppression of conflict as implicated in the larger project of the Western rhetorical tradition helps us to understand not only how implicated we are in that tradition but also the exclusions that that tradition necessarily entails.

Put another way, reading AA/AI in terms of its place in the field of composition studies as well as in the rhetorical tradition, as we have just done, requires us to acknowledge the extent to which our essay both inhabits and expresses what Lynn Worsham terms our field's modernist commitment "to the Enlightenment dreams of communication and consensus, emancipation and empowerment" (100). That we now question some aspects of these dreams is evident in our desire to interrogate AA/AI in order to reveal at least some of its exclusions and repressions. These exclusions and repressions need to be acknowledged, we believe, if (as both writers and teachers) we are to work effectively to further those goals that we remain unwilling to relinquish. For with Stanley Aronowitz and Henry Giroux we believe that "those ideals of the project of modernity that link memory, agency, and reason to the construction of a democratic public sphere need to be defended" (59).

Our understanding of what it means to work to further the goals of democratic education has changed, however, since we wrote AA/AI. We have learned to be suspicious, for instance, of claims to empower or do something "for" others, especially when that claim entails representations that may essentialize those on whose behalf these claims are made. (Current arguments about basic writing programs turn at least in part on this issue.) We have also learned to reassess what it means to be "successful" as both writers and teachers, and we have become aware of the ways in which "success" disciplines and shapes what we are allowed—generically, theoretically, pedagogically—to do. Perhaps most importantly, we now know in our bones that there is no pure or separate space from which we may write or teach. Representation, of ourselves as well as of those audiences that we both invoke and address, can never be innocent—whether that representation involves writing an essay (such as the one you are now reading) or teaching a class. Nevertheless, without representation we cannot engage in discourse, nor can we create spaces that, potentially at least, enable others—as well as ourselves—to speak. And without representation, we cannot teach writing or reading, for those acts depend absolutely on a willingness to represent and be represented.

Coda

In this rereading of AA/AI, we have attempted to engage in a series of reflections about what it means to represent audience, and, in doing so, to raise some questions about "successful" discourse, disciplinary critique, and progress. We have looked at AA/AI as an example of "successful" discourse and attempted to examine the nature of that success. In so doing, we have tried to indicate that "success" is—in every case—more charged with tensions, competing motives, and tradeoffs than we had imagined, tensions that, we have been at pains to suggest, can and should inform our teacherly and writerly practices.

In writing this essay we have also attempted to resist the impulse to engage in traditional academic critique by overturning our previous work. We have done so primarily because we have come to feel that such critical maneuvers, while necessary and helpful in many ways, make it particularly easy for us to forget how multiple, heterodox, and situated both teaching and writing are. They also contribute to a rhetoric of disciplinary progress that tends to exempt those effecting critique from inquiry into their own ethical responsibilities and choices. No critical reading can ensure or guarantee that our field will effect positive pedagogical change, and we have no doubt that our analysis has failed to illuminate some of the ethical responsibilities and choices implicit in our earlier work. Nor do we doubt that the essay presented here could be effectively subjected to the same kind of positioning and exploration and critique. (Indeed, some of our reviewers have provided us with the beginnings of such a critique.)

What seems finally most important to us, however, is not the particular product of a particular critique of the intensely self-reflective kind attempted here, but the process, the intellectual habit of mind, necessary to doing so. In the long run, we have written (not to mention rewritten and rewritten) this essay over a period of some two years now because we are trying to enact a practice that can inform our teaching as well as our scholarship. What, after all, do we have to offer our students if we cannot pass out universal laws of correctness, absolute textual meanings, and guarantees of communicative success along with our syllabi? What we have to offer, we believe, is a way of being in language and a way of both inhabiting and shaping knowledge structures, ways that strive to be critically self-reflective, multiperspectival, and complex.

In short, what we have been trying to do here is consonant with what Don Bialostosky argues we must teach our students to do: to interrogate not only the discourses of schooling but personal, communal, and professional discourses as well. For students, the cultivation of such habits of mind can lead, Bialostosky believes, to the development of "double-voiced" texts that are self-reflexive, aware of the situated nature of the words they write and speak (18). Such a pedagogy should, Bialostosky implies, not stop with students' awareness of their own situatedness but instead move toward a commitment to representing themselves as fully and ethically as possible—and toward an increased responsibility for their written and spoken words.

We should not, however, expect our students, as Bialostosky says, "to examine the words they arrive with" unless we ourselves are also engaged in just such an ongoing project (17). It is, we know from experience, much easier to call for scholarly and pedagogical changes than to enact such changes. In a footnote to "Beyond the Personal: Theorizing a Politics of Location in Composition Research," for instance, Kirsch and Ritchie acknowledge "the irony of the text . . . [they] have produced: a relatively univocal, coherent text that argues for experimental, multivocal writing" (27). And we can certainly find similar examples of such unintended discursive irony in texts we have authored or coauthored and in much other "successful" work in our field. Part of the burden of this essay has been to question the grounds of such discursive "success," but to do so in ways that suggest the possibility of non-agonistic disciplinary critique, a critique that we believe necessarily entails self-critique and self-reflection. We are not, however, arguing for the imposition of some "new" singular norm of scholarly practice. Rather, we hope that others will join us in articulating the multiple ways in which scholars may productively "examine the words they arrive with" whenever they engage in the representation of self and audience.

Acknowledgments

We are grateful to friends and colleagues who responded to sometimes wildly varying drafts of this essay: Sharon Crowley, Russell Durst, Tom Fox, Suzanne Clark, Vicki Collins, Cheryl Glenn, Anita Helle, and Gesa Kirsch.

Notes

1. In "Wearing a Pith Helmet at a Sly Angle: or, Can Writing Researchers Do Ethnography in a Postmodern Era?" Ralph Cintron comments, for instance, on the extent to which "academic debates are to a significant degree performances. Differences—and they do exist—push themselves forward by creating caricatures of each other. Although it may seem paradoxical, differences are deeply relational: To denounce the other's position is to announce one's own" (376).

2. Many feminist scholars are working to challenge the generic constraints associated with the traditional academic essay and are claiming the essay, in fact, as a site of intense struggle and exploration. The student writer we invoke in AA/AI is involved in no such struggle, seeking instead to inhabit traditional genres "successfully."

3. We have been particularly aided in recognizing the potential conflicts and contradictions inherent in inhabiting various writerly identities by reading the many works of bell hooks—whose reflections on audience in particular (see, in this regard *Talking Back: Thinking Feminist, Thinking Black*) and literacy in general reflect her powerful understanding of how much is at stake in acts of reading and writing. We are aware of other projects that will help illuminate our understanding of these issues, such as Juanita Comfort's dissertation, "Negotiating Identity in Academic Writing: Experiences of African American Women Doctoral Students."

4. In "On Race and Voice: Challenges for Liberal Education in the 1990s," Chandra Talpade Mohanty makes a similar point when she observes that "if complex structural experiences of domination and resistance can be ideologically reformulated as individual behaviors and attitudes, they can be managed while carrying on business as usual" (157).

Works Cited

Aristotle. *The Rhetoric of Aristotle.* Trans. and ed. Lane Cooper. Englewood Cliffs: Prentice, 1932.

Aronowitz, Stanley, and Henry A. Giroux. *Postmodern Education: Politics, Culture, and Social Criticism.* Minneapolis: U of Minnesota P, 1991.

Bialostosky, Don H. "Liberal Education, Writing, and the Dialogic Self." *Contending with Words: Composition and Rhetoric in a Postmodern Age.* Ed. Patricia Harkin and John Schilb. New York: MLA, 1991. 11–22.

Burke, Kenneth. *Language as Symbolic Action: Essays on Life, Literature, and Method*. Berkeley: U of California P, 1966.

Cintron, Ralph. "Wearing a Pith Helmet at a Sly Angle: or, Can Writing Researchers Do Ethnography in a Postmodern Era?" *Written Communication* 10 (1993): 371–412.

Comfort, Juanita. "Negotiating Identity in Academic Writing: Experiences of African American Women Doctoral Students." Diss. Ohio State U, 1995.

Ede, Lisa, and Andrea Lunsford. "Audience Addressed/Audience Invoked: The Role of Audience in Composition Theory and Pedagogy." *CCC* 35 (1984): 155–71.

Harris, Joseph. "CCC in the 90s." *CCC* 45 (1994): 7–9.

hooks, bell. *Talking Back: Thinking Feminist, Thinking Black*. Boston: South End, 1989.

———. *Yearning: Race, Gender, and Cultural Politics*. Boston: South End, 1990.

Kirsch, Gesa E., and Joy S. Ritchie. "Beyond the Personal: Theorizing a Politics of Location in Composition Research." *CCC* 46 (1995): 7–29.

Long, Russell C. "Writer-Audience Relationships: Analysis or Invention?" *CCC* 31 (1980): 221–26.

Mitchell, Ruth, and Mary Taylor. "The Integrating Perspective: An Audience-Response Model for Writing." *College English* 41 (1979): 247–71.

Mohanty, Chandra Talpade. "On Race and Voice: Challenges for Liberal Education in the 1990s." *Between Borders*. Ed. Henry A. Giroux and Peter McLaren. New York: Routledge, 1994. 145–66.

Ong, Walter J. "The Writer's Audience Is Always a Fiction." *PMLA* 90 (1975): 9–21.

Richards, I. A. *The Philosophy of Rhetoric*. London: Oxford UP, 1936.

Shaughnessy, Mina P. *Errors and Expectations*. New York: Oxford UP, 1977.

Worsham, Lynn. "Writing against Writing: The Predicament of *Ecriture Feminine* in Composition Studies." *Contending with Words: Composition and Rhetoric in a Postmodern Age*. Ed. Patricia Harkin and John Schilb. New York: MLA, 1991. 82–104.

CHAPTER THREE

Among the Audience: On Audience in an Age of New Literacies

ANDREA A. LUNSFORD
Stanford University

LISA EDE
Oregon State University

With participatory media, the boundaries between audiences and creators become blurred and often invisible. In the words of David Sifry, the founder of Technorati, a search engine for blogs, one-to-many "lectures" (i.e., from media companies to their audiences) are transformed into "conversations" among "the people formerly known as the audience."
　　　　　　　—Andrew Kluth, "Among the Audience:
　　　　　　　A Survey of New Media." *The Economist* (4)

Critics argue that privacy does not matter to children who were raised in a wired celebrity culture that promises a niche audience for everyone. Why hide when you can perform? But even if young people are performing, many are clueless about the size of their audience.
　　　　　　　—Ari Melber, "About Facebook." *The Nation* (23)

W hen we wrote "Audience Addressed/Audience Invoked: The Role of Audience in Composition Theory and Pedagogy" (hereafter AA/AI), which was published in *College Composition and Communication* in 1984, we little realized the life that it would have. As the editors of this volume argue, however, much has changed in the teaching of writing—and in the technologies of communication—since then. Much has changed, as well, in our culture and cultural awareness. So much so, in fact, that we saw the need in 1996 to critique our earlier essay, calling attention to several unexamined assumptions that we wished to expose and challenge. In "Representing Audience: Successful Discourse and Disciplinary Critique," published in *College Composition and Communication* in 1996, we observed, for instance, that although we intended our essay "to invoke and address a broad range of audiences, it speaks most strongly to those whose identifications and experiences mirror our own, while turning away from the potential difficulties and costs often inherent in the effort to achieve the kind of academic 'success' that our essay takes for granted as well as from those who would wish to subvert such 'success'" (175).

A dozen years later still, we see the need to reflect yet again on the role of audience in composition theory and pedagogy. In this regard, we are particularly interested in the role that new literacies are playing in expanding the possibilities of agency, while at the same time challenging older notions of both author-ship and audience. In addition, observations of and talks with students—as well as changes in our own reading, writing, and researching practices—have alerted us to new understandings and enactments of textual production and ownership. As a result, our goal in this chapter is both theoretical and pedagogical. We wish to subject the concept of audience to renewed inquiry, attempting to account for the way texts develop and work in the world in the twenty-first century. We hope, as well, that the resulting analysis will be useful in our classrooms. As we conduct this exploration, we will address the following questions:

♦ In a world of participatory media—of Facebook, MySpace, Wikipedia, Twitter, and Del.icio.us—what relevance does the term *audience* hold?

♦ How can we best understand the relationships between text, author, medium, context, and audience today? How can we usefully describe the dynamic of this relationship?

◆ To what extent do the invoked and addressed audiences that we describe in our 1984 essay need to be revised and expanded? What other terms, metaphors, or images might prove productive? What difference might answers to these questions make to twenty-first-century teachers and students?

On New Media and New Literacies

Before turning to these questions, we would like to situate our discussion in the context of recent research on new media and new literacies, for how we view their relationship matters a good deal to our understanding of both audience and authorship. Are new literacies "new" simply because they rely upon new media, or is the relationship more complex? This is a question that Michele Knobel and Colin Lankshear raise in the introduction to their collection, *A New Literacies Sampler*. Knobel and Lankshear argue that the latter is the case. While acknowledging that new media have certainly played an important role in the development of new literacies, they argue that what they term *paradigm cases* of new literacies have, as they put it, both "new 'technical stuff'" and "new 'ethos' stuff" (7). Central to the development of new literacies, in other words, is the mobilization of "very different kinds of values and priorities and sensibilities than the literacies we are familiar with" (7). New literacies, they argue, are "more 'participatory,' 'collaborative,' and 'distributed' in nature than conventional literacies. That is, they are less 'published,' 'individuated,' and 'author-centric' than conventional literacies." They are also "less 'expert-dominated' than conventional literacies" (9).

New literacies involve, in other words, a different kind of mindset than literacies traditionally associated with print media. In their introduction to *A New Literacies Sampler*, Knobel and Lankshear contrast what they refer to as a "physical-industrial" mindset—the mindset that the two of us certainly grew up with throughout our schooling and a good deal of our working lives—with a "cyberspatial-postindustrial mindset" (10). According to Knobel and Lankshear, those whose experience grounds them primarily in a physical-industrial mindset tend to see the individual person as "the unit of production, competence, intelligence." They also identify expertise and authority as "located in individuals and institutions" (11). Those who inhabit a "cyberspatial-postindustrial mindset," in contrast, increasingly focus on "collectives as the unit of production, competence, intelligence" and tend to view expertise, authority, and agency as "distributed and collective" (11). In a "cyberspatial-postindustrial mindset," in other words, the distinction between author and audience is much less clear than in that of the physical-industrial mindset of print literacy.

Those familiar with research in our field on new media and new literacies—research undertaken by scholars such as Cynthia Selfe, Gail Hawisher, Anne Wysocki, Johndan Johnson-Eilola, the New London Group, and others—will recognize that the distinction that Knobel and Lankshear draw has been made before. (They will recognize, as well, the value of complicating this binary, helpful as it is in a general sense.) The insights these and other scholars in our field have generated have been enriched by research in such related areas as literacy, cultural, and Internet studies. In works ranging from Gunther Kress's *Literacy in the New Media Age* to Howard Rheingold's *Smart Mobs: The Next Social Revolution,* Henry Jenkins's *Convergence Culture: Where Old and New Media Collide,* Lisa Nakamura's *Digitizing Race: Visual Cultures of the Internet,* Keith Sawyer's *Group Genius,* and Clay Shirky's *Here Comes Everybody,* those studying online and digital literacies—particularly Web 2.0 literacies—are challenging conventional understandings of both authorship and audience.[1]

As we have engaged this literature and have attempted to better understand what it means to be a reader and writer in the twenty-first century, we have come to see that what we thought of as two separate strands of our scholarly work—one on collaboration, the other on audience—have in fact become one. As writers and audience merge and shift places in online environments, participating in both brief and extended collaborations, it is more obvious than ever that writers seldom, if ever, write alone.

The End of Audience?

In our contemporary world of digital and online literacies, it seems important to question the status and usefulness of the concept of *audience.* Are the changes brought about by new media and new literacies so substantial that it is more accurate to refer to those who participate in Web 2.0 as "the people formerly known as the audience," as David Sifry suggests in the first epigraph to this chapter?

Even before the explosion of such social networking sites as blogs, Facebook, and YouTube, some scholars in the field of rhetoric and writing argued that the term *audience* may have outlived its usefulness. Some suggested, for instance, that the term *discourse community* better reflects social constructionist understandings of communication. This is the position that James Porter espouses in his 1992 *Audience and Rhetoric: An Archaeological Composition of the Discourse Community*. Others have wondered whether the term *public*, as articulated and developed by Jürgen Habermas and explored and extended in Michael Warner's *Publics and Counterpublics*, might not be just as useful as (or more useful than) the term *audience*. In *Citizen Critics: Literary Public Spheres*, for instance, Rosa Eberly argues that the term *public* is more helpful than the terms *reader* or *audience* for her study of letters to the editor about four controversial literary texts—two published early in the twentieth century and two published later.

These and other efforts to reexamine and problematize the concept of audience reflect developments in the field over the last several decades. In the early 1980s when we were talking, thinking, and writing about audience, the need for such problematization was anything but apparent to us. Our context was different. At that time, we were immersed in research on the contemporary relevance of the classical rhetorical tradition, as our 1984 essay "On Distinctions between Classical and Modern Rhetoric" attests. That same year saw the publication of our coedited *Essays on Classical Rhetoric and Modern Discourse*.

In the years since we published AA/AI, we have come to recognize the limitations, as well as the strengths, of the classical (and more broadly Western) rhetorical tradition. In our 1996 reflection on AA/AI, "Representing Audience," for example, we acknowledge the individualism inherent in this tradition. We also point out that the rhetorical tradition's commitment to *successful* communication has exacted a high hidden price, particularly in terms of efforts to address the ethics of diversity: "For how better to avoid misunderstanding and failure (and to make 'successful' communication more likely) than to exclude, to disenfranchise those who by their very presence in the arena of discourse raise increased possibilities for communicative failures" (174). The rhetorical tradition, as a consequence, risks indifference or hostility to issues of difference, to "audiences ignored, rejected, excluded, or denied" (174).

Does this mean that we wish to reject the term *audience?* No, it does not. We believe that *audience*, like such other terms as *discourse community* or *public*, is inevitably overdetermined, but is still (as is the case with these other terms) in many contexts both helpful and productive. Finally, terms such as *audience, reader, discourse community*, and *public* gesture toward and evoke differing concerns, traditions, and interests. The emphasis on the reader in reader response criticism, for instance, was clearly a salutary response to the emphasis on the text in formalist new criticism.[2]

We continue to believe, then, that the concept of audience provides a helpful theoretical and practical grounding for efforts to understand how texts (and writers and readers) work in today's world. We also believe, as we stated in AA/AI, that a productive way to conceive of audience "is as an overdetermined or unusually rich concept, one which may perhaps be best specified through the analysis of precise, concrete situations" (168). Indeed, in rereading AA/AI we are struck by the powerful role that the analysis of such situations plays in our own essay. As readers may already realize, in remaining committed to the term *audience* we remain committed to rhetoric and to the rhetorical tradition. Our understanding of the rhetorical tradition has changed since we first wrote AA/AI, but we continue to find rhetoric's emphasis on the rhetorical situation to be theoretically and pedagogically enabling.

The "Rhetorical Triangle" Revisited

In AA/AI we described our own experiences with varying audiences, arguing that "the elements [of invoked and addressed audience roles] shift and merge, depending on the particular rhetorical situation, the writer's aim, and the genre chosen" (168). Thus we embedded our discussion of audience in the classical conception of the "rhetorical triangle," the set of relationships between text, author, and audience out of which meaning grows. Twenty-five years ago, while our work attempted to complicate these sets of relationships, this basic understanding served us simply and well. Today, however, we need a more flexible and robust way of understanding these traditional elements of discourse and the dynamic at work among them.

As a result, we now use the following figure (Figure 3.1) to portray the basic elements of the rhetorical situation.

This figure not only specifies medium as an element of the rhetorical situation but also includes context. This element of the rhetorical situation calls attention to the diverse and multiple factors that writers must consider when they compose—from generic or situational constraints to ideologies that make some writerly choices seem obvious and "natural," while others are "unnatural" or entirely hidden from view.

As this figure suggests, the relationship between writer and message and medium (or media) is complex and full of reciprocity. In a digital world, and especially in the world of Web 2.0, speakers and audiences communicate in multiple ways and across multiple channels, often reciprocally. And this momentous shift has challenged not only traditional models of communication but also the relationship between "creators" of messages and those who receive them. Today, as we have pointed out, the roles of writers and audiences often conflate, merge, and shift.

The deeply participatory nature of electronic forms of communication provides new opportunities for writerly agency, even as it challenges notions of intellectual property that have held sway now for more than three hundred years, leading—as we have been at pains to point out in our research on collaboration and collaborative writing—both to diverse forms of multiple authorship and to the kind of mass authorship that characterizes sites such as Wikipedia and Google News. To say that the music and film industries, along with some print-based companies, are resisting such shifts in authorship and its embeddedness in traditional intellectual property regimes is an understatement. While these entities will continue to cling to regimes of the past, it seems clear that new ways of managing the relationship between texts, "authors," media, contexts, and audiences are emerging. In this regard, consider the alternative rock group Radiohead's decision

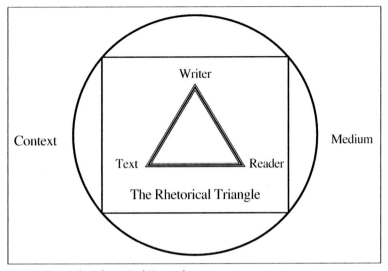

FIGURE 3.1. *The Rhetorical Triangle.*

to release its seventh album, *In Rainbows*, as a digital download on the Internet. Fans of this group could purchase the DVD on the Web—and they were completely free to pay whatever price they wished for the album.[3]

In *The Economics of Attention*, Richard Lanham argues that we have moved from what he calls a "stuff economy" (one based on material goods) to a "fluff economy" (one based on immaterial information). With his typical humor and verve, Lanham shows that while in a "stuff" economy scarcity is the major economic principle at work, that principle utterly fails in a "fluff" economy, where information is anything but scarce. In fact, as Lanham points out, we are drowning in it. In such an economy, what is needed, according to Lanham, is *attention*—that is, a way of attending sensibly to the information pouring in:

> In an attention economy, the center of gravity for property shifts from real property to intellectual property. This shift has plunged us into confusions about the ownership of such property . . . that it will take some time to sort out. . . . Information, unlike stuff, can be both kept and given away at the same time. As long as the means of notation were fixed in physicality as books, reported, painted images, we could gloss over this major

obstacle: that "possession" means something different from a private property in stuff. Now, with information expressed on a digital screen, with its new means of dissemination, we can no longer continue this gloss. Hence the current agonies in the music and film business. They have been caught in a vise, squeezed between the macro and the micro economics of attention. (259)

We too are caught between the macro and micro economies of attention, since we cannot ignore the world of "stuff." But we are clearly in what Lanham calls a "revisionist" way of thinking. "Our locus of reality has shifted," he argues. "We have not left the physical world behind and become creatures of pure attention. Neither has wealth become totally disembodied. Our view is now bi-stable. We must always be ready to move from one view of the world to another. They are always competing with each other. We are learning to live in two worlds at once" (258). In a time of transition, some workers are differentially advantaged or disadvantaged—a fact which reminds us that in an attention economy we also need to be aware of possible inequities and of differing degrees of access to that economy.

As Lanham's discussion suggests, writers who want and need to shift among worlds must be able to hold flexible views of the real and potential relationships between text, context, author, medium, and audience. They must be able to negotiate distinctions between writing and reading, between author and audience that refuse to remain stable; they must also be able to sort out the competing claims of words, images, and sounds in choosing the best medium or media of communication. And they must also become comfortable with new ways of thinking about property, about ownership of the messages that are created amidst the dynamic interaction of writers, audiences, and media.

In many ways, our students are already experienced inhabitors of Lanham's two worlds, and they are increasingly comfortable with new ways of thinking about textual ownership. Such new ways began to emerge in interviews with students conducted during the Stanford Study of Writing (SSW), when researchers asked the students about their views on intellectual property. These interviews, which took place between 2001 and 2006, revealed what at first felt like a hard-to-describe, nebulous change: the best the researchers could say was that something seemed to be happening to the way students thought about intellectual property and ownership. But more recent analyses of the transcripts of some 150 interviews indicate the kind of flexible shifting back and forth described above.

Perhaps one vivid example will serve to limn this shift in understanding and attitude. One participant in the study, Mark Otuteye, wrote a poem during the first weeks of his frosh year. Titled "The Admit Letter," this poem was performed by Mark later that year during Parents' Weekend: it opens with a "so-called friend" saying to Mark, "Oh sure, you got into Stanford: you're Black." What follows is Mark's imagining of what his "so-called friend" thought his admit letter might have said. The two imaginary versions of the admit letter that Mark performs are biting—and very, very funny; together, they not only put the so-called friend in his place but also manage to send up the university as well. On the Stanford campus, news of this poem spread like proverbial wildfire, and Mark was called on to perform it in numerous venues. In one such venue, the poem changed significantly: now it was performed by Mark and a Chicana student, who powerfully wove together versions of their "admit letters."

"The Admit Letter" went through additional permutations during Mark's college career, and during one of the interviews with him SSW researchers asked him, "So is this poem yours? Do you own it?" In a lengthy conversation, Mark said that he considered the poem to be his—but not exclusively his; in fact, he said, his work is usually written and performed collaboratively, and he sees it as part of a large poetic commons. In short, this student was already effectively moving between the information and the attention world, and he was comfortable writing with as well as for others, in a range of media. For Mark, and for many other students in this study, what has seemed at times to us the perplexing fluidity and even tension between writer, text, context, medium, and audience feels to them like home turf. This home turf is not without its potential dangers and challenges, however. As we discuss in a later section of this chapter, problems can arise if students fail to differentiate between the constraints and opportunities inherent in their self-sponsored writing and those of the academic rhetorical situation.

Taxonomizing Audiences

When we wrote AA/AI, we literally could not have imagined the textual and material world we inhabit today. At that time, we were attempting to intervene in a then-contemporary debate over audience. In our effort to understand and give coherence to this debate, we grouped various scholars' work on audience under two constructs, that of audience invoked and audience addressed. (Since AA/AI is included in this collection, we will not summarize these positions here.) If reprintings and references to AA/AI are any indication, others have found the constructs of audience addressed/invoked useful. But we are also aware that the impulse to taxonomize—to create binaries and various other sorts of categories—has disadvantages as well as advantages. Indeed, the felt need to go beyond addressed and invoked audiences to acknowledge audiences that are "ignored, rejected, excluded, or denied" motivated our effort to look again at AA/AI when we wrote "Representing Audience" (174).

A quarter of a century after AA/AI was published, we want to look again at these two constructs to determine what relevance they hold in an age of new media and new literacies.[4] When we look at our earlier work, we continue to value the way that the constructs of audience addressed and audience invoked enable us to call attention to "(1) the fluid, dynamic character of rhetorical situations; and (2) the integrated, interdependent nature of reading and writing" (156). We value as well the extent to which they discourage overly stark binaries—such as those that posit sharp dichotomies between speaking and writing. In AA/AI we point out, for instance, that Walter Ong's representative situations (in "The Writer's Audience Is Always a Fiction") of "the orator addressing a mass audience versus a writer alone in a room" will always "oversimplify the potential range and diversity of both oral and written communication situations" (161).

If this statement was true in 1984, it is even more compelling today with the proliferation of electronic and online media and social networking programs. Increasingly, for instance, students in our writing classes post messages to course blogs and/or contribute to wikis. When they compose academic texts, they may well insert images and sound, or provide tables or spreadsheets with supporting information. When we turn from students' academic writing to their self-sponsored communication, the possibilities explode—including everything from instant messaging and texting to blogging, creating text and images on Facebook and MySpace (and commenting on others' pages) to posting photos on Flickr and sharing tags on del.icio.us.

As we noted earlier in this chapter, these kinds of participatory communications challenge conventional understandings of both authorship and audience, even as they provide an opportunity for anyone and everyone to become both author and audience, writer and reader.[5] But do they invalidate the general constructs of audience addressed and audience invoked that we established in AA/AI? In the most general sense, the kinds of participatory communication that we have just described can, we believe, be encompassed within these two categories—which, we argue in AA/AI, are best understood as a dialogic pair.

Consider, in this regard, our experience writing this chapter. Rather than relying on the technologies of telephone, electric correcting typewriter, and photocopy machines (technologies essential to the composition of AA/AI), we relied on contemporary electronic technologies, particularly email and the Web. Yet our experience composing this text still required us to negotiate both addressed and invoked audiences. In short, we find that the categories of invoked and addressed audiences still inform the much more complex online communicating we do today. As we post to listservs, look for items on YouTube that we can use in our classes, or participate in a wiki devoted to developing an accreditation report for one of our institutions, we are conscious of both addressed and invoked audiences. In the case of the accreditation report, some thirty members of a task force are contributing to this document, which is addressed directly to the accreditation board. In a more indirect way, this document is also addressed to all members of our team and to our upper administrators as well. But to address these audiences, and especially the first one, we must invoke the accreditation board, which we have done very carefully and cautiously: a lot is at stake in our getting this particular invocation right.

Having said this, we need to acknowledge that precisely because the constructs of audience addressed and audience invoked are so broad and encompassing, they can only take us so far in our understanding of audience, including contemporary online and electronic audiences.[6] Thus while we hope that the constructs of audience addressed and audience invoked will continue to prove useful as a means of understanding the rich and overdetermined concept of audience, we find ourselves with many questions about audiences as they are addressed and invoked today. What motivates someone who has read Barbara Kingsolver's *The Poisonwood Bible* to write a review and add it to the 1,398 customer reviews that, at the time we wrote this chapter, were posted on Amazon.com—and what audiences does such a review address and/or invoke? How can we best understand the relationships among the photographers who as of that same day had posted 27,569 photos of black Labs on Flickr, tagging them so that other audiences with a similar passion for this breed of dog can easily find them?[7] What kind of a relationship (if any) might we be forming with a photographer who has contributed photos and tags to Flickr if we click on his or her contacts, profile, or public groups, or if we comment on a photo that we find particularly compelling? How do we envision or invoke this photographer, and how is such an invocation related to a decision to address the photographer directly or not?

How can we best understand what Henry Jenkins in *Fans, Bloggers, and Gamers: Exploring Participatory Culture* refers to as "the interactive audience" (136)? Those communicating with such audiences must necessarily both address and invoke each other. But having said that, what more might we add? How does the technology of gaming or blogging, for example, ignore or exclude certain audiences? What ideological positions may be unspoken in such activities? How can we avoid the utopian/dystopian ways in which audiences and members of new online communities are often framed, both in the popular press and in more serious scholarly work? In attempting to answer this last question, Jenkins observes that "the interactive audience is more than a marketing concept and less than a 'semiotic democracy'" (136). Jenkins's comment suggests that interactive or participatory audiences fall somewhere along a continuum, from those who consume media and content on the Web in fairly traditional ways to the full shared agency characteristic of many online communities.

We have additional issues and questions as well. In an online, participatory culture, the concerns that we articulated in "Representing Audience" about audiences "ignored, rejected, excluded, or denied" become even more salient (174).[8] As we will discuss more fully in the next section, many students easily forget that when they post something on the Web, they may encounter unwanted audiences—such as an employer checking their Facebook or MySpace entries or a researcher checking on their use of his or her scholarly work.

These questions suggest potential limitations of the constructs of audience addressed and audience invoked. We believe that these constructs can usefully remind us of the rich complexity of any form of communication, written or spoken, print or online. But as we have suggested, they are too general to directly address questions such as the ones we have just articulated. These questions require the kind of "analysis of precise, concrete situations" that we call for near the end of AA/AI (168).[9] Such work is currently being done, most often in qualitative studies that require the depth and breadth of ethnography. One powerful example of such work occurs in Angela Thomas's chapter "Blurring and Breaking through the Boundaries of Narrative, Literacy, and Identity in Adolescent Fan Fiction" in Knobel and Lankshear's *New Literacies Sampler*. In this four-year ethnographic study, Thomas explores the experiences of two adolescent females: "Tiana, aged 14 years, and Jandalf, aged 17 years, friends who met online and who have been collaboratively writing fan fiction for over a year" (139). These two young authors prove to be exceptional in a number of ways, including the degree of self-reflexivity and flexibility that they exhibit. In characterizing their writing, both individual and collaborative, Thomas observes that Tiana and Jandalf move successfully "in and out of media type, text type, form, style, and literary device with an ease and poetry of linguistic dexterity that is truly exceptional" (151). In doing so, they assume a range of audience roles for each other, taking turns, for example, at role-playing as they develop the outlines of plots and of characters for their fan fiction. Tiana explains: "when I transcribe over, I sort of become two people—Tiana and a narrator. I make myself see things from a third-person POV [point of view] while still writing as my characters" (144). In describing the many kinds of writing the pair undertakes, Thomas mentions "the role-playing, the out-of-character discussions occurring synchronously within the role-playing, the character journals, the artwork, the careful plotting out of story lines, the forum discussions, the descriptions of worlds and cultures, the invention of language, the playful spoofing, the in-role poetry, the metatextual allusions to sound effects, movie techniques" (145).[10] As this example suggests, understanding the complexity of writing processes, audience awareness, and participation calls for a much more specific, grounded, and nuanced analysis than the binary of addressed and invoked audiences can provide.

Teaching Audience in the Twenty-First Century

Imagine this: A student in a required writing class composes a research-based argument and then presents an oral version of the argument as part of a panel at an in-class "conference" held at the end of the term. The teacher of the class creates a website and posts all of the student arguments on it, inviting response. Two years later, the teacher gets a response from a professor at another university, pointing out that the student's argument drew on the professor's work, citing that work but often failing to enclose directly quoted passages within quotation marks. The professor demands that the student's argument be taken off the website, accusing the student of sloppy habits at best, plagiarism at worst. Notified of this turn of events, the student—now a prospective graduating senior—is completely surprised: he had not meant to plagiarize, and he certainly had not imagined that one of his sources would go to the trouble of accessing his essay.

Like many others, this student experiences the Internet and many of its sites as fairly private, when the reality is that audiences are there all the time, browsing, searching, engaging, responding, sometimes accusing. Many have commented on the breakdown between private and public today and on the somewhat contradictory attitudes students hold: they often say they are comfortable being in public and that a public stance comes with the territory of digital communication. But they also sometimes view sites—especially social networking sites such as Facebook—as relatively private, away from the prying eyes of parents and other unwanted audiences. We had these students in mind when we quoted Ari Melber at the opening of this chapter: "Critics argue that privacy does not matter to children who were raised in a wired celebrity culture that promises a niche audience for everyone. Why hide when you can perform? But even if young people are performing, many are clueless about the size of their audience" (23).

Clearly, even though many of our students are digital natives, they nevertheless need to become more knowledgeable about the nature and complexity of the audiences for whom they perform, particularly as they shift back and forth from self-sponsored online writing to academic writing. The first lesson we draw from grappling with the questions we pose in this chapter, then, is that we have a responsibility to join with our students in rich and detailed explorations of just what "audience" can mean in their writing and in their lives. Such explorations might well begin with unpacking the problematics of viewing the teacher as the audience for student writing. As the real-life example earlier suggests, the teacher remains *an* audience for student texts, but by no means the only audience, especially when student writing is posted on the Web. Even if it is not posted, student writing often invokes and addresses audiences well beyond the teacher (who is also, often, both addressed and invoked).

Beyond unpacking the concept of teacher as audience, teachers can help students understand the contemporary complexities of audience by providing case studies that exemplify various kinds of audiences. The participatory audience of peer review, for instance, can be theorized and interrogated by students in their composition classes: that is, rather than simply responding to one another, they can take time to get to know these real-life audiences, along with the assumptions and values they bring to their fellow students' texts, literally examining where these members of the audience are coming from. Or students can create a genealogy of audiences for a particular social networking site, exploring the many diverse individuals and groups that have access to the site and asking which audiences the site invokes and which it seems to address. Students could examine the many issues raised, for instance, by various Pro Ana (pro anorexia) sites on the Web. Who are the sponsors of these sites? Just what kind of collaborative relationships are being invoked and addressed by those who post to and read this site?

As we have noted in this chapter, what began for us as two different strands of research—one on audience, another on collaboration—have all but merged during the last couple of years as we have seen how frequently writers become audiences and vice versa. Yet more often than not, students resist collaboration in their schoolwork even as they collaborate constantly in their out-of-class online writing. There are reasons for this seeming contradiction or tension: school writing is part of a deeply individualistic system that rewards individual students through a system of grades and points and values the individual GPA; working collaboratively runs counter to that system. But while we work to change the hyper-individualistic base of higher education in the United States, we need also to engage students in intense discussions of this issue. As we have been arguing for some time, we know that most of the innovative work that gets done in the world today gets done in collaborative groups (see Sawyer, Tapscott and Williams, Sunstein, Ede and Lunsford)—including, increasingly, teams that work primarily online. And we know that colleges and universities, for reasons mentioned earlier, are doing very little to prepare students to thrive in such an environment (see Bok, Light). We need to do more, then, than *assign* collaborative projects: we need to provide a theoretical rationale for such projects along with data to support it. In addition, we need to craft collaborative projects that will engage every member of the group and guide the group in analyzing their work together from beginning to end. And we need to join with students in exploring the use of free collaborative writing tools such as Google Docs or Writeboard.

We also need to consider the impact that new literacies are having—and should have—in our teaching. Such literacies often call for producing new texts, often referred to as "new media" texts. The question of whether and how to teach such new media writing poses significant challenges to teachers of writing today. Thanks to the work of Anne Wysocki, Johndan Johnson Eilola, Cynthia Selfe, and Geoffrey Sirc, we have excellent examples of the kinds of new media writing students are doing today, both inside and outside of the classroom. In one chapter in the collaborative *Writing New Media,* Cynthia Selfe points out the double-edged sword that comes along with new media texts as she tells the story of David, a young man who teaches himself to produce effective new media texts only to fail his college classes because of his inability to create acceptable traditional print texts. The point Selfe makes is one all teachers of writing need to heed: we must help our students to learn to conceive and produce a repertoire of texts, from the convincing academic argument to the compelling website or memorable radio essay. (Selfe has also recently published a helpful guide for teachers: *Multimodal Composition: Resources for Teachers.*)

It is important to acknowledge the difficulties inherent in taking on such a task. At Stanford, when the Faculty Senate mandated that the Program in Writing and Rhetoric (PWR) develop a new second-level course that would go beyond academic writing to embrace oral presentations with multimedia support, the PWR teaching staff responded with great enthusiasm. By the time they began piloting courses to equally enthusiastic students, the sky seemed to be the limit: students wanted to write and produce hour-long documentaries; to produce NPR-quality audio essays; to design, write, and produce online magazines; not to mention creating texts to be performed in a wide range of settings. By the end of the second quarter of the pilot, however, both teachers and students realized that their reach had clearly exceeded their grasp. Most notably, the writing that students were doing as they worked their way toward new media texts was declining in quality—and everyone saw it. As a result, before the new course was fully implemented, the teaching staff, working in conjunction with the Undergraduate Advisory Board, pulled back from some of their ambitions, focusing the course first on producing a research-based argument and then working the rest of the term to "translate" that argument into various genres and media.

In answer to our question, "What difference might answers to [the three questions we pose at the beginning of this chapter] make to twenty-first-century teachers and students?" we can sum up by saying, "A lot, a whole lot." In this section of our essay, we have explored several important implications for teaching the concept of audience in the twenty-first century, the most important of which is to engage our students in analyzing and theorizing the new literacies themselves, especially as they call for collaboration, for new understandings of audience, and for a robust ethics of communication. But as this discussion has suggested, we are simply not at a point where we can draw absolute conclusions about what writing teachers should do in this age of new literacies.

Ethics and Participatory Literacies

As we have worked on this chapter, we have found ourselves meditating on audiences across the millennia—the audiences who gathered before the ancient Greek rhapsodes, who "read" the scriptures along with literate scribes in the medieval period, who sat among the groundlings at the Globe and other Elizabethan theaters, who waited in rapt anticipation for the next issue of the latest Dickens novel, who gathered at whistle-stops throughout the United States to engage with political hopefuls, who cheered their teams to victory, and who today log on to check in with Facebook friends or read and comment on their favorite blog. In some ways, there has always been a relational or participatory quality to audiences. Yet it seems clear that changes in technology and other material conditions that have brought us to the present moment have opened avenues for audiences to take on agency and to become participants and creators/shapers of discourse in more profound ways than ever before.

In making this comment, we do not intend to join those who characterize the Web and social networking sites in utopian terms. If there is one thing we have learned from our study of the rhetorical tradition, it is that the nature and consequence of any act of communication can never be determined in advance and that inquiry into issues such as these requires a deeply situated, finely tuned analysis. When consumers post reviews to Amazon. com, for instance, are they expanding their possibilities for agency and for collaborations with others or are they serving as unpaid volunteer workers for this ever-expanding company? There are no simple, decontextualized answers to questions such as these.

Our engagement with the rhetorical tradition, as well as our study of the history of communicative technologies, thus reminds us that both utopian and dystopian views of our current moment are likely to oversimplify. They also remind us of how difficult it is to predict how various communication technologies will be employed. The earliest graphic symbols, it is good to remember, were used for accounting, not writing. We might consider in this regard Twitter, a free online social networking program that allows individuals to send brief, frequent messages to each other. Twitter limits these messages to 140 characters and suggests that those employing this software post regularly in response to this question: "What are you doing?" The intended use of Twitter is fairly obvious: those who want to keep in touch can quickly and easily use this program to do so. Who would have expected, then, that some users of Twitter would decide that this program provides the perfect online space to write haiku, much less that the haiku created on Twitter would hail an avid audience? Just how much interest is there in the world today in Twitter haiku? We can't know for sure, but a quick check on Google instantly pulled up 269,000 hits. In searching the Web, we have also found numerous references to Twitter contests. One frequent challenge invites writers to compose micro-essays and micro-stories limited to Twitter's 140 characters. In case you're interested, a search on Google using the term *Twitter contests* generated 554,000 hits. Here's what one Twitter user, Calvin Jones, posted to his website Digital Marketing Success about his fascination with Twitter: "I love the way twitter makes you condense your writing, squeezing the maximum out of every character. Here's my swiftly penned missive: She paused, shivering involuntarily; the wave of adrenalin surged through her, leaving her giddy and disoriented. It was quiet. He was gone!" Twitter was released to the public in October 2006, and we conducted these Google searches in late May 2008. Thus does a software program designed to help friends, coworkers, and family members keep in touch devolve in lightning speed on the Web, making a space for readers to become writers who then become invoked and addressed audience members for still other writer/readers.

What if a friend or family member prefers not to know what someone close (or not so close) to them is doing throughout the day? Twitter.com addresses this at the level of software architecture—one must sign up for Twitter to receive messages—and via its settings feature. But surely ethical issues remain. Twitter can be used to help groups gather quickly, whether for positive purposes (engaging in civic discussion or action) or negative. How can those interested in participating in this social networking site best understand their responsibilities as writers and audiences for others?

At its strongest and most productive moments, the rhetorical tradition has acknowledged the potentially powerful ethical implications inherent in any act of communication. As we conclude this discussion of audience in an age of new literacies, then, we turn to several other ethical questions that seem most compelling to us as teachers and scholars. Perhaps most important, in a world of participatory media, it seems essential for teachers and students to consider the multiple reciprocal responsibilities entailed in writer-audience relationships. What does a student writer posting to Facebook owe to all the potential audiences of that post, from a former partner to a potential employer? And what responsibilities do audiences have toward those whose messages they receive, seek, reject, or encounter? One goal of future research on audience must surely be to explore the ethical dimensions of such relationships.

It seems equally important for scholars, teachers, and students to collaboratively explore the increasingly complex issue of plagiarism/patchwriting in an online world.[11] As the example earlier, about the professor who found his work used without proper attribution in a student essay on a class website, demonstrates, the ease of cutting and pasting and the wide availability of a multitude of sources make holding to traditional norms of scholarly citation increasingly difficult or even problematic. While students we know roundly condemn buying or downloading a paper wholesale from a website as unacceptable cheating, they are much more ambivalent about using a form of sampling in their writing, and they are downright resistant to the need for what they often think of as excessive (or even obsessive) citation: if you go to the Web with a question and get thousands of "hits" in answer to it, they say, shouldn't that answer be considered as common knowledge that doesn't need to be cited? And even if we answer "no" to that question, which one of the thousands of sources should be *the* one to be cited? These questions and the issues they raise suggest that we must not only continue to explore student understandings of intellectual property but also to engage them in a full discussion of where academic citation practices came from, why they have been so deeply valued, and what is at stake in developing alternative practices—such as a much broader definition of "common knowledge" or ways of distributing citation credit across a wide range of contributor/authors.

Another potential ethical problem that contemporary audiences must address has quite diverse origins and implications: what are the consequences for civic discourse of a world in which those interested in a specific topic or audience can easily find sites where they can communicate with like-minded individuals, where our culture seems to promise, as Ari Melbur observes, "a niche audience for everyone" (23)? Is our culture likely to fragment into what legal scholar Cass R. Sunstein refers to as "information cocoons" (9), and how can we best understand and enact an appropriate relationship between privacy and free speech on the Web? One place to turn in exploring this set of ethical issues is the extensive work on public discourse being pursued by many scholars in rhetoric and communication studies.[12] Another strategy is to encourage (even inspire) students to build bridges between the seemingly private voices they inhabit online and the public ones they can establish, to move from the kind of personal opinions found ubiquitously online to a truly public opinion they can help to create and sustain.

In his 2007 "Vision of the Future," Howard Rheingold notes the need for parents and students alike to take responsibility for the ethical and moral choices they make in reading and writing online. Rheingold is primarily interested in how young people can get beyond the small niches of the Web to participate most effectively in online settings. Noting that while students today are "naturals" when it comes to point-and-click explorations yet "there's nothing innate about knowing how to apply their skills to the processes of democracy" (4), Rheingold calls on teachers to help students make connections "between the literacies students pick up simply by being young in the 21st century and those best learned through reading and discussing texts" (5). We can help students make such connections, Rheingold argues, by allowing them to move "from a private to a public voice" that will help them "turn their self-expression into a form of public participation" (5). Public voice, Rheingold insists, is "learnable, a matter of consciously engaging with an active public rather than broadcasting to a passive audience" (5).

Thus, while Rheingold recognizes the potential for fragmentation, for performing only for small niche audiences, and for existing "information cocoons," he also sees the potential for developing participatory public opinion that can "be an essential instrument of democratic self-governance." We believe that Rheingold is right to argue that if we want such public voices to arise, we must teach to and for them. And along with Rheingold, we recognize that teaching to and for new publics and public voices calls for "a whole new way of looking at learning and teaching" (7) that will, we believe, require close attention to the ethical issues raised by new literacies and new media. It will also call for resisting the dichotomy between those who dream utopian dreams of a vast collective and participatory democracy enabled by Web 2.0 and those who bemoan a collapse into fragmentation and solipsism that can come from talking only with those who already think just as you do.

At its strongest moments, the Western rhetorical tradition, however flawed, has encouraged both writers and teachers of writing to take a deeply situated perspective on communication—and thus to challenge the kind of binaries that we have just described. Whenever we write, read, speak, or (as Krista Ratcliffe has so eloquently reminded us) listen, there are no guarantees that either the process or the outcome will be ethical. This is an understanding that we can—and should—bring with us when we enter our classrooms, especially our first-year writing classrooms. For there we have the opportunity to help our students experience the intellectual stimulation and excitement, as well as the responsibility, of engaging and collaborating with multiple audiences from peers to professors, as well as addressed and invoked audiences of all kinds.

Notes

1. We use the term *Web 2.0* here and elsewhere recognizing that some

have argued that this term is inaccurate and/or hyperbolic. In an interview posted on IBM's developerWorks site, for instance, Tim Berners-Lee argues that Web 2.0 is "a piece of jargon, nobody even knows what it means. If Web 2.0 for you is blogs and wikis, then that is people to people [as opposed to Web 1, which is sometimes described as computer to computer]. . . . But that was what the Web was supposed to be all along." Berners-Lee prefers to use the term *Semantic Web* rather than Web 2.0.

2. Two recent monographs helpfully remind us of the differing concerns, traditions, and interests that scholars have brought to the concept of audience. The first study, Mary Jo Rieff's 1994 *Approaches to Audience: An Overview of the Major Perspectives*, chronicles the development of research on audience within English studies in general and rhetoric and writing in particular. The second study, Denis McQuail's 1997 monograph *Audience Analysis*, is written from the perspective of communication studies, particularly mass communication and cultural studies.

3. After making their album available on the Web, Radiohead also released their music as a conventional CD.

4. Other scholars have also examined these constructs in helpful ways. We would particularly like to call attention to Robert Johnson's "Audience Involved: Toward a Participatory Model of Writing," Jack Selzer's "More Meanings of Audience," Rosa Eberly's "From Writers, Audiences, and Communities to Publics: Writing Classrooms as Protopublic Spaces," Mary Jo Reiff's "Rereading 'Invoked' and 'Addressed' Readers through a Social Lens: Toward a Recognition of Multiple Audiences," and the essays published in Gesa Kirsch and Duane H. Roen's edited collection *A Sense of Audience in Written Communication*. Though space limitations do not allow us to discuss these studies, we have benefited from these authors' analyses and critiques.

5. In "Agency and Authority in Role-Playing Texts," Jessica Hammer identifies three kinds of authorship in video games: primary, secondary, and tertiary. As Hammer notes, "The primary author develops a world and a set of rules," while "the secondary author takes the work of the primary author and uses it to construct a specific situation or scenario[;] . . . . the tertiary authors, then, 'write' the text of the game in play" (71).

6. In *Audience Analysis,* for instance, Denis McQuail helpfully identifies the following dimensions of audience: "degree of activity or passivity; degree of interactivity and interchangeability; size and duration; located-ness in space; group character (social/cultural identity); simultaneity of contact with source; heterogeneity of composition; social relations be-

tween sender and receiver; message versus social/behavioral definition of situation; degree of 'social presence'; sociability of context of use" (150).

7. Such tagging is, of course, an imprecise art. On the day that we searched Flickr with the term *black labs*, the sixth photo that appeared was of a black Lab cookie. The twenty-third and twenty-fourth photos were titled "Black Phoenix Alchemy Lab" and "Black and White Photo Lab." Neither photo was of a black Labrador retriever. And needless to say, these anomalous photos undoubtedly address and invoke different audiences than do those of real live black Labs.

8. In *Rhetorical Refusals: Defying Audiences' Expectations*, John Schilb examines cases in which speakers and writers intentionally defy audience expectations.

9. Scholars in such areas as media and cultural studies, communication, sociology, and anthropology have undertaken research in media reception and audience ethnography. For an introduction to this interdisciplinary body of work, see Pertti Alasuutari's *Rethinking the Media Audience: The New Agenda*. Representative studies include Virginia Nightingale's *Studying Audiences: The Shock of the Real*, S. Elizabeth Bird's *The Audience in Everyday Life: Living in a Media World*, and Will Brooker and Deborah Jermyn's *The Audience Studies Reader*.

10. Thomas goes on to observe that "[i]n addition to exploring the scope of the narrative worlds of the fan fiction, it is important to note that the girls also produce multimodal texts to enhance their fan fiction, making avatars (images to represent themselves) for role-playing, making visual signatures as can be seen at the side and end of each post on the forum . . . , finding icons to reflect mood, creating music bytes, making fan fiction posters in the form of an advertisement and teaser, and creating mini movie trailers using their own spliced-together combination of existing movie clips, music, voiceovers, and text. They also draw maps and room plans of their world, draw and paint scenery, and sketch images of their many characters. As well as hand-drawn sketches, they create digital images, digital colorizations or enhancements of their sketches, or purely digitally created images" (150–51).

11. Rebecca Howard has written extensively and compellingly about the developmental nature of what she calls "patchwriting" as well as about the ways in which students and teachers understand (and often misunderstand) plagiarism.

12. Several essays in Section IV of *The Sage Handbook of Rhetorical Studies* explore such issues; see, especially, Gurak and Antonijevic and Beasley.

Works Cited

Alasuutari, Pertti, Ed. *Rethinking the Media Audience: The New Agenda.* London: Sage, 1999.

Ang, Ien. *Livingroom Wars: Rethinking Audiences for a Postmodern World.* New York: Routledge, 1995.

Beasley, Vanessa. "Between Touchstones and Touchscreens: What Counts as Contemporary Political Rhetoric." *The Sage Handbook of Rhetorical Studies.* Ed. Andrea A. Lunsford, Kirt Wilson, and Rosa Eberly. Thousand Oaks, CA: Sage P, 2009.

Bird, S. Elizabeth. *The Audience in Everyday Life: Living in a Media World.* New York: Routledge, 2003.

Bok, Derek. *Our Underachieving Colleges.* Princeton, NJ: Princeton UP, 2006.

Brooker, Will, and Deborah Jermyn, eds. *The Audience Studies Reader.* London: Routledge, 2003.

Eberly, Rosa. *Citizen Critics: Literary Public Spheres.* Urbana, IL: U Illinois P, 2000.

Ede, Lisa, and Andrea A. Lunsford. *Singular Texts / Plural Authors: Perspectives on Collaborative Writing.* Carbondale, IL: Southern Illinois UP, 2000.

Gurak, Laura, and Smiljana Antonijevic. "Digital Rhetoric and Public Discourse." *The Sage Handbook of Rhetorical Studies.* Ed. Andrea A. Lunsford, Kirt Wilson, and Rosa Eberly. Thousand Oaks, CA: Sage P, 2009.

Hammer, Jessica. "Agency and Authority in Role-Playing Texts." *A New Literacies Sampler.* Ed. Michele Knobel and Colin Lankshear. New York: Peter Lang, 2007. 67–94.

Howard, Rebecca Moore. *Standing in the Shadow of Giants: Plagiarists, Authors, Collaborators.* Stamford, CT: Ablex, 1999.

Jones, Calvin. "Twitter Story Competition." Blog entry.23 May 2008. Digital Marketing Success. 5 June 2008 <http://www.digitalmarketingsuccess.com/twitter-story-competition/ >.

Kluth, Andrew. "Among the Audience: A Survey of New Media." *The Economist* 20 Apr. 2006.

Knobel, Michele, and Colin Lankshear. *A New Literacies Sampler*. New York: Peter Lang, 2007.

Kress, Gunther. *Literacy in the New Media Age*. New York: Routledge, 2003.

Lanham, Richard A. *The Economics of Attention: Style and Substance in the Age of Information*. Chicago: U Chicago P, 2006.

Laningham, Scott. "Interview with Tim Berners-Lee." 22 August 2006. Podcast. 5 June 2008 developerWorks Interviews. <http://www.ibm.com/developerworks/podcast/all.html>.

Light, Richard J. *Making the Most of College*. Cambridge: Harvard UP, 2004.

Lunsford, Andrea A., and Lisa Ede. "On Distinctions between Classical and Modern Rhetoric." *Essays on Classical Rhetoric and Modern Discourse*. Carbondale, IL: Southern Illinois UP, 1984: 37–49.

McLuhan, Marshall, and Quentin Fiore. *The Medium Is the Massage*. New York: Bantam, 1967

McQuail, Dennis. *Audience Analysis*. Thousand Oaks, CA: Sage P, 1997.

Melber, Ari. "About Facebook." *The Nation* 20 Dec. 2007: 23.

Nightingale, Virginia. *Studying Audiences: The Shock of the Real*. London: Routledge, 1996.

Porter, James. *Audience and Rhetoric: An Archaeological Composition of the Discourse Community*. Englewood Cliffs, NJ: Prentice Hall, 1992.

Ratcliffe, Krista. *Rhetorical Listening: Identification, Gender, Whiteness*. Carbondale, IL: Southern Illinois UP, 2005.

Reiff, Mary Jo. *Approaches to Audience: An Overview of the Major Perspectives*. Superior, WI: Parlay P, 2004.

Rheingold, Howard. "Vision of the Future." *Education.au Seminar*. Melbourne, Australia, October 2, 2007. <http://www.educationau.Edu/au/jahia/webdav/site/myjahiasite/shared/seminars/Rheingold_Melbourne_Speech.pdf>.

Sawyer, Keith. *Group Genius: The Creative Power of Collaboration*. New York: Basic Books, 2007.

Schilb, John. *Rhetorical Refusals: Defying Audiences' Expectations*. Carbondale, IL: Southern Illinois UP, 2007.

Selfe, Cynthia. *Multimodal Composition: Resources for Teachers.* Cresskill, NJ: Hampton P, 2007.

Sunstein, Cass R. *Infotopia: How Many Minds Produce Knowledge.* Oxford: Oxford UP, 2006.

Tapscott, Don, and Anthony D. Williams. *Wikinomics: How Mass Collaboration Changes Everything.* New York: Penguin, 2006.

Warner, Michael. *Publics and Counterpublics.* New York: Zone Books, 2005.

Wysocki, Anne, Johndan Johnson Eilola, Cynthia Selfe, and Geoffrey Sirc. *Writing New Media: Theory and Applications for Expanding the Teaching of Composition.* Logan, UT: Utah State UP, 2004.

II

THEORY STREAMS: EBBS AND FLOWS OF AUDIENCE THROUGH COMPOSITION AND COMMUNICATION

Placing Ede and Lunsford's Work into Contemporary Conversation

Chapter Four

Authors, Audiences, and the Gaps Between

Traci A. Zimmerman
James Madison University

An audience is always warming but it must never be necessary to your work.

—Gertrude Stein

The reader! You, dogged, uninsultable, print-oriented bastard . . .

—John Barth

So that the jest is clearly to be seen, Not in the words—but in the gap between . . .

—William Cowper

Michel Foucault frames his essay "What Is an Author?" (1969) with a quotation from Samuel Beckett: "'What does it matter who is speaking,' someone said, 'what does it matter who is speaking'" (141). Foucault does so to challenge our concept of the author (and our understanding of "authorship") as something solid; instead he makes it clear that the author is not simply a person but a socially, culturally, and historically constituted *subject*. He wonders at our tendency to think of authors as "individualized" heroic figures and looks to examine the relationship between text and author, "the manner in which the text points to the 'figure' [the author] that, at least in appearance, is outside it and antecedes it" (141). Following Karl Marx and his crucial insight that it is history that makes man and not man that makes history, Foucault implicitly argues that an author does not exist prior to or outside of the language which creates him. But what of the audience? Is it not bound by the self-same language? By the same narrow role (as reader)? And if, as Foucault argues, the author is not the "genial creator" of an "inexhaustible world of significations," but is instead "a certain functional principle by which, in our culture, one limits, excludes, and chooses," an "ideological figure by which one marks the manner in which we fear the proliferation of meaning" (159), could not these same fears be applicable to the audience as part of that same system which serves to limit or restrict meaning? Have we not already proven so, when we (paradoxically) read a text to open its meaning, but almost immediately close the process by looking for "authorial intent"—limiting what we *might* say about the text, what *could* be said—marking some interpretations as dead before they have a chance to be born?

In so doing, we get caught in a vicious, fruitless cycle: we construct an author out of our reading of her and then we use this fiction to limit our reading of the text. Thus we deny the meanings which (always already) lie beneath the structure of language. Can we, then, be as glib as Gertrude Stein and insist that audiences are nice but not necessary? And when we teach students to "write with an audience in mind," do we note that, often times, those audiences have more power to shape meaning than they the writers do? Audiences might get cues from authors about how to read, but they can manipulate context, ignoring some details and highlighting others, to achieve the meaning they want.

Perhaps a better question would be "which comes first, the author or the audience, the writer or the reader?" One certainly cannot exist without the other. We do not write without an audience in mind—be it "addressed" or "invoked," real or imaginary, public or private. And certainly the call to write, the "urge to discourse" as Foucault might say, is not precipitated in a vacuum, and is much more than an urge to dialogue with an audience: it is a desire to create in language that which cannot be created in real life—the desire to talk about what cannot be talked about, to desire what is forbidden. The call to read might take as many forms. Beckett's question could just as easily become "What does it matter who is reading? Or listening?" and Foucault's question could just as easily be asked as "What Is an Audience?"

But asking Beckett's question differently has interesting implications. After all, this is a man who, when asked about the meaning of *Waiting for Godot*, insisted that he "take[s] no sides in that . . . [that] it means what it says" (Croall 44, 91). When his questioner pressed the issue and elaborated on what he took Beckett's play to mean, Beckett replied, "well . . . if you think that's what my play's about, I expect that's what it's about" (87).

In the seeming indifference of Beckett's question (and in light of Beckett's own position as an author), it might be more appropriate to say "*all* that matters is who is reading." Or, as he has said, "language is all we have." When we read, we are certainly not just decoding or translating letters into words or words into sentences, just as when we write we are not just taking dictation, copying down a kind of written representation of our speech. We interpret symbols. We argue about what those symbols mean and how they mean. We know that texts, very rarely (if ever) "mean what they say." Where meaning resides is certainly a more complicated question, made even more so when we turn our attention to the ways in which we teach, learn, model, assess, talk about, and theorize writing in the university.

In many ways, the careful study of authorship and its origins reveals a complex, multilayered understanding of the prominence that audience has had in determining a text's meaning and the role it has had in defining (and even "killing") the author. Indeed, Roland Barthes, who declared the "death of the author," did so to proclaim "the birth of the reader" (130). For Barthes, it is in the reader (or the audience) that meaning resides; he even goes so far as to say that, without the audience, the text would not exist:

> Thus is revealed the total existence of a writing: a text is made up of multiple writings, drawn from many cultures and entering into mutual relations of dialogue, parody, contestation, but there is one place where this multiplicity is focused and that place is the reader, not the author. The reader is the space upon which all the quotations that make up a writing are inscribed

without any of them being lost; a text's unity lies not in its origin, but in its destination. (129)

Thus, the audience occupies a rather interesting space: it is the place where writing is made to *mean*, not merely the point at which a message is delivered, or the group for which a message is designed. The author's message (like sound itself) can only be heard when it bounces off the surface of an audience. Authors can imagine and plan arguments for their audiences, but it is those audiences who will ultimately decide its value. As Horace wrote in his *Epistles*, "*Et Semel Emissum volat irrevocabile verbum* (and once sent out, a word takes wing irrevocably)*.*" Theories of authorship connect and complicate theories of audience and these intersections provide numerous challenges for both writing teachers and writing students alike. One of these challenges is understanding the distinction between *author* and *writer*. In this chapter, I use the two terms interchangeably and rather paradoxically so: I find that it is precisely the attempts to distinguish between the two terms that inextricably link them together. As Foucault points out, "A private letter may well have a signer—it does not have an author; a contract may well have a guarantor—it does not have an author. An anonymous text posted on a wall probably has a writer—but not an author" (148).

Alexander Nehamas deftly explores the author/writer distinction in his article "What an Author Is." He argues that treating "writers as authors" signals a fundamental shift in the way we understand their texts: "to treat writers as authors, therefore, is to take a particular attitude toward their texts: it is to ask of them a certain type of question and to expect a certain type of answer" (685). The "attitude" is implicitly linked to interpretation. Those texts that can be duly (literarily) interpreted to have a meaning "beneath" or "beyond" the words on the page are "authored" texts; those that do not require such interpretation are considered "written" texts (686).

What this can mean for the teaching of writing is that we, as teachers, implicitly discourage our students from being "authors," not because their writing does or does not conform to a specific genre, but because our attitude toward their texts is one that privileges a kind of noninterpretive, informational stance. That is to say, student writers are "actual individuals, firmly located in history, efficient causes of their texts" (686); as such we read their papers to determine what they have to say and how they are saying it. By the same token, we could argue the opposite: that we, as teachers, implicitly encourage our students to be "authors," so that we can determine what the text ultimately means or, more to the point, what grade it will receive. As authors, student writers can "be understood to have produced a particular text *as we interpret it*" (686, emphasis added), not as they "intended" it.

The student writer operates in an economy that they do not control, where they have no real currency, and where they must feign "authority" without being "authors." They must "appropriate (or be appropriated by) a specialized discourse, and they have to do this as though they were easily and comfortably one with their audience, as though they were members of the academy" (Bartholomae 511). In many ways, the author is just as much of a fiction as the audience: "the problem of audience awareness, then, is a problem of power and finesse. It cannot be addressed, as it is in most classroom exercises, by giving students privilege and denying the situation of the classroom" (515). Thus the dynamic of the classroom is one in which students are asked to play a game in which they pretend they can write for various audiences, and teachers pretend that they can be those audiences. In the end, though, the house always wins. Student writers, asked to "assume privilege without having any," cannot effectively participate in a discourse that both eludes and excludes them.

Whether or not we study authorship theory, we are affected by it as teachers of writing; it affects our understanding of the student writer and shapes the way we regulate, even "police," the way writing is produced in the classroom. Lisa Ede and Andrea Lunsford have recognized this tendency in several of their articles, most notably "Audience Addressed/Audience Invoked," which reflects the then-very-nascent understanding of how we understand, teach, and theorize "audience" in the composition classroom. Ede and Lunsford begin their essay with questions that look very much like the kind Foucault and Barthes were leveling at the author. "How can we best define the audience of a written discourse? What does it mean to address an audience? To what degree should teachers stress audience in their assignments and discussions? What *is* the best way to help students recognize the significance of this critical element in any rhetorical situation?" (155). Their call to write comes from their observation that, given the lack of scholarship on the topic, most teachers of writing find the task of defining, addressing, and teaching audience "limited to a single option—to be for or against an emphasis on audience in composition courses" (155). The problems with understanding audience in the poles of two extremes are numerous, and so Ede and Lunsford set forth in their article to "demonstrate that the arguments advocated by each side oversimplify the act of making meaning through written discourse" (156)—and then to propose an "alternative formulation," a model that will "more accurately reflect the richness of 'audience' as a concept" (156).

In proposing this model, however, Ede and Lunsford run into the same kinds of problems as do Foucault and Barthes: how to define their terms in a practical way, instead of moving "over-simplified" and "limited" terms into the realm of indeterminacy. The inclusion of Walter Ong's 1975 essay "The Writer's Audience Is Always a Fiction" is most interesting to me, as it reflects Ede and Lunsford's rather prophetic understanding that in order to understand "writing," we need to have an interdisciplinary approach. They argue that Ong's essay "has had a significant impact on composition studies, despite the fact that its major emphasis is on fictional narrative rather than expository writing" (160) and in so doing, they implicitly argue for an understanding of writing that reaches beyond genre and discipline.

In that vein, I would look to include alternative theories of audience. Certainly, most of the groundbreaking work on authorship had been done prior to 1984. Marxist and Foucaldian theories have infiltrated much of literary study; as such, "teachers of literary studies can no longer fall back on a standardised, received, methodology" (Bennett vii). Nor can teachers of writing. Even though post-structuralist theories of "the author" seem to lend themselves more to deconstruction than to practical models for teaching audience, I have found that they do offer a kind of base from which we can complicate the term much more richly than if we limit our analysis to mere "real world writing" versus "imagined world writing."

Ede and Lunsford's treatment of audience lends itself to this understanding as well. As examples of the kind of "book-ending" going on in the pedagogy of audience, Ede and Lunsford use the terms *audience addressed* and *audience invoked*. Each term tends toward a kind of mutually exclusive isolation: too much emphasis on audience and the writer is powerless; too much emphasis on the writer and the audience is insignificant. It is in this gap, between author and audience, between writer and reader, that we need to teach.

The *writer* model is too limiting because it defines writing as mere "self-expression" or "fidelity to fact," which seems to explicitly argue that the writer is the "only potential judge of effective discourse" (157, 158). The *written product* model is too narrow because it assumes an importance and stability centered on "intrinsic features [such as a] lack of comma splices and fragments" as if teachers of writing have, could, or ever will agree on precisely which of these intrinsic features characterize good writing (157).

Instead of the writer having the sole power of evaluating writing (as in the writer model), or the audience having the sole power of evaluating (as implied in the written product model), Ede and Lunsford note Mitchell and Taylor's audience/response model, but they go on to argue that it merely substitutes "audience" for the evaluating role, thus creating a "similar distortion" (158). Ede and Lunsford write:

> In their model, the audience has the sole power of evaluating writing, the success of which "will be judged by the audience's reaction: 'good' translates into 'effective,' 'bad' into 'ineffective.'" Mitchell and Taylor go on to note that "the audience not only judges writing; it also motivates it" (250), thus suggesting that the writer has less control than the audience over both evaluation and motivation. (158)

Though Ede and Lunsford imply otherwise, in a writing class, this lack of control is true. Regardless of how we ask students to address (or invoke) their audiences, we, their teachers, *are* the audience. Ultimately, we are the ones who design the assignments, evaluate their efficacy, and look for authorial transgressions like inappropriate collaboration and plagiarism. It is not just in taking tests that the student as writer is constrained, where she faces a "single audience, the teacher" (163). These constraints become "academic conventions," which often function as a kind of elusive subtext, especially in writing classrooms.

Ede and Lunsford's model asserts that audiences can be "either addressed or invoked," that writers can effectively "establish a range of potential roles an audience may play," and that that audience "may, of course, accept or reject the role or roles the writer wishes them to adopt in responding to a text" (165–66). On the one hand, this is a rich interpretation of the gaps between author and reader and text; on the other, the audience still retains the ultimate "veto" power, which has important resonances whether the writer is James Frey or a first-year college student. In both examples, the power to make writing "mean" seems more in the hands of the consumer, not the creator.

Lunsford and Ede's 1994 article "Collaborative Authorship and the Teaching of Writing" further questions this balance of power, looking at the ways in which our myth of the "author" has radically revised not only our understanding of the "traditional" relationship between writers and their audience, but also our understanding of what form that writing should take. They admit that "real world writing" is quite synonymous with collaborative writing; as such, they argue for a "reconstructed pedagogy that will allow for collaborative authorship" (418). Where they experience some difficultly is in understanding how that collaborative effort is to be evaluated. "Where," they ask, "does the responsibility lie? Who stands behind the words of a report written by fifteen people?" (418).

It is precisely these kinds of questions that motivated Michel Foucault to interrogate the concept of "the author" through the lens of the "author-function." One of the first characteristics he notes about this function is its relationship to ownership and appropriation: "texts, books, and discourses really began to have authors (other than mythical, 'sacralized,' and 'sacralizing' figures) to the extent that authors became subject to punishment, that is, to the extent discourses could be transgressive" (148). Indeed, this concept of "transgression" influences the way that we evaluate student writing, the way that we develop assignments, the way we explicitly privilege solo authored creations devoid of the scourge of "plagiarism." But even before that, "transgression" influences the dynamic of power in the classroom. Lunsford and Ede, quoting Richard Ohmann, acknowledge the problem of student "powerlessness" in writing classes: "the writer's situation is heavy with contradictions. She is . . . invited both to assume responsibility for her education and to trust the college's plan for it; to build her competence and to follow a myriad of rules and instructions; to see herself as an autonomous individual and to be incessantly judged" (434). Turnitin.com (and the other iterations of plagiarism software) and the policies that we use to police our authors in the classroom are only one manifestation of this kind of "judgment"; yet "judgment" is certainly not limited to "autonomous individuals." David Bartholomae deftly explores how this power imbalance extends to questions of discourse and access to that discourse. He argues that

> our colleges and universities, by and large, have failed to involve basic writing students in scholarly projects, projects that would allow them to act as though they were colleagues in an academic enterprise. Much of the work they do . . . places them outside the working discourse of the academic community, where they are expected to admire and report on what we do, rather than inside that discourse, where they can do its work and participate in a common enterprise. This is a failure of teachers and curriculum designers who, even if they speak of writing as a mode of learning, all too often represent writing as a "tool" to be used by an (hopefully) educated mind. (517)

What is interesting in this admonition is what is absent: there are no basic writers involved in his essay, though he reviewed "500 [student] essays" and cited quite a few. Ironically, a large part of the challenge of developing a "pedagogy of collaboration" lies in determining how to actually go about collaborating.

So how can we teach audience in the twenty-first century? How can we understand the whos, whats, and hows of audience in a culture where the "boundaries between audiences and creators [are] blurred and often invisible," as Ede and Lunsford quote Andrew Kluth in "Among the Audience" (42)? Perhaps the first step would be to blur those boundaries in our own classes by interrogating some of the misunderstandings that influence and often inhibit our teaching of reading and writing, author and audience, writer and message.

Participatory Media Is New

The title of the introductory writing course I teach at James Madison University is GWRIT 103: "Critical Reading and Writing." Active reading implicitly blurs the line between audience and author because it involves interpretation and interaction with the words on the page. If we can effectively teach active reading, then we can better address the gaps between reader and text, between writer and reader, between word and meaning.

Students are well-trained to read for information (what I call "reading with a little *r*"); they are not as skilled in reading for meaning (or "reading with a capital *R*"). My advice to students as we begin the process of creating a writing community is to understand the difference. When you are putting together a piece of furniture, you have to read for information (what goes where, in what order to assemble the pieces, how to use the enclosed hardware). As students work on their reading assignments for class, I remind them: "You aren't putting together a bookshelf." Instead of reading for bits of information to highlight and memorize, students have to inhabit a different role, one that is necessarily participatory, in order to understand what the piece means, what it seems to argue, how it is argued, why it is argued that way. This is interpretation, and it is participatory and collaborative. The only way the text exists (as Barthes would claim) is when a reader reads it. And once she has, the meaning is not conveyed in some simple act of translation, as if taking down and transcribing that which was dictated long ago. The reader never reads alone: she has to negotiate the message with the "voices" in her head, those influences that shape how she will understand certain arguments or devalue others. We are always reading (and writing) "under the influence"; understanding these influences is one step closer to understanding our audiences.

T. S. Eliot's "Tradition and the Individual Talent" and Harold Bloom's "Anxiety of Influence," though focused on literary theory (and primarily on poetry), were well ahead of their time in recognizing the kinds of negotiations that have to take place in order to create "original" work in the face of the vast and overwhelming influence of history. Originality, it seems, can only come from a deep understanding of "origins;" that is, where and what and how we come to find our own voice in the sea of voices that precede us. This seems an even more relevant observation when our attention turns to the origins of our new media and the attendant controversies they inspire. Walter Ong's "Writing Is a Technology that Restructures Thought" also offers insight into these origins by reminding us that we have so "interiorized the technology of writing . . . that without tremendous effort [we] cannot separate it from ourselves or even recognize its presence and influence" (19). He goes on to show us what we have forgotten, the "obvious truth" that has been rendered invisible "so deeply has the fixity of the written word taking possession of our consciousness" (20):

> Writing was an intrusion, though an invaluable intrusion, into the early human lifeworld, much as computers are today. It has lately become fashionable in some linguistic circles to refer to Plato's condemnation of writing in the *Phaedrus* and the Seventh Letter. What is seldom, if ever noticed, however, is that Plato's objections against writing are essentially the very same objections commonly urged today against computers by those who object to them. Writing, Plato has Socrates say in the *Phaedrus*, is inhuman, pretending to establish outside the mind what in reality can only be in the mind. Writing is simply a thing, something to be manipulated, something inhuman, artificial, a manufactured product. We recognize here the same complaint that is made against computers: they are artificial contrivances, foreign to human life. . . . Technologies are artificial, but—paradox again—artificiality is natural to human beings. (21, 24)

By examining the new media as a kind of "naturally artificial" tool (instead of an unnatural threat) in our classrooms, we can better explore how it helps and hinders the connections we make with ourselves and our audiences. Perhaps Google is not making us "stoopid" after all; some have observed that hypertext more closely resembles the organization of information in human memory than do linear texts. James Paul Gee has written extensively on the ways in which even new media like videogames strengthen agency, identity, and interaction. If anything, Lunsford and Ede's new article might well stand as a central point of inquiry in our budding understanding of new media (and new media literacies): "what does it mean to be a reader and writer in the twenty-first century?"("Among the Audience" 45)

Students These Days Are So Much More Collaborative

By now we all know that books are old-fashioned and isolating, and reading them is an equally solitary task. But Facebook has some strikingly similar tendencies. Technology has the power to connect and to isolate simultaneously whether that technology is a pencil or pixel. So while it may seem "more obvious than ever that writers [in the twenty-first century] seldom write alone" ("Among the Audience" 45), it might prove more complicated an observation. Many writers are indeed writing alone in terms of where they are located in physical space and time (in front of computer screens or over phone keypads—texting, creating Facebook pages, adding to Wikis, authoring blogs), but, paradoxically, they are and have never been "alone"; making meaning has always been collaborative. The new media merely ensures that there are always people "out there" watching, reading, writing, copying, and stalking the presence you have created online. "Among" this kind of audience, there is a distinct blur between what is collaborative and cautionary, between what is intended and unwanted.

Lunsford and Ede address this imbalance, noting that "more often than not, students resist collaboration in their schoolwork even as they collaborate constantly in their out-of-class online writing" ("Among the Audience" 58). But this seems to be a more complicated relationship than this binary would suggest. Students certainly resist a simplistic understanding of collaboration in classrooms (like "group work" where the few will do the work for the many and all will get the same grade). And while students are making attempts to "communicate" constantly in their out-of-class writing, it is not necessarily "collaborative." What they do most often outside of class and resist in class is dialogue, plain and simple. They might resist having a dialogue with an essay, they might resist having a dialogue with me or a feisty classmate or a guest speaker, but they will dialogue the rest of the day quite happily. How much they are actually listening in these exchanges is debatable; that is the crucial piece of any interaction, be it reading, writing, or texting. Posting is not discussing.

Lunsford and Ede note as much when they write that "one place to turn . . . is the extensive work on public discourse being pursued by many scholars in rhetoric and communication studies" (63). They go on to suggest (as a classroom strategy) to "encourage . . . students to build bridges between the seemingly *private voices they inhabit online* and the public ones they can establish" (63, emphasis added). What is interesting about this suggestion is the explicit observation that, for all of the talk of participatory, collaborative, and public media, the voices that students inhabit online are seen as private. This is easy to conceive if you visualize how most online exchanges take place: one student sitting in front of her own computer or Blackberry screen, alone. Thus the ethical elements of which Ede and Lunsford write gain a new sense of urgency. They ask, "What does a student writer posting to Facebook owe to all the potential audiences of that post, from a former partner to a potential employer?" (62) "All the potential audiences" could also realistically include online stalkers, pedophiles, hackers, and scam artists. Not all audiences are rhetorical. The concept of audience in the twenty-first century is harder to grasp precisely because of the sheer scope and range of online communication—anyone with an internet connection is in the "potential audience" base.

Despite their interest in the Internet, "many students may easily forget that when they post something on the Web, they may encounter unwanted audiences" ("Among the Audience" 55). Students who are increasingly described as savvy online communicators can nonetheless "forget" how many hits they get on Google, or how large of a pond they swim in on a daily basis. When they do most of their composing in private it becomes difficult to envision the public for whom they (inadvertently) write. The paradox of anonymity is that we feel most anonymous when we are surrounded by others. The line between public and private has never been so thin; thus it seems that the negotiation between "private voice and public voice" is a crucial one to deal with in our classrooms (63–64).

2 Ponder 4 Later

In AA/AI, Ede and Lunsford work to understand the gap between writer and audience by exploring the gaps between those who understood "audience" as something that could be realistically conceptualized and those who understood "audience" as something necessarily fabricated. What they discover is that "audience" is too complex of a concept to live happily in either place. Their "reconstructed pedagogy" is not to be taken lightly. If collaboration is to succeed in a writing classroom, it needs to infuse the course from day one. A good friend of mine goes so far as to have her introductory biology students create the syllabus for her course, deciding points for projects and even the number and frequency of exams. There are numerous resources out there on collaborative learning and learner-centered teaching that can help in re-visioning a collaborative pedagogy. Of course, the kinds of revisions to a course need not be so radical: in my introductory writing course, I challenge students to create the assignments for each essay, to create rubrics around which those essays will be evaluated, and to take primary control and responsibility for directing our writing workshops. This is not done without a great deal of preparation and forethought. Part of my role in a collaborative classroom is to facilitate the kinds of learning that will create conditions in which students can succeed at these tasks. A main goal of the process is to build a shared vocabulary around which we can talk about writing and be relatively sure that we are literally, figuratively, and virtually "on the same page."

Ultimately what this kind of collaborative work teaches is self-assessment. If students are able to talk about writing and the writing process in a way that allows them to deconstruct the myth of the "solitary genius recollecting in tranquility" or the mystery of how essays are graded, they ultimately gain agency and authority over their own work. If students are always looking outside for validation—looking for some "expert" to tell them that "this is good" or "this isn't"—then their lives will always be narrated to them, rather than created by them. Collaborative work, especially in a writing course, gives students the chance to create knowledge about what makes for good writing and why, rather than consume "picky writing rules" or static, formulaic, and overly simplistic versions of what makes for good writing. It allows them some degree of control over the audience they also form a part of. Collaborative writing classrooms reinforce the fact that writing is a dynamic process—that the best essays begin with good questions, rather than absolute positions—that starting with a hypothesis is even better than starting with a thesis because it allows time and opportunity to sift through research and listen to it, to participate in the conversation instead of eavesdropping and using only the best-suited parts.

More than anything, a study of authorship, be it individual or collaborative, brings us back to the point at which we started: "What does it matter who is speaking?" The answer seems less to do with the "who" and more to do with the "whom"; that is, "what does it matter to whom you are speaking?"—a salient question in the composition classroom. Having the power to determine what constitutes "transgression," teachers may find themselves reinforcing, rather than dismantling, the very structures of power they purport to challenge with collaborative writing assignments that too simplistically posit a peer audience.

Works Cited

Barthes, Roland. "The Death of the Author." *Authorship: From Plato to the Postmodern.* Ed Sean Burke. Edinburgh: Edinburg UP, 2004.

Bartholomae, David. "Inventing the University." *Cross-Talk in Comp Theory: A Reader.* 2nd ed. Ed. Victor Villanueva, Jr. Urbana, IL, NCTE, 1997. 623–654. Rpt. in "Inventing the University." *Literacy: A Critical Sourcebook.* Ed. Ellen Cushman, Eugene R. Kintgen, Barry M. Kroll, and Mike Rose. Boston: Bedford, 2001. 511–524.

Bennett, Andrew. Ed. *Readers and Reading.* London: Longman Group Limited, 1995.

Croall, Jonathan. *The Coming of Godot: A Short History of a Masterpiece.* New York: Consortium Book Sales and Distribution, 2006.

Culler, Jonathan. *Literary Theory: A Very Short Introduction.* Oxford: Oxford UP, 1997.

Ede, Lisa, and Andrea Lunsford. "Audience Addressed/Audience Invoked: The Role of Audience in Composition Theory and Pedagogy." *CCC* 35 (1984): 155–171.

Elbow, Peter. "The Pedagogy of the Bamboozled." *Embracing Contraries: Explorations of Learning and Teaching.* New York: Oxford UP, 1986. 87–98.

Foucault, Michel. "What Is an Author?" *Textual Strategies: Perspectives in Post-Structuralist Criticism.* Ed. Josue V. Harari. Ithaca, NY: Cornell UP, 1979. 141–160.

Howard, Rebecca Moore. *Standing in the Shadow of Giants: Plagiarists, Authors, Collaborators.* Stamford, CT: Ablex Publishing Corporation, 1999.

Lunsford, Andrea A., and Lisa Ede. "Among the Audience: On Audience in an Age of New Literacies." *Engaging Audience: Writing in an Age of New Literacies.* Ed. Elizabeth Weiser, Brian Fehler, and Angela González. Urbana, IL: NCTE, 2009. 42–69.

Lunsford, Andrea, and Lisa Ede. "Collaborative Authorship and the Teaching of Writing." *The Construction of Authorship: Textual Appropriation in Law and Literature.* Ed. Martha Woodmansee and Peter Jaszi. Durham, NC: Duke UP, 1994. 417–438.

Nehamas, Alexander. "What an Author Is." *The Journal of Philosophy* 83.11 (1986): 685–691.

Ricoeur, Paul. "What Is a Text? Explanation and Understanding." *Hermeneutics and the Human Sciences.* Thompson, John B. Ed. Trans. Cambridge: Cambridge UP, 1981. 145–164.

Woodmansee, Martha. "On the Author Effect: Recovering Collectivity." *The Construction of Authorship: Textual Appropriation in Law and Literature.* Ed. Martha Woodmansee and Peter Jaszi. Durham, NC: Duke UP, 1994. 15–28.

CHAPTER FIVE

Communicating with the Audience

DAVID BEARD

University of Minnesota-Duluth

Audience in Composition Studies: An Opportunity Lost

The initial explorations of audience in the composition community in the 1980s held much promise, crystallized by Lisa Ede's provocative claim in 1984 that "composition teachers can achieve a sophisticated, complex understanding of the nature and role of audience in written discourse only if they are aware of both empirical and theoretical research in their own and other disciplines" (140). Ede proceeded to cite Aristotle's *Rhetoric* as a seminal text and to cite the twentieth-century works in rhetorical theory (Donald Bryant, Douglas Ehninger, Karl Wallace) that "refine, rather than reject [Aristotle's] basic strategy" (141). As such, Ede offered a central critique of the speech communication tradition for audience analysis: she identified the limitations inherent in the preference to see audience as reducible to demographics. Russell C. Long, in "The Writer's Audience: Fact or Fiction," makes concrete the criticism of the demographic perspective:

> A specific reader may be white, 45-years-old, have a college degree, be married with one adolescent child, have voted the straight Democratic ticket in the last three elections, be making payments on his own home, have two cars, take at least one two-week vacation each year, and be a member of the Methodist church. . . . There is almost nothing here that would allow the writer to shape or mold a particular piece of writing to fit the reader's specific needs or tastes. (80)

Clearly, the demographic tradition had some substantial limitations and was ripe for criticism and supplement.

In her efforts to undermine the reduction of audience analysis to a collection of demographic data, Ede pulls us toward Edwin Black's "second persona" and to Walter Ong's fictionalized audience as an alternative (143). In "The Writer's Audience Is Always a Fiction," Ong tells us that "if the writer succeeds in writing, it is generally because he can fictionalize in his imagination an audience he has learned to know not from daily life but from earlier writers" (*An Ong Reader* 410). Black and Ong (and later, Wander, Anderson and Charland) focus on the audience as a product of the text.

In establishing a tradition of audience analysis as either demographically centered or as generated as a product of the text (as *audience addressed* vs. *audience invoked*), Ede and Andrea Lunsford set the paradigm for audience studies in composition for decades. Yet within ten years, research on audience in composition studies had slipped from the center of disciplinary discourse. The paradigm was set; the difference between the audience invoked and the audience addressed became *the* integral distinction in audience studies. As a result, Ede's initial call went unmet: compositionists ceased to look outside composition to understand audience. But audience remained a central area of investigation in other fields, quickly outpacing the state of the art in audience studies in composition.

This anthology marks an opportunity to reopen that conversation between audience as a concept within rhetoric and composition and audience as a conceptual field in other disciplines. Lunsford and Ede, in "Among the Audience," note that the distinction between author and audience is much less clear in disciplinary work outside composition.

This chapter revisits Ede's contribution of twenty-five years ago—bringing "empirical and theoretical research" in other disciplines into composition. I turn, in particular, to interpersonal communication and mass communication literature, in which the empirical study of audience has continued unabated since Lunsford and Ede reviewed that literature in the 1980s. Where we could once oppose the demographic audience (the reader) and the invoked audience with confidence, we now recognize that audiences are even more complex, multivalent entities. Helping students appreciate that will improve their abilities as writers, the final goal of this chapter and this collection.

Core Claim: Audiences Are Active

Among the most energetic areas of contemporary audience research is new media studies. New media can be configured to mirror "old media" (think, for example, of websites that simply stream traditional television content or allow the download of songs that used to be purchased as singles; Bolter and Grusin call this kind of transfer and transfiguration "remediation"). New media can also be configured to enable radical dialogue and extreme interactivity. This field gives us an initial schema for understanding the levels of audience interaction with a text. Rob Cover outlines three levels of audience interactivity useful to composition:

> 1. At the first level, "interactive engagement is minimal, and is set within the context of a single, central broadcaster and multiple receivers on the periphery" ("Audience Inter/Active" 142). This level of interactivity is the one that we traditionally envision for the passive media audience—the listeners huddled around the radio.

> 2. Audience interactivity can be configured as "*consultation*, which occurs in the use of a database, such as a CD-Rom or a World-Wide-Website, where a user actively searches for pre-provided information" (142). Here, the user is more active, in that they *search* for something rather than passively *consume*, but the interaction is still minimal.

> 3. Finally, "*conversational interactivity* . . . occurs when individuals interact directly with each other" (142). This last level of interactivity is both metaphorical and literal. It is literal in that in some circumstances, direct dialogue is possible. It is metaphorical in that readers can produce texts that respond to texts, even if the authors are geographically distant.

Current research in audience in composition tends to fall within the first two categories. On the one hand, audiences have always been cognitive puzzlers, attempting to "puzzle through" the meaning of texts. Following reader-response theory, compositionists have spoken of the transaction of the reader and the writer (see Joseph J. Comprone). This model corresponds to the first level precisely because of the primacy it gives the author as "central broadcaster" and reader as receiver. On the other hand, readers have been configured as "users." Craig Stroupe, in "The Rhetoric of Irritation," notes that configuring the audience as a user implies that texts should be designed "as unambiguously and conventionally as airports" (255). As easily as travelers find their gates, so should someone interacting with a text in what we will call a "consultation" model find their information. Both of these models are common in contemporary composition and professional writing, but, like Stroupe, I find the model for the audience as a user too limited, restricting audience interactivity with a text.

The research discussed in this chapter, then, takes conversational interactivity as the norm in audience interactivity with a text. This research presumes that readers do active, engaged, and creative things to a text, far beyond the kind of activity discussed in the invoked/addressed paradigm. As Aeron Davis phrased it, "the research question has become more a matter of what audiences do with their media rather than what the media do to them" (305). The third, conversational level of interactivity articulated by Cover is my foot in the door to answer Davis's question.

I begin by consulting research in interpersonal communication to explore the ways that audiences actively interpret a text. Listening research can be the root of a schema of those processes as they might apply to composition teaching and research. Next, I consult research in mass communication to explore the ways that an audience relates to a text and to the narrative voice within it. Mass communication research offers a schema of those relationships as they might apply to the teaching voice or *ethos* in composition. Finally, I explore the most active uses of a text by an audience for the creation of a community and of new texts—a full example of conversational activity—and the challenges that that research might pose to composition research and pedagogy.

The Audience Listens: Listening Research Applied to the Reading Audience

The building blocks of a fully conversational interaction with a text should begin with an examination of interpersonal communication. Listening, formally defined by the International Listening Association as "the process of receiving, constructing meaning from, and responding to spoken and/or nonverbal messages," can, by analogy, help us elaborate on what Cover means by conversational interaction with texts. Further, it will enrich our ability to describe genres for our students.

Research into Listening Style Preference (LSP) initiated by Watson and Barker in 1992 gives us a schema for describing how people listen. A summary of the research into LSP follows.

- ◆ *People-oriented listeners* are perceived as nurturing and caring; they search for common interests and goals. They place a premium on understanding the emotional state of the speaker as part of understanding their claims. Weaver associated this listening style with extroversion; Weaver, Watson & Barker see some correlation between gender and this listening style, in that women tend to self-report a "people-orientation" in their listening behaviors. This may correspond to what sociolinguist Deborah Tannen has popularly called "rapport-talk" in *You Just Don't Understand.*

- ◆ *Action-oriented listeners* focus on solving problems. They listen with an eye toward finding information that will enable them to make a decision, and they can be disoriented or impatient with speakers who don't speak with the same focus in mind. Worthington connected this listening style to the Myers-Briggs personality indicator's "Thinking and Judging."

- ◆ *Content-oriented listeners* listen for critical evaluation of arguments, evidence, and claims. They are comfortable listening to complex or technical messages because they take some pleasure in puzzling them through. Weaver also associated this listening style with extroversion.

- ◆ *Time-oriented listeners* engage in what Worthington called "communicative time management." They will push others along toward a quicker resolution of the conversation. Few people identify primarily as a time-oriented listener; this orientation typically inflects or complements another orientation.

As we explore a conversational model for audience interaction with a text, the distinctions developed in the listening literature can be helpful. Instead of the audience as cognitive puzzle solver (a content orientation, perhaps) or as user (an action orientation), we can see a greater spectrum of audience behaviors. Action-oriented audiences approach a text with a different agenda than people-oriented listeners; they pick apart the text in different ways.

We can connect those behaviors to demographic and personality data—a real step forward in understanding who will read our text and ways to accommodate them. The strong tradition in communication research for correlating variables (for demonstrating correlations between listening style and personality type, gender, education level, learning style, etc.) can help research in composition studies.

The Audience Relates: Mass Communication Research Applied to the Voice of a Writer

As teachers of written communication, we agree that the act of writing is defined by the rhetorical situation as a complex of intertwining factors. Maddeningly, though, compositionists have sometimes pulled aspects of the rhetorical situation apart for analysis, despite Flower and Hayes's admonishment, in 1980, that "Good writers respond to all aspects of the rhetorical problem" (71). Research in mass communication can help us reintegrate the rhetorical situation, including voice and persona.

Compositionists' interest in "voice" took root in the 1980s, at roughly the same time that research on audience was reaching its height. Voice was defined as "style, persona, stance, or ethos" (Bowden 173). Research on voice was supported, on the one hand, by Bahktinian calls to polyvocality. Joy S. Ritchie could write about a student who "tried on different voices and identities" as part of drafting essays in a composition class (140). On the other hand, some explored *authentic* voice—"'voice' as embodying the distinctive expression of an individual writer" (hooks 54). Roger D. Cherry, writing in "*Ethos* Versus Persona," even borrows the continuum Ede and Lunsford advance in describing audience addressed and audience invoked to describe the distinction between "ethos" and "persona." By Cherry's argument, *ethos* refers to the demographic, material self of the author, while *persona* is as fictionalized an authorial self as the audience invoked is a fictionalized reader (98).

Too often, the literature on voice, *persona,* and *ethos* in composition courses focused on voice as a tool for building credibility. Without the classical rhetorical inflection, this scholarship that was derived from the Elbow tradition of composition placed a high value on authenticity as essential to effective writing. Such models placed much value on the audience as a co-creator of meaning with a rich variety of reasons for reading a text. The reader simply voted, as in a plebiscite, whether the text was persuasive or not; voice was a contributing factor in that evaluation.

In order to more richly understand the ways that audiences might respond to voice in composition, we need to understand the mass communication research on audience relationships with characters in television shows and other media (both fictional and real). Some of the possible relationships include the following:

- ◆ Readers can respond to voice in terms of *"Authority Relationship."* That authority relationship is most related to what we understand as credibility in composition research. In mass communication, it has been studied in the United States by Geoffrey Raymond, for example, who talks about the construction of authority in newscasting. It has been assessed internationally by Auter, Arafa, and Al-Jaber in "Identifying with Arabic Journalists." In both cases, the newscasters are constructed as authority figures and the viewer's relationship to them is defined by that position.

- ◆ *Homophilous Identification* relationships refer to "sharing a character's perspective and vicariously participating in the character's experiences" (Eyal and Rubin 80). Early research into mass media audiences studied audience identification with Archie Bunker in *All in the Family.* Viewers who had a high tendency to identify with Archie did not always claim to enjoy the television series. Clearly, Bunker's struggles with a changing world became struggles for the audience who identified with him. As we think about "voice" and ethos in composition, we can ask whether the voice of the writer is one that encourages homophilous identification.

◆ *Wishful Identification* is a refinement on the homophilous model in that the audience member does not, as they are now, identify with the fictional character but instead "looks up to" that character and identifies wishfully (Hoffner and Buchanan). We can see this in fictional writing, as young adults aspire to be more like Harry Potter. But we can also see it in political rhetoric.

◆ *Parasocial Interaction* is the experience of a relationship between a recurring media character and an audience member. Eyal and Rubin (81) emphasize "perceived intimacy" with the characters and figures on television. Recall the tendency of talk-show hosts to thank audiences, in the early days of TV, for allowing them into their living room. Wicks notes that viewers call Peter Jennings, Oprah Winfrey, and Rush Limbaugh by their first names, indicating a "feeling of kinship" (167). Can the voice of an author engage the reader in "parasocial interaction," especially in ongoing writing situations like journalistic columns? (Was Mike Royko a friend to readers of his syndicated column? How about Studs Terkel?)

This list is by no means exhaustive and its categories by no means exclusive. It is possible, for example, for a newscaster to be both an authority figure and the object of parasocial interaction. Precisely because media figures can be the object of wishful identification, they may have some authority relationship with their audience. These categories, however, are useful because the "voice" of an essay—*persona* or *ethos*—is just as much the potential object of these relationships as a newscaster or character in a sitcom. For example, Ann Burnett and Rhea Reinhardt Beto have successfully explored parasocial relationships in romance novels.

With the measures introduced by mass communication research, we can ask our students: what does it mean to construct a speaker, an essayist's *ethos* or *persona*, which might encourage or allow for one of these relationships? In technical writing, we construct a manual primarily from the voice of authority, but is it possible to speak from a perspective potentially homophilous with the audience? (Perhaps the Apple computer manuals exemplify this blended relationship.) Public or political discourse can be analyzed from the perspective of authority, to be sure. But how much richer would such analysis be if the student in an advanced composition course could differentiate between a president who seeks to create a relationship of authority with the

American people and a president whose text fosters a parasocial relationship with the American people? I am thinking, for example, of the "fireside chats" so historically important to FDR; do contemporary weekly presidential radio broadcasts (like those archived at http://www.whitehouse.gov/news/radio/) also enable a parasocial relationship? And could students, over the course of several assignments, craft a narrative voice which not only persuaded or argued effectively, but also enabled a parasocial interaction with the audience? These are the opportunities that open to a compositionist who possesses a richer conceptualization of audience enabled by media studies research.

The Audience Responds: Convergence Culture in the Writing Classroom

While the previous two sections of this chapter use communication research to enhance our ability to teach how audiences consume texts, this final section moves into the most controversial arena of communication research: what the audience creates in response to a text. Lunsford and Ede begin to explore this literature in "Among the Audience," examining the writings of Henry Jenkins and others to talk about the ways that the audience also becomes the author. This is the culmination of the conversational model for audience interaction. For the act of writing or speech to become a conversation, there must be the possibility of response. Here, I mean more than the "response" implied by reader response theory; that notion of response is still centered entirely around the consumption of a text. I mean the possibility to speak back—to construct something meaningful.

Research into the ways that media audiences "write back" was pioneered by Jenkins in *Textual Poachers* and has become important for cultural and media studies scholars. Scholars in this tradition use qualitative research methods (ethnography, interviewing) to explore

> forms of interactivity in which the text or its content is affected, resequenced, altered, customized or re-narrated in the interactive process of audiencehood. This is the sort of interactivity in

which content is affected not only at the 'nodal point' at which it becomes textual—a set of points which includes broadcast or release time or other forms of digital dissemination—but also and particularly the point at which a text leaves the hands or immediate, real-time control of an author or content creator and becomes available to alteration in some way by a reader or content-user. Such interactivity . . . has resulted in new tensions in the author-text-audience relationship, predominantly by blurring the distinction between author and audience. (Cover 140)

The blurred distinction between audience and author has crept into our culture slowly: Melissa Wall tells us about the ways that the "audience as co-creators is seen . . . in game shows that allow audiences to supply answers, in much reality programming, in audiences who supply the questions for call-in radio shows" (167). In an age in which access to publication is as simple as nickels for a photocopier or use of a computer from a public Internet connection, the possibilities of audiences as co-creators in dialogue with the original media text explode. Jenkins calls the larger historical moment characterized by this blurring "convergence culture."

I divide this body of research into two steps that help us unpack its challenges for the composition classroom. First, I examine the ways that audiences construct community from a text. Then, I examine the ways that audiences engage in a dialogue with the original texts and produce new ones. This is the fullest manifestation of Cover's conversational paradigm.

Audiences Respond: Forming Community in Response to a Text

Media research has shown that, contrary to traditional beliefs, viewing television need not be a zombie-like activity, and watching television in a group need not be collective zombification. Finucane and Horvath note that, while conversation decreases while couples watch TV, "nonverbal communication such as increased touching increases" (312). This kind of interactive co-viewing serves to support relationships. Couples who watched TV together experienced *increased affiliation*, or the sense that time spent watching TV counted as relationship maintenance.

They also experienced *communication facilitation*; couples that watched TV together discuss and process the viewing experience together, sometimes initiating conversations that might not have arisen without the TV (Finucane and Horvath 316). This last finding is consonant with Hobson's findings that soap operas and other television programming open opportunities for conversation among viewers—sometimes around difficult topics.

If texts (television or otherwise) support relationships among audience members, they can become the foundation of community. Fans constitute the kind of community most often discussed in media studies. As Jenkins put it in "Star Trek Rerun, Reread, Rewritten," "one becomes a fan not by being a regular viewer of a particular program but by translating that viewing into some kind of cultural activity, by sharing feelings and thoughts about the program content with friends, by joining a 'community' of other fans who share common interests" (41). In *Convergence Culture*, Jenkins tells us that communities form around media if three conditions are met. Members of the community must be able to pool knowledge with others in a collaborative enterprise, to make connections across scattered pieces of information, and to share and compare value systems by evaluating ethical dramas. Jenkins's examples (the community of fans that coalesce around *Survivor*, for example) pool knowledge about *Survivor* to guess where it will be filmed next season. Fans of television shows like *Heroes* and *Lost* make connections across scattered pieces of information to guess how mysteries will be solved and plotlines will be resolved. And finally, in discussing the behaviors of players on a game show or characters on a fictional show (evaluating whether a character behaves appropriately when faced with a challenge), the fans of a television show compare value systems in evaluating "ethical dramas."

The first challenge that this study of audience behavior offers the composition classroom involves the difficulty posed in understanding the processes by which a community of readers (or fans) coalesce in response to a text. Typically, when composition instructors teach about audience, they do so in a way that presumes that the community exists prior to the act of composition (*addressed*) or that the audience is *invoked* by the text as part of the process of consumption. Certainly, there is some measure of audience addressed in *Star Trek*, for example. Gene Roddenberry needed to be able to articulate an identifiable demographic audience to sell the show to the network. There is also a measure of "audience invoked," in that certain features of the show (for example, the stipulation of a racially integrated future) invoked an audience with a kind of value set that was only coming into being in the United States in the 1960s. This strand of media research takes us further.

The study of fan communities reminds us that readers coalesce around a text in ways that are outside what we typically understand as authorial control. The signature example of such a community is the Gaylactic Network, Inc., a community of gay, lesbian, and bisexual science fiction fans (discussed in Jenkins's *Fans, Bloggers, and Gamers*). At no point did Gene Roddenberry imagine *Star Trek* addressing an audience composed in this way, but they coalesced around the text, imagining their values and visions within the *Star Trek* universe in ways not explicit in the text.

Audiences Respond: Drafting Texts in Response to a Text

The communities that coalesce around a text become forums for the production of new texts. Traditionally, photocopied fanzines were the medium of fan text production—a place where criticism of the primary text, and fiction adapting or invoking the primary text found their own readers. But these small-circulation publications lacked the reach that is possible in today's online fan community forums. Online fan communities range in audience and purpose. They can be as limited as TheForce.net (a *Star Wars* fan fiction site) or as broad as FanFiction.net (which catalogs films, TV shows, books, comics, and games written by inspired fans).

Fan authors pick up a pen and carry the stories in their own way. Their desire to publish, according to Jenkins, results from the fan's unique relationship to the text: "Fan critics pull characters and narrative issues from the margins; they focus on details that are excessive or peripheral to the primary plots but gain significance within the fans' own conceptions of the series" (*Textual Poachers* 155). Characters conceived as supporting in the original text may become significant keys to interpret the narrative in fan criticism or become the protagonists of their own stories in fan fiction. The elements of the original text are refocused and realigned in the new text. The classic example of this realignment is *slash* fan fiction, a term derived from the use of a slash to designate the characters featured in the story (for example, Buffy/Angel or Kirk/Spock). Slash fiction is sexual by definition, taking Buffy the vampire slayer and Angel the vampire into a relationship that the TV shows did not allow, or taking Kirk and Spock into a homoerotic relationship that Gene Roddenberry never expected.

Slash fiction is an extreme example of the multimedia age truism that changes in technology have made every text open for appropriation, adaptation, and transformation. Such transformation may be at the hands of an audience with malicious, mischievous, or argumentative intent: this would include video remixes of George W. Bush on YouTube. One such film, sequencing clips from various speeches to make it appear that Bush is singing the U2 song "Sunday, Bloody Sunday," makes its point through irony. And the Gaylaxians remind us that not even every friendly (critical or creative) transformation of a text is welcome. The Gaylaxians may hold nothing but reverence for Gene Roddenberry's creation, yet Henry Jenkins and John Campbell's analysis of Paramount's resistance to Gaylaxian petitions to place a gay character on the Enterprise reminds us that not all friendly appropriations are welcome. The authors of the original texts, in the final analysis, can argue against readings of the texts that they do not like. And they can, via appeals to authorial intent or legal authority, attempt to suppress readings that they do not like. But those readings cannot be controlled; nothing could be done to preclude a homoerotic reading of a *Star Trek* episode.

The lesson that this final and perhaps most prominent strand of media research gives the composition instructor undercuts what may be the goal of the study of audience analysis in some composition courses: the implicit assumption that a better understanding of audience will lead to a better text. Indeed, the promise of a better text was the way that I couched the significance of listening and mass communication research in the first two sections of this chapter. And "better" is typically measured by the effect that the text has on the reader: the reader is persuaded, the reader learns, the reader understands, the reader is moved to action. This implicit assumption is important; it helps us defend the importance of composition courses to administrators and it helps us motivate students. They will work harder if they believe that the goal of a richer understanding of audience is the production of texts that *do work* upon an audience.

But a truly conversational understanding of an audience's interaction with a text means that we must, at some level, release control. We must understand that, once let loose in the world, any response to our text is possible. This includes responses that are contrary to our intentions or desires. To close this chapter, I will note that this strand of media research makes manifest a tension between two composition theories and the pedagogies that follow from them: *dialectical* theories of argument and *paralogic* theories of rhetoric. These are the tensions between engaging a rational conversation with the audience and recognizing that real conversations have lives of their own.

The Dialectical Program and Paralogic Paradigm

The drafting of an argument, under the most cutting edge of research on argumentation theory, takes this conversational relationship between author and audience as paradigmatic of the writing situation. Ralph Johnson talks about the ways that arguments both prove a point and address an audience through the *illative core* and the *dialectical tier*.

> An argument is a type of discourse or text—the distillate of the practice of argumentation—in which the arguer seeks to persuade the Other(s) of the truth of a thesis by producing the reasons that support it. In addition to this illative core, an argument possesses a dialectical tier in which the arguer discharges his dialectical obligations. (168)

The illative core is nothing new; it looks very much like traditional studies of argument, with an emphasis on form, on validity, and on truth. Syllogisms are, in many ways, purely illative core. The dialectical tier is the innovation, because it takes the argument's role as conversation seriously.

To more fully outline the effects of the dialectical tier upon argument construction, Johnson develops four criteria for assessment of the dialectical obligations of an argument. The arguer, to fulfill these obligations, must:

- ◆ Anticipate an objection to a premise (206)
- ◆ Anticipate other criticisms (206)
- ◆ Deal with alternative positions (207)
- ◆ Anticipate the consequences and implications (208)

An argument which does not satisfy these conditions has not satisfied the dialectical tier, and can be negatively evaluated because of this limitation, regardless of the logical soundness of the argument.

Johnson gives the teacher of composition a set of criteria for evaluating argumentative writing which is fully informed by current research into audience. Furthermore, it functions systematically, in a way that also translates immediately into a grading rubric. The limitation of the dialectical paradigm, however, is precisely its grounding in rationality. It presumes that, if the argument is well constructed, the audience's assent is likely, predictable, rational. If the most cutting edge of audience research has taught us anything, it's that audience response to a text is not sure to be rational.

Thomas Kent provides us with the foundation for paralogic rhetoric. Kent believes that "most writing and reading courses" assume that "discourse hooks on to the world in a predictable way" (35), much like Johnson's dialectical paradigm presumes. From the paralogic position, in contrast, "neither a writer's knowledge of a writing process—any process—nor her ability to employ a process will ensure that she will communicate effectively" (36). In the paralogic perspective, "writing and reading cannot be reduced to systemic processes" (37), and, corollary to that claim, we cannot teach students to write more effectively if that means writing to dominate or control the interpretive work of the reader. There is no art of rhetoric, no dialectical paradigm, in Kent's perspective, that can guarantee that much control over our own discourse.

Kent focused specifically on the philosophical investigation of the instability of language as carrier of meaning to justify his claims. Empirical research in audience gives us qualitative data rooted in real human interpretive activity. We know, from the amazing variety of communities that form around texts, that no theory of audience (addressed, invoked, or otherwise) can completely explain the dynamics of the reception of a text as described by media research into fan communities. We know, from the astounding diversity of interpretations, appropriations, and transformations of media texts that fans produce, that it may be impossible to learn to write in a way that restricts those interpretations. The paralogic perspective, the thread of post-process theory that most radically challenges all of the assumptions we have about the possibility of writing classes to make effective writers by teaching them analytic tools and systems, is validated by this empirical research. Studies of fan culture let us look at the actual reception of texts and see that what Kent told us was true by virtue of philosophy is equally true empirically: that, fundamentally, if we hold conversation as the model for audience interaction with texts, we must admit that our texts, no matter how well designed, are subject to the idiosyncrasies of others. And no measure of rhetorical theory can predict or account for that.

In the classroom, this cannot play out, as Johnson's position can, directly in the rubric. We can't draft miscommunication, misunderstanding, and forcible reinterpretation of texts into our syllabi. But as we manage activities like peer review, response writing, and even in-classroom debates, we can keep this perspective in mind. Not every misreading is an error, not every misunderstanding is unproductive, and in many cases, they can yield an important new product: a sense of community, coalesced around an interpretation of a text.

Conclusion

When Ede claimed that "composition teachers can achieve a sophisticated, complex understanding of the nature and role of audience in written discourse only if they are aware of both empirical and theoretical research in their own and other disciplines" (140), she opened a door to research on audience within the composition tradition. I close this chapter by illustrating exactly how correct Ede was. Studying research in communication studies does yield a sophisticated and complex understanding of audience precisely because it both validates and undermines the implicit foundations of our work.

Research in listening and in the relationships that audiences have with media texts, on the one hand, gives us the tools to clarify student understanding of genre and of "voice." Armed with research on listening styles, we can discuss the ways that readers process various genres of text. Armed with research on authority, identification, and parasocial relationships, composition teachers can better explain the multiple functions of voice in a text.

On the other hand, research into convergence culture blurs the lines between production and consumption of a text in a way that fully manifests a conversational interaction between audience and author. It grounds a new way of teaching argumentation (and evaluating arguments in the composition classroom, the dialectical paradigm), yet calls into question the initial impulse behind audience research in the 1980s. That is, it invites doubts about the assumption that a more thorough understanding of audience will yield greater skill at writing more effective texts. The paralogic perspective articulates this skepticism from a philosophical perspective; convergence culture research gives empirical ground to the same claims. Audiences simply don't always behave in the ways that theories predict; therefore they cannot be controlled by adherence to such theories.

This twin discovery—that research in another discipline can at once improve the conception of audience at the center of composition pedagogy while at the same time destabilizing the implicit assumptions of that pedagogy—constitutes a complex and sophisticated contribution to answer Ede's call. The more richly we understand audience, the more it enables us to improve while it invites us to rethink our work.

Works Cited

Adorno, Theodor, and Max Horkheimer. *Dialectic of Enlightenment.* London: Verso, 1979.

Anderson, Benedict. *Imagined Communities: Reflections on the Origin and Growth of Nationalism.* New York: Verso, 1991.

Auter, Philip J., Mohamed Arafa, and Khalid Al-Jaber. "Identifying with Arabic Journalists: How Al-Jazeera Tapped Parasocial Interaction Gratifications in the Arab World." *Gazette* 67.2: 189–204.

Black, Edwin. "The Second Persona." *Quarterly Journal of Speech* 56 (1970): 109–119.

Bolter, Jay David, and Richard Grusin. *Remediation: Understanding New Media.* Cambridge, MA: MIT P, 2000.

Bowden, Darsie. "The Rise of a Metaphor: 'Voice' in Composition Pedagogy." *Rhetoric Review* 14.1 (Autumn 1995): 173–188.

Burnett, Ann and Rhea Reinhardt Beto. "Reading Romance Novels: An Application of Parasocial Relationship Theory." *North Dakota Journal of Speech & Theatre.* 2000. 13 January 2007 <http://www2.edutech.nodak.edu/ndsta/beto.htm>.

Charland, Maurice. "Constitutive Rhetoric: The Case of the *Peuple Quebecois.*" *Quarterly Journal of Speech* 73.2 (May 1987): 133–50.

Cherry, Roger D. "Ethos Versus Persona." *Landmark Essays in Voice and Writing.* Ed. Peter Elbow. Mahwah, NJ: Hermagoras P, 1994.

Comprone, Joseph J. "Recent Research in Reading and Its Implications for the College Composition Curriculum." *Rhetoric Review* 1 (1983): 122–137.

Cover, Rob. "Audience Inter/Active: Interactive Media, Narrative Control and Reconceiving Audience History." *New Media & Society* 18.1: 139–158.

Davis, Aeron. "Media Effects and the Active Elite Audience: A Study of Communications in the London Stock Exchange." *European Journal of Communication* 20.3: 303–326.

Ede, Lisa. "Audience: An Introduction to Research." *CCC* 35 (1984): 140–54.

Ede, Lisa, and Andrea Lunsford. "Audience Addressed/Audience Invoked: The Role of Audience in Composition Theory and Pedagogy." *CCC* 35 (1984): 155–171.

Eyal, Keren, and Alan M. Rubin. "Viewer Aggression and Homophily, Identification, and Parasocial Relationships with Television Characters." *Journal of Broadcasting and Electronic Media* 47.1 (2003): 77–98.

Finucane, Margaret O., and Cary W. Horvath. "Lazy Leisure: A Qualitative Investigation of the Relational Uses of Television in Marriage." *Communication Quarterly* 48.3 (Summer 2000): 311–321.

Flower, Linda, and John R. Hayes. "The Cognition of Discovery." *Landmark Essays on the Writing Process.* Ed. Sondra Perl. Mahwah, NJ: Hermagoras P, 1994.

Hobson, Dorothy. "Soap Operas at Work." *Remote Control: Television, Audiences, and Cultural Power.* Ed. E. Seiter, H. Borchers, G. Kreutzner, and E. W. Warth. London: Routledge, 1999. 150–167.

———. "Women, Audiences, and the Workplace." *Televison and Women's Culture: The Politics of the Popular.* Ed. M. E. Brown. Thousand Oaks, CA: Sage, 1990. 61–74.

Hoffner, Cynthia, and Martha Buchanan. "Young Adults' Wishful Identification With Television Characters: The Role of Perceived Similarity and Character Attributes." *Media Psychology* 7: 325–351.

hooks, bell. "When I Was a Young Soldier for the Revolution: Coming to Voice." *Landmark Essays in Voice and Writing.* Ed. Peter Elbow. Mahwah, NJ: Hermagoras P, 1994.

International Listening Association. January 2007. <http//:www.listen.org>.

Jenkins, Henry. *Convergence Culture: Where Old and New Media Collide.* New York: New York UP, 2006.

———. *Textual Poachers.* New York: Routledge, 1992.

———. Ed. *Fans, Bloggers, and Gamers: Media Consumers in a Digital Age.* New York: New York UP, 2006.

Jenkins, Henry, and John Campbell. "Out of the Closet and into the Universe." *Fans, Bloggers, and Gamers: Media Consumers in a Digital Age.* New York: New York UP, 2006. 89–112.

Johnson, Ralph. *Manifest Rationality.* Mahwah, NJ: Erlbaum, 2000.

Kent, Thomas. "Paralogic Hermeneutics and the Possibilities of Rhetoric." *Rhetoric Review* 8.1 (Autumn 1989): 24–42.

Long, Russell C. "The Writer's Audience: Fact or Fiction?" *A Sense of Audience in Written Communication*. Ed. Gesa Kirsch and Duane H. Roen. Newbury Park, CA: Sage, 1990. 73–84.

Lunsford, Andrea A., and Lisa Ede. "Among the Audience: On Audience in an Age of New Literacies." *Engaging Audience: Writing in an Age of New Literacies*. Ed. Elizabeth Weiser, Brian Fehler, and Angela González. Urbana, IL: NCTE, 2009. 42–69.

Lunsford, Andrea, and Lisa Ede. "Representing Audience: 'Successful' Discourse and Disciplinary Critique." *CCC* 47:2. (May, 1996): 167–179.

Mallard, Kina S. "Lending an Ear: The Chair's Role as Listener." *The Department Chair* 9.3 (Winter 1999). January 2007. <http://www. cccu.org/resourcecenter/resID.2262,parentCatID.270/rc_detail. asp>.

Ong, Walter. "The Writer's Audience Is Always a Fiction." *PMLA* 90 (1975): 9–22.

Raymond, Geoffrey. "The Voice of Authority: The Local Accomplishment of Authoritative Discourse in Live News Broadcasts." *Discourse Studies* 2 (2000): 354–379.

Ritchie, Joy S. "Beginning Writers: Diverse Voices and Individual Identity." *Landmark Essays on Bakhtin, Rhetoric, and Writing*. Ed. Frank Farmer. Mahwah, NJ: Hermagoras P, 1998.

Stroupe, Craig. "Rhetoric of Irritation." *Defining Visual Rhetorics*. Ed. Charles A. Hill and Marguerite Helmers. Mahwah, NJ: Lawrence Erlbaum Associates, 2004. 243–258.

Tannen, Deborah. *You Just Don't Understand*. New York: Ballantine. 1990.

Wall, Melissa. "'Blogs of War': Weblogs as News." *Journalism* 6.2: 153–172.

Walzer, Arthur E. "Articles from the "California Divorce Project": A Case Study of the Concept of Audience." *CCC* 36:2 (May, 1985): 150–159.

Wander, Phillip. "The Third Persona: An Ideological Turn in Rhetorical Theory." *Central States Speech Journal* 35 (1984): 197–216.

Watson, Kittie, and Larry Barker. "Comparison of the ETS National Teacher Examination Listening Model with Models Used in Two Standardized Tests." *Journal of the International Listening Association* 6: 32–44.

Weaver, James B. "Personality and Self-Perceptions about Communication." *Communication at Personality*. Ed. J. C. McCroskey, J. A. Daly, M. M. Martin, and M. J. Beatty. Cresskill, NJ: Hampton P, 1998. 95–117.

Weaver, James B., Kittie Watson, & Larry Barker. "Personality and Listening Preferences: Do You Hear What I Hear?" *Personality and Individual Differences* 20: 381–387.

Wicks, Robert H. *Understanding Audiences: Learning to Use the Media Constructively*. Mahwah, NJ: LEA, 2001.

Worthington, Debra. "Exploring Juror Listening Processes: The Effect of Listening Style Preference on Juror Decision Making." *International Journal of Listening* 15: 20–35.

———. "Exploring the Relationship between Listening Style Preference and Personality." *International Journal of Listening* 17: 68–87.

---III---

PRAXIS STREAMS: AUDIENCE WENDING THROUGH CLASSROOMS AND COMMUNITIES

*Scholars Respond to Audiences Addressed
and Invoked, Diverse, and Interactive*

CHAPTER SIX

New Media's Personas and Scenarios

DAVID DAYTON
Towson University

If we ask instructors of technical communication to list the top precepts about writing that they teach, most will mention the axiom of rhetoric, both ancient and modern: "Know your audience." If we then ask the instructors how they teach students to discover and represent knowledge about an audience, most of what they tell us will be covered by this short list of general techniques:

- Worksheets for classifying the audience into primary and secondary readers as well as into types of readers defined by job roles;

- Heuristics for getting students to think about their readers' background and education, their likely attitudes toward the subject, and their interests and goals related to the information;

- Suggestions for seeking insights by consulting people in the intended audience, or people who can be regarded as proxies for audience members.

These methods reflect the theory of audience that emerged and quickly stabilized during the 1980s as the teaching of technical writing took a rhetorical turn and became a distinct subdiscipline of composition and rhetoric. Emphasizing Lisa Ede and Andrea Lunsford's audience addressed, "the concrete reality of the writer's audience" ("AA/AI" 156), this approach assumes that "knowledge of this audience's attitudes, beliefs, and expectations is not only possible (via observation and analysis) but essential" (156). Audience invoked, the once-rival view of a writer's audience that Ede and Lunsford reconceptualize as complementary, receives attention from technical communication teachers and textbooks indirectly through the basics of document design, workplace and technical writing style, and common genres such as memo and letter reports, how-to instructions, mechanism and process descriptions, formal reports, and others.

This standard approach to treating audience addressed/audience invoked works best with students who have already had work experience that involved substantial writing. The approach is far less successful with students who have only experienced writing in academic contexts because they tend to reify the audience addressed and to use generic outlines as rigidly formulaic templates, invoking in their texts an abstractly conceived, stereotypical representation of the intended audience. How can technical communication instructors help students to imagine their intended audience vividly and concretely and then remain continuously mindful of that audience while planning, drafting, and revising? This is exceedingly difficult for students to accomplish when they are not writing to real audiences and when the only proxies for their imagined audiences are fellow students and their instructor.

In most important workplace writing tasks, a feedback loop informs adjustments to the writing and design of the text; this process helps to bring the audience invoked by a text into sync with the most likely attitudes, perceptions, and reactions of the audience addressed. Toward the end of their landmark essay, Ede and Lunsford describe a feedback loop common in scholarly writing. To provide students in technical communication courses with a semblance of that kind of constructive feedback, instructors of technical communication critique drafts and assign peer reviews—each reviewer acting as a stand-in for the audience addressed in evaluating the matchup with the audience invoked by the text. That is asking a lot of instructors and peer reviewers: to keep a student author's abstractly imagined audience clearly in mind while evaluating the author's draft.

In designing assignments for my courses, to make the audience addressed/invoked more real for writers, their peer reviewers, and me—the ultimate evaluator of students' writing performances—I have adopted the practice of having students create image- and detail-rich stories of vividly imagined persons who represent their intended audience. These visual-verbal representations of key audience groups originated and evolved as design artifacts in the world of website designers; they are called by names familiar to scholars of rhetoric and writing: personas and scenarios. I learned to create and value these types of personas and scenarios from experts in plain language writing and information design, consultants who themselves learned to create them while working with multidisciplinary teams to develop websites for large organizations and government agencies.

Interaction designer Alan Cooper is credited with popularizing personas and scenarios, which are now considered standard elements of a user-centered design process for creating all manner of interactive information products. Cooper championed their use in his popular polemic arguing for user-centered technology design, *The Inmates Are Running the Asylum: Why High-Tech Products Drive Us Crazy and How to Restore the Sanity.*

> Personas are not real people, but they represent them throughout the design process. They are hypothetical archetypes of actual users. Although they are imaginary, they are defined with significant rigor and precision. Actually, we don't so much "make up" our personas as discover them as a byproduct of the investigation process. We do, however, make up their names and personal details. (Cooper, *Inmates* 123)

It is now common for teams developing websites and high-tech products to invent personas based on market segmentation data and findings from user research. They distinguish personas based on sets of distinct goals related to the product being designed. After composing the persona documents, which usually include a photograph or illustration, the teams turn their attention to imagining the persona interacting successfully with their product-in-the-making; these brief but detailed narratives are scenarios. By Cooper's definition, "A scenario is a concise description of a persona using a software-based product to achieve a goal" (*Inmates* 179).

Personas and scenarios have only recently entered the conceptual vocabulary of technical communication, and they have not yet appeared in our textbooks. But they will soon, initially in textbooks teaching user-centered design of websites and online documentation. I have found benefits in using personas and scenarios in all significant information design projects involving advanced undergraduate and graduate students. I have found that having students compose personas and scenarios invigorates their invention and discovery work and enriches their sense of audience throughout the process of writing and design—particularly when they are working in teams.

A Short History of Personas and Scenarios

Alan Cooper developed personas in 1983 as a tool for defining software-user requirements ("Origins"). To gather requirements for a project management application, he interviewed people representing the type of knowledge worker with a use for the tool he envisioned. These interviews were apparently somewhat intense, for Cooper reports that during breaks from writing code he spontaneously began to dialogue with the invoked mental representations of these people. One in particular seemed the perfect archetype of the users he needed to win over with his application, and his play-acting episodes began to focus on conversations with her. She became the prototype for the formalized fictional representations that Cooper later began to develop as a standard procedure for analyzing user groups and their goals. He taught associates of his consulting company to create personas, and in 1998 he revealed this method to the world in *The Inmates Are Running the Asylum.*

Microsoft researchers Jonathan Grudin and John Pruitt note that personas have their roots in "the abstract user representations" (3) commonly used by marketing analysts; they credit Cooper with enriching the concept and adapting it for design of software and websites. Cooper admits that there are similarities between his personas and the traditional archetypes created by marketers to represent the targeted audiences for products; however, he insists that his personas are distinct in their focus on user goals and in the richness of realistic detail and narrative drama that go into creating them ("Origins"). Everyone agrees that Cooper's book (*Inmates*) created a tipping point in the spread of personas as a design technique among information architects and interaction/interface designers.

The use of scenarios to describe user requirements developed in the early 1990s, promoted by members of that part of the software development community that goes by the name of human-computer interaction (HCI). At an international HCI conference in 1993, Bill Verplank and colleagues urged designers to use scenarios to expand and explore what they knew from their empirical observations of users' experiences by role-playing through the characters in scenarios, which were defined as "fictional stories, with characters, events, products, and environments" (36). Verplank and colleagues taught that "scenarios put us in another person's shoes. By developing stories about characters with different characteristics from our own, we are forced to think about the experience of using things from a different point of view" (36). They also stressed the need to make scenarios visual: "The stories always have a visual element—because they are the vehicle for expressing visual design ideas and interactions between people and things" (36). These descriptions of design scenarios by Verplank and colleagues prefigure the development of the personas and scenarios widely used today in the design of websites and many types of products requiring users to interact with computerized information interfaces such as cell phones, MP3 players, and myriad high-end appliances and devices.

When Grudin and Pruitt decided to experiment with persona-centered interface design at Microsoft, they began with Cooper's concept of personas but tied the selection of user groups and the creation of personas to a rigorous examination of user research data, both quantitative and qualitative. They recorded extensive detailed information about each persona in a central document containing "copious footnotes, comments on specific data, and links to research reports that support and explain the personas' characteristics" (5). Their "persona team" orchestrated a communication campaign about personas to the entire product development team through "posters, flyers, handouts, and giveaways (e.g., squeeze toys with persona images and information)" (6). They also used email, including email sent to developers from the personas themselves. Grudin and Pruitt admit that such campaigns can lead to "persona mania," and warn against their overuse: "Personas are not a panacea. They should augment and enhance—augment existing design processes and enhance user focus" (8).

Echoing both Cooper and Verplank and colleagues, Grudin and Pruitt compare the persona-driven design process to method acting. "A character is fiction, but the behavior is based on real data" (149). Whitney Quesenbery, influential information design consultant and past president of the Usability Professionals' Association, who has a bachelor's degree in theatre, teaches a persona-centered approach to user-centered design that has much in common with the one developed at Microsoft. I follow the general outline of her method in teaching personas and scenarios to my students. The interaction design textbook by Cooper and Reimann presents essentially the same steps:

- ♦ Collecting and analyzing data on users, their tasks, and their contexts of use

- ♦ Identifying primary and secondary user groups based on differences such as job function, level of experience, usage patterns, and, especially, the most important goals in using the product

- ♦ Creating the profile of a single user who will represent each user group: one set of distinct demographic, attitudinal, and behavioral characteristics

- ♦ Adding a realistic life story to create personas based on the user profiles, checking the accretion of details against data from the real users in the group the persona is meant to represent as an archetype

- ♦ Creating vivid mini-stories depicting the personas using the product

Why Personas and Scenarios Have Caught on

Real-world design teams use personas and scenarios because they

- ♦ Condense, organize, and clarify findings from marketing and user research into a coherent vision of users and their goals

- ♦ Allow that vision to be communicated compellingly to everyone with a stake in making the product a success

◆ Articulate clearly all key assumptions affecting design so they can be validated through research and discussion

Quesenbery notes that the chronological structure and agent-action thrust of storytelling help us encapsulate our understanding of causality and correlations. "As a communication tool, stories let one person persuade many. . . . Storytelling ignites the listener's creativity" (6). In commenting on the power of storytelling as a design tool, Grudin and Pruitt note how naturally and well it fits with our everyday ways of thinking collectively:

> From birth or soon thereafter, every day of our lives, we use partial knowledge to draw inferences, make predictions, and form expectations about the people around us. We are not always right, but we learn from experience. We continue to extrapolate. Personas evoke this universal capability and bring it into the design process. (4)

Another Synthesis for the Addressed/Invoked Dialectic

Personas and scenarios encapsulate the dialectic about real and imaginary readers that forms a leitmotif running through our field's theorizing about a writer's sense of audience. Personas and scenarios reconcile the dialectic between audience addressed and audience invoked, a thesis-antithesis whose synthesis is direct communication with users: Robert R. Johnson's "audience involved." Personas and scenarios synthesize all three views of audience; using them, writers enter the world of user-experience design:

◆ Involving the audience in the planning stage through user research, including contextual inquiry and other methods involving firsthand observation and communication

◆ Addressing the needs and interests of niche audiences through concretely felt identification with distinct personas and their specific goals

◆ Invoking these representatives of targeted audience subgroups in every aspect of information and interaction design

Audience theory in technical communication has already conceived of personas on both sides of our texts and hypertexts. Coney and Steehouder wrote of the need for Web designers to consider the best match between a site's authorial persona and the primary user personas. Jonathan Price also describes this persona-to-persona approach to writing and information design (32–34), a perspective certain to become more prominent in technical communication as Web content development becomes a core component of our curricula.

Textbooks in Web writing, website design, and human-computer interaction have already begun to include step-by-step instructions in how to create personas and scenarios, including examples (Redish; Cooper and Reimann; Garrett; Wodtke; Brinck, Gergle, and Wood). Professors teaching Web design, online documentation, and multimedia will naturally be among the early adopters of this innovative audience-analysis method. Some of us are already having our students compose personas and scenarios in these types of classes. We need studies looking into the impact of these methods on students' experience of the audience analysis method and how the method appears to affect the information products they design.

Will this method, or some variation of it, benefit students analyzing audiences in business and technical writing service courses? Can the method be adapted for use in courses focused on certain genres of expository writing, such as science writing, environmental writing, and advanced technical writing? These and sundry other provocative questions await reports from teacher–researchers.

In technical communication, we already teach our students to identify actual members of the target audience, gather information about these people and relate it to their goals for the information being designed, and observe, if at all possible, members of the intended audience doing the work that requires the information being designed. What has been missing from our approach to analyzing audiences is the middle of the three approaches elaborated by Karen Schriver in *Dynamics in Document Design*: classification-driven, intuition-driven, and feedback-driven. In our teaching of audience in technical communication, we have added the feedback-driven approach to the classification-driven approach, but we lack easily describable methods and tools for linking the audiences that our students define through heuristic procedures to the projected audiences created by their texts, the fitness of which can be reliably validated only by gathering feedback from actual members of the target audience. I conceive of both audience addressed and audience invoked as operative only through the intuition-driven approach; in both cases, the material that the imagination and intuition work on is knowledge distilled from observation and experience.

Putting It into Practice: The MiViP Handout Assignment

In my current position, I teach a course each fall semester introducing master's students to technical writing and information design. In a recent version of the course, I had the students work in groups on the first of three projects and then gave them the option of working alone or together on the other two projects. (Only one student out of the ten chose to go solo on the other two projects.) The first project was to create a handout about the Microsystems-based Visual Prosthesis, or MiViP (Delbeke and colleagues). I provided all the source information for the handout: a PDF copy of a no-longer-available website about the MiViP, a conference proceedings paper, and a more recent two-page fact sheet with an illustration of the MiViP concept.

The audience for the handout to be developed by the students consisted of people attending a technical presentation by one of the MiViP project scientists; his talk was slated to precede a panel discussion on biomedical ethics. That context, my instructions for the assignment noted, would attract many people with minimal interest in the technical details about the MiViP but with some interest in understanding generally how the device works and in knowing key facts about the project. The purpose of the handout was to give an overview of the MiViP project before the presentation and follow-up panel discussion got under way.

I introduced the class to the project by distributing a one-page description of the case problem, which we read together to spark a discussion aimed at clarifying their understanding of the rhetorical situation. We considered a number of reasonable assumptions about the audience and production constraints: the pros and cons of various formats and software options; what images could be obtained and how they might be modified; the use of color, images, and printing methods. Working in groups of three or four, the students then met to exchange contact information and figure out how they would collaborate online.

The first project milestone I set was to create at least two personas with corresponding scenarios. Each group decided to have at least two group members create a draft persona and scenario, which those students posted to the course website and discussed in the following week's class meeting. I had lectured on personas and scenarios and had provided them with links to Web pages and PDF documents containing a variety of sample personas and scenarios, most of which are available on the Web—nonacademic instructional texts for specialists in usability and user-experience design.

I divided the class of ten students into three groups (four, three, and three). Group A (four students) and group C decided to produce a three-fold brochure for the MiViP handout, while Group B went with an unfolded page printed on both sides. While the draft personas and scenarios created by all three groups demonstrated basic understanding of those artifacts' generic elements, some personas were short on specific details, which is often the case with first efforts at writing personas. To Cooper, details are essential for effective personas:

> That's because personas lose elasticity as they become specific. For example, we don't just say that Emilee uses business software. We say that Emilee uses WordPerfect version 5.1 to write letters to Gramma. . . . As we isolate Emilee with specific, idiosyncratic detail, a remarkable thing happens: She becomes a real person in the minds of the designers and programmers. We can refer to her by name, and she assumes a tangible solidity that puts all of our design assumptions in perspective. As she loses her elasticity, we can identify her skills, her motivations, and what she wants to achieve. (*Inmates* 128)

Real-world persona writers often do not place as much emphasis on concrete details as Cooper advocates. Indeed, the personas and scenarios produced by information architects, interaction designers, and usability professionals are quite varied, suggesting that the genre-formation of these design artifacts would make an interesting study. I encourage my students to follow the persona and scenario guidelines and examples developed by Quesenbery. However, I expose students to a variety of examples illustrating different levels of detail, organization, and visual display in personas and scenarios.

I have found that students tend to like writing personas more than they like writing scenarios; they find it easier to put themselves in creative writing mode when describing the characters representing subgroups of their audience than they do in writing brief narratives depicting these people using the information product being designed. Their first efforts at writing a scenario are often sketchy descriptions of what the persona would expect, or they may opt for a model of a persona in which the scenario is replaced by a bullet-point list of goals and expectations relative to the information product.

In reviewing students' draft personas and scenarios, I encourage them to think like fiction writers. I stress that their goal is to make their personas realistically compelling and to tie the personas' goals directly to specific aspects of the design concept that the group has begun to flesh out. All three groups in the master's class produced solid personas and scenarios, though the personas were more detailed and persuasive than the scenarios. Figure 6.1 presents an image of a sample persona created by a student for the MiViP project. I have added a scenario to illustrate the type of mini-story that I encourage students to emulate when writing scenarios to go with the personas they create.

In addition to the portfolio of projects that groups handed in at the end of the course, each student delivered an individually composed essay reporting and reflecting on what they experienced and learned from the projects. In the first part of this essay, they summarized what they experienced with regard to group dynamics, interaction, and division of responsibilities. They also recounted the story behind the development of each of the three projects and compared their group's products to those presented by the other groups. They ended the essay with a reflective account of what they most valued about what they had learned, what had caused them the most frustration, how they thought they might

Background

- 46 years old, married
- BS in Biology from University of Oregon and PhD in Biomedical Engineering from The Johns Hopkins School of Medicine
- Appointed to a two-year term as senior researcher under the Director of the National Institutes of Health
- Responsible for collecting and disseminating information about high-risk/high-payoff projects that could merit funding from NIH

Persona: Joseph Tufano

Joseph Tufano's passion is biomedical engineering, a passion sparked in the mid-seventies by the television series *The Six Million Dollar Man*. The show captivated Joseph, spurring a profound interest in the melding of flesh and machine to benefit those who have been incapacitated by injury or disease. Friends often joke about Joseph's penchant for reaching into the world of science fiction to predict the future of healthcare.

Joseph studied Biomedical Engineering at The Johns Hopkins University's Whitaker Institute. The education had a profound effect on Joseph's world-view of what was possible within his field, leading to a dissertation that focused on the relay of electrical charges from an artificial system to living tissue of the human nervous system. Joseph has spent most of his postdoctoral years working on interpreters that transmit electrical charges from the central nervous system to artificial limbs.

Scenario

Recently, Joseph accepted a position at the National Institutes of Health (NIH) under a two-year appointment by the director. One of his responsibilities is to investigate projects not currently receiving funds from NIH that could merit special consideration for support. A colleague suggested he attend the symposium at Towson University to get the latest information on the Microsystems-Based Visual Prosthesis (MiViP) being developed by an international consortium of researchers.

When Joseph arrives at the auditorium where the symposium is being held, he is greeted at the main doorway by a young man in a business suit. "Good evening, welcome to Towson University," says the student usher, handing Joseph a program.

After taking a seat in a rear corner where he can watch for people he might know, Joseph opens the program and finds, tucked inside, an attractive three-fold brochure about the MiViP. He opens it hoping to find more recent information about the project than he was able to find on the project's rather messy website.

He is surprised to find a colorful illustration of the MiViP that includes both a simplified schematic of key components and a cartoon-like portrait of a person wearing the device. Both parts of the illustration are clearly labeled with numbers that connect the parts to a simplified technical description. *Nice*, he thinks, *they should put this on the website*. After reading through the brochure, he makes a mental note to ask an usher on his way out if he can get extra copies of the brochure.

FIGURE 6.1. *A sample persona created by a student.*

apply what they had learned, and what future learning goals, if any, the course had led them to set for themselves.

My guidance for writing this essay directed students to provide details about how the teams divided the work on each project. Though the assignment instructions did not mention personas and scenarios, the students' reports mentioned them frequently because drafting the personas and scenarios had been the first step in the design process I had them follow. All but one of the ten students reported taking a turn at creating personas and scenarios, and some students reported having specialized in this task. To my surprise, none of the students expressed the slightest skepticism about the usefulness of this method for analyzing audiences. That contrasts with previous experiences I had had teaching online documentation and Web design classes in which students worked alone on a major project. In those classes, students' first reactions to personas and scenarios were marked by muted resistance, grudgingly accepting them as part of the formal planning report—which itself seemed mainly to be seen as an academic ritual of procedural correctness.

One student from a Web design class I taught wrote the following in a formal online discussion about personas, after the class had been through the experience of creating personas for their planning reports:

> In every course I've taken in technical communication, I have been told the following things, incidentally, that I already knew: research and analyze your audience before creating any communication and if the information gathered can be qualified and quantified, that would be optimum. The creating of personas and scenarios appears to fly in the face of this preemptive TCOM doctrine, so I had to question this. Isn't it better to find and design for real people in real, everyday situations at the outset, rather than to design fictional people in fictional contexts at the outset?

Though many students in those previous classes seemed initially skeptical about the method's value, I received no negative feedback about personas and scenarios after students had actually created them, and I received numerous positive comments about them, both in classroom conversations and in messages posted to the bulletin board in the Web design class, which was taught online. In fact, the student whose skeptical question is quoted above made a turnabout in attitude that was typical. After creating and using personas and scenarios in designing a website for an actual client, she became convinced of their value. She ended her post this way: "When all is said and done, the use of personas and scenarios is very useful for me as I approach my website designs in this class. It forces me to focus on prospective users and not solely on designer assumptions."

I have observed two general patterns about students' reactions to creating personas and scenarios. First, the more workplace writing experience students have, the more skeptical they are likely to be about the usefulness of creating personas and scenarios. And second, students working in pairs or groups on a project come to see the value of personas and scenarios more quickly than those working alone.

The strongly skeptical statement quoted above, for example, was written by a student who had been a broadcast journalist for a major news network; she had years of writing experience in journalism, public relations, and marketing. Her initial skepticism contrasts sharply with the attitude described below by a student who had little experience in writing for real-world audiences:

> When I first started working with the MiViP material, I felt overwhelmed because the content was very technical. I wasn't sure what to include in the brochure because there was so much information. Fortunately though, the personas came in handy, and I learned my first important skill: selecting appropriate content for the target audience. My past writing experiences didn't really require that I select details for a particular audience; usually, I selected details to meet a specific purpose. I am distinguishing the two because this project forced me to consider what information the reader needed and wanted to know, whereas my previous writing tasks focused around answering a question the way I saw fit. With these [project] documents, however, it wasn't about answering a question or proving a point; it was about presenting material that meets the audience members' needs.

In the class experienced by the student just quoted, the personas and scenarios proved particularly effective at getting teams to construct a shared vision of key audience groups and keeping teams focused on meeting the needs of their personas. The students in that class recognized how personas and scenarios helped MiViP project teams in particular, as shown by these excerpts from two end-of-term reports:

1. The first decision we made for the MiViP handout was to determine who our audience was. Day and I both created two personas and the group picked the best two out of the four. These ended up being an advocate for the blind and a student of ophthalmology. Then we started to design a handout that met the needs of both of our personas. . . . As a group, we were very pleased with how the brochure turned out. This handout meets the requirements of the professor and the needs of our personas.

2. Lori and Chris wrote the final MiViP personas that we used. I suggested the National Institutes of Health (NIH) as the place of employment for one of the personas. I looked up NIH online to make sure it was still in business. Chris then created Tufano, an NIH researcher. . . . As a usability test, I took the prototype to work with me and got some feedback from a respected colleague, who is in the targeted age bracket as our personas. His ideas were useful and confirmed my feelings about the brochure. I felt that we were on the right track.

Creating personas and scenarios is a way to bring imagination and intuition more forcefully into our analysis and invention of audiences. To try out this new storytelling paradigm, we must teach our students to think more like novelists and psychologists and less like accountants and engineers as they articulate who they think their audiences are and what those people would expect and want. By teaching our students to create personas and scenarios, we motivate them to break out of stereotypical thinking and imagine, instead of *types*, real people—unique, interesting, emotional, and ultimately interested only in getting quickly whatever it is they wanted that brought them to the interface or document that we have so thoughtfully designed especially for them.

Works Cited

Brinck, Tom, Darren Gergle, and Scott D. Wood. *Usability for the Web: Designing Web Sites That Work*. San Francisco: Morgan Kaufmann Publishers, 2002.

Carroll, John M., Ed. *Scenario-Based Design: Envisioning Work and Technology in System Development*. New York: John Wiley & Sons, 1995.

Coney, Mary B., and Michael Steehouder. "Role Playing on the Web: Guidelines for Designing and Evaluating Personas Online." *Technical Communication* 47 (2000): 327–340.

Cooper, Alan. *The Inmates Are Running the Asylum*. New York: McMillan Computer Publishing, 1999.

———. "The Origin of Personas." *Cooper Newsletters on Personas*. 5 February 2007. <http://www.cooper.com/content/insights/newsletters/2003_08/Origin_of_Personas.asp>.

Cooper, Alan, and Robert M. Reimann. *About Face 2.0: The Essentials of Interaction Design*. New York: John Wiley & Sons, 2003.

Dubrulle, Pierre. *MiViP: Microsystems-Based Visual Prosthesis*. 14 April 2003. 5 February 2007. <http://www.md.ucl.ac.be/gren/mivipresult.html>.

Ede, Lisa, and Andrea Lunsford. "Audience Addressed/Audience Invoked: The Role of Audience in Composition Theory and Pedagogy." *CCC* 35 (1984): 155–171.

Garrett, Jesse James. *The Elements of User Experience: User-Centered Design for the Web*. Indianapolis: New Riders, 2003.

Grudin, J., and John Pruitt. "Personas, Participatory Design, and Product Development: An Infrastructure for Engagement." *PDC 2002: Proceedings of the Participatory Design Conference*. June 23–25, Malmö, Sweden, 2002. 144–161.

Houser, Rob. "What is the Value of Audience to Technical Communicators? A Survey of Audience Research." *Crossroads in Communication*: IPCC 97 Proceedings, Salt Lake City, 22–25 October 1997. 155–166. Online reprint. *User Assistance Group*. 26 October 2008. <http://www.userassistance.com/presentations/audience.htm>.

Johnson, Robert R. "Audience Involved: Toward a Participatory Model of Writing." *Computers and Composition* 14.3 (1997): 361–376.

Lunsford, Andrea A., and Lisa Ede. "Among the Audience: On Audience in an Age of New Literacies." *Engaging Audience: Writing in an Age of New Literacies*. Ed. Elizabeth Weiser, Brian Fehler, and Angela González. Urbana, IL: NCTE, 2009. 42–69.

Ong, Walter. "The Writer's Audience Is Always a Fiction." *PMLA* 90 (1975): 9–22.

Price, Jonathan, and Lisa Price. *Hot Text: Web Writing That Works.* Indianapolis: New Riders, 2002.

Quesenbery, Whitney. "Storytelling: Using Narrative to Make Users Come Alive." *Workshop for the STC TransAlpine Chapter* November 2001. <http://www.cognetics.com/papers/whitney/storytelling+personas-tac.pdf>.

Schriver, Karen. *Dynamics in Document Design.* New York: John Wiley & Sons, 1997.

Verplank, Bill, Jane Fulton, Allison Black, and Bill Moggridge. "Observation and Invention: Use of Scenarios in Interaction Design." *Conference on Human Factors in Computing Systems INTERCHI'93.* Tutorial Notes. Amsterdam, The Netherlands, April 24–29, 1993. New York: ACM Press, 1993. 36.

Wodtke, Cristina. *Information Architecture: Blueprints for the Web.* Indianapolis: New Riders, 2003.

CHAPTER SEVEN

Tactician and Strategist

BOB BATCHELOR
University of South Florida

Jessica is a typical new student in "Writing for Public Relations," a foundational skills-based course in the three-semester public relations sequence at the University of South Florida (USF). She excelled in the introductory mass communications courses and eagerly anticipates finally digging deeper into her major. As a matter of fact, she earned an "A" in both the required writing courses—"Writing for Mass Media" and "Beginning Reporting"—further solidifying her decision to major in public relations, since she knows writing skills are critical for her future success in the profession.

Despite her enthusiasm, two weeks into the course, Jessica is dejected. She appreciates the constructive criticism and deep edits she receives on her papers but is puzzled by the thematic comments, such as "whose story are you telling here?" and "tell the organization's story." Jessica wonders if she somehow missed an important lecture in one of the introductory writing classes. Her confidence wanes. She doubts if she really has what it takes to make it as a public relations writer. At home that night, after thinking over the challenge all day, she jots a quick email to her professor requesting a conference during tomorrow's office hours. Jessica is determined to become a professional-level writer, the kind that any organization would love to hire.

In their meeting the next morning, the professor reviews some of the comments made on Jessica's early assignments. From her command of grammar and language, he realizes that Jessica is one of this semester's strongest writing students, so while fixing the challenge will take a bit of time and effort, the end result will be well worth it. Her problem is the same one he fights every semester with nearly every student regardless of ability level—Jessica does not understand the notion of audience as it applies to public relations writing.

Jessica's previous classes concentrated on addressing issues from a journalistic perspective, so the transition to looking at an issue from a company point of view runs counter to what she learned earlier. A short while later, however, after talking through the idea of audience, or more bluntly, the "publics" that make up public relations, the concept clicks into place and a beaming smile breaks out across Jessica's face.

Jessica's teacher addressed the change she needed to make within the broader theme of storytelling. He advised that she continue to write using journalistic techniques, but begin to analyze issues from the perspective of an organization's representative who is advocating on its behalf. Jessica's goal should be to remember the style (inverted pyramid, fact-based, etc.) that she learned in "Beginning Reporting," but consider that she is now strategically telling the company's story. Jessica assures her professor that she "gets it" and leaves the meeting revitalized. Her journey down the path to becoming a professional public relations writer is under way.

Excellent Writing Skills Required

A student entering public relations must possess exceptional writing skills. Every job ad, internship call, and piece of career literature emphasizes superior writing talents. When confronted with a number of highly qualified individuals, hiring managers routinely rank candidates based on their writing samples, as well as a writing test they often administer as part of the interview process. The challenge is that public relations students in introductory "Writing for Public Relations" courses face a steep learning curve, particularly in understanding audience.

Audience is at the core of every writing task students face, because at the heart of public relations is the goal of influencing human behavior. Organizations have short- and long-term objectives in communicating with audiences, or the numerous labels practitioners attach to them, such as "publics," "stakeholders," "customers," "consumers," and so on. In public relations, the practitioner has multiple audiences in mind when developing strategies and tactics to achieve objectives. The next logical step, therefore, is producing a variety of documents that reaches these audiences at the point of contact with them.

Every piece of information generated in a communications campaign begins with some targeted audience or several audience segments. For example, when IBM develops a quarterly earnings press release, it is aimed at current shareholders, as well as the media, potential shareholders, employees, vendors, customers, and future customers, among others. Thomas H. Bivins defines a target audience as the "end users of your information—the people you most want to be affected by your writing" (22). Since most public relations writing is designed to be informative or persuasive, the professional must understand the audience's goals, aspirations, and mindsets intimately.

The practitioner then makes careful decisions about how to reach a particular audience. Doug Newsom and Jim Haynes explain that the need for understanding a public goes beyond basic demographic or gut-level information to the broader use of psychographics, or classifying people "by what they think, how they behave, and what they think about—their special interests" (9). Grasping how the media, employees, activist groups, share-holders, and other groups come together to form an audience is a difficult issue for mass communications students beginning the public relations major to understand. Overcoming the challenge, however, is critical to their success as writing students and future professionals.

A primary concern is that the student's past coursework is journalism-based, which teaches them to think and write like journalists. As future public relations professionals, however, they must quickly learn to think and write like representatives of organizations, whether large corporations or nonprofit agencies. In actuality, students have to initially "unlearn" what they have been taught about audience in basic journalism and mass communications writing classes but retain the journalistic writing style, which guides both professions. The student's understanding of audience is at the heart of this transformation. From the start, they must learn to tell the client's or organization's "story" rather than gather and report news.

Teaching Audience

Teaching audience to public relations students begins with a word that scares them beyond most others—"research." When students hear the dreaded R-word, they imagine dusty card catalogs and cobwebbed reference books stored in the library basement. In fact, though, the idea of researching a public relations challenge is vastly different. Students soon even realize (gasp!) that public relations research is fun, because it is multifaceted and critical in building an overall plan that solves an organization's problem. For example, common research tools, such as focus groups, surveys, and interviews, enable communications professionals to speak directly to and with their publics and are far removed from the initial scary thoughts students have about research.

The combination of primary and secondary research conducted at the initial stage of program planning enables public relations writers to build a comprehensive understanding of what is challenging a company and who needs to be informed to change the situation. The fact-based nature of this information allows a communications plan to be built on more than gut instinct or intuition.

Most important, research helps ferret out a great deal about audiences and potential audiences. In examining secondary research for a technology company, for example, a practitioner learns much about marketplace competitors and the kinds of articles written about the industry. Often, one finds details within the research that open up a new audience that might have been otherwise overlooked. According to Bivins, "Knowing the audience for whom you're writing is probably the most important factor in planning your message. The success of your writing will be determined, to a great extent, on how well you've aimed your message" (23). In "Audience Addressed/Audience Invoked," Ede and Lunsford acknowledge the challenge in reaching audiences due to the varying thoughts and opinions within seemingly uniform demographic groups. Writers have "no recipes," the authors explain, that account for the uniqueness of each "rhetorical situation," which forces "the writer, catalyzed and guided by a strong sense of purpose, to reanalyze and reinvent solution" (164). Student communicators address this challenge by learning to use a variety of writing tools, from press releases to social media tactics, to connect to audiences, though they certainly realize that hitting everyone within a target group is virtually impossible. Professionals who understand the interaction between messages and audiences evaluate their work at different points across the continuum of a strategic plan to assess how the message is assimilated, as Ede and Lunsford encourage. In this way, according to the authors, "writers conjure their vision . . . by using all the resources of language available to them to establish a broad, and ideally coherent, range of cues for the reader" (167).

Tactician and Strategist

While thinking about potential audiences and how to reach them, public relations students are learning to be tacticians, honing their writing and critical thinking skills. These abilities are valued most when students move into entry-level positions—the "worker bee" part of their careers, when they will distinguish themselves based on their foundational skills. However, as they learn how to communicate professionally, they must also begin to cultivate higher-level strategic thinking and senior-level counseling abilities, which enable them to move up the job ladder later in their careers.

The best way for students to develop their tactical skills is through practice and real-world application at internships and/or volunteer positions. It is difficult, though, to replicate the stakes or culture at a public relations agency or corporation in the classroom. My colleagues and I at the University of South Florida attempt to overcome this deficiency by implementing service-learning projects, essentially pairing an entire class with a real organization. These efforts provide the writing students with exposure to realistic assignments that force them to consider audience as they craft messages and documents for an organization.

The energy created when students begin researching and drafting content for service-learning clients is exhilarating. Not only does it require them to constantly consider the organization's goals and aspirations, but crafting pieces that reach targeted audiences solidifies the writing lessons the students learn in the classroom.

Service-learning projects also help students better understand diversity and cultural sensitivity in a real-world setting. For many organizations, targeting a particular audience segment based on ethnicity or lifestyle is an important aspect of the overall communications plan. For example, one semester students worked for a client that provided health-care services to the working poor in one of Florida's large counties between Tampa and Miami. Much of its communications effort was directed at Hispanic workers, who could not afford or were not provided adequate health care.

Based on the client's need to communicate with this audience, the class conducted extensive research on the Hispanic community in the area. Since the client identified increasing Hispanic awareness of its facilities as a primary strategy, the students developed specific tactics to fulfill the objective, including reaching out to Spanish-language media and writing newsletter articles focusing on successes the organization had in delivering care to Hispanic patients. Providing this kind of service-learning project broadens the skills of student writers and gives them greater appreciation of concepts like diversity that they may or may not internalize by reading the textbook.

The process of creating written work further establishes students as tacticians. At the same time, however, they realize how public relations professionals influence behavior through strategic planning, which is the ability business executives value as tacticians transform into strategists. Working primarily with nonprofit clients and sensing their passion provides student writers with a better understanding of the link between a strategic communications plan and the steps needed to implement the plan. Therefore, service-learning projects reveal that students have learned the practical skills necessary for successfully entering the profession and, at the same time, help them better comprehend the role of strategic thinking.

Smartest Person in the Room

Few professionals in the business world are responsible for a more complex and vital function than those in communications. Just examining audience alone, a communicator must be mindful of all the external and internal touch points where someone may intersect with the organization, whether it is a customer, vendor, employee, reporter, or governmental official. A practitioner's list of potential "publics" is endless, particularly as social media websites, bloggers, and citizen journalists make the news cycle instant. As a result of the totality of the communicator's role, I tell my students that their goal as a professional should be to be the smartest person in the room.

Outside of actually serving as a chief executive officer, what other role combines psychological insight, writing ability, critical/strategic thinking skills, historical knowledge, interpersonal talents, and management all in one? Professional communicators are the eyes and ears of an organization internally and externally, as well as the keepers of its culture.

On top of being cognizant of these influences, practitioners then have to communicate with all these different groups in the way that the members want to receive information, which in written context alone may take the form of a press release, feature article, website content, speech, or fact sheet.

Social Media Transformation

Technology drives change. Often corporations are at the helm, pushing innovations out into the wider public, but sometimes, a groundswell of popularity surrounding a new technology bubbles up from below, propelled by users, before the business world leaps in and attempts to "monetize" the innovation. In today's tech-heavy environment, the Internet (particularly the Web 2.0/social media craze) is intensifying the push/pull nature of consumer marketing, as well as the notion of what constitutes an audience for communications professionals. Lunsford and Ede provide guidance for understanding audience in a social media environment in their essay "Among the Audience." While some critics may question whether "audience" still exists in the Web 2.0 world, the authors show that the term is still "helpful and productive" but expands to include a more nuanced understanding of medium and context (47). Perhaps the most significant change, however, is how the audience interacts with the writer. Lunsford and Ede explain, "In a digital world, and especially in the world of Web 2.0, speakers and audiences communicate in multiple ways and across multiple channels, often reciprocally" (48). This "momentous shift" toward reciprocity, the authors outline, adds a complex dimension to the work conducted by communications practitioners. At what point, for example, do roles switch as audience members respond to a chief executive's corporate blog by posting counterarguments and their own thoughts and opinions?

I am less convinced than Lunsford and Ede, however, that college students truly understand this shift. Although an overwhelming majority of students use social media tools, they do not necessarily know how to use them as a professional would as part of a strategic campaign. Teaching students to use social media as a practitioner is essential, though, because their future bosses will expect that they possess these skills. The case studies that follow will illuminate this point.

For example, since its launching in 2004, more than 110 million people have joined MySpace. Each day, it receives one billion page views, making it one of the top Internet properties in the world. MySpace fills an interesting void. The site allows people with computer access to become the star of their own show, a kind of mini-celebrity, attracting "friends," who are then listed on the Web page. Journalists have dubbed the most popular users "MySpace celebrities," some of whom have acquired more than one million friends. Many of these Web friends actually are better described as fans. Like an exaggerated, online version of the high school cafeteria, MySpace provides otherwise ordinary people with a taste of celebrity. Individual users then become their own brand, with friends serving as their enduring fans.

MySpace is also an increasingly commercial space for marketers to interact with massive numbers of consumers and for people to find content, whether a video from a little-known indie band or the television show *24*. A number of national advertisers are signed with the site, including Coke, Honda, and Procter & Gamble. An ad on the homepage can cost $500,000 a day. Countless corporations, including Wendy's and Unilever, have their own MySpace pages, which cost $100,000 or more. Several companies have already run successful viral marketing campaigns on MySpace. P&G, for example, launched a "Miss Irresistible" page for a new Crest toothpaste and drew almost 40,000 friends and more than three million page views (Sellers 73–4).

In October 2006, search engine behemoth Google made headlines by purchasing year-and-a-half-old YouTube for $1.6 billion. Though at the time wildly popular among teenagers and Web-savvy hipsters, YouTube was certainly no household name. Critics scoffed at the steep price. Since then, YouTube has shown no signs of slowing down. In January 2008 alone, for example, seventy-nine million users watched three billion videos.

Given YouTube's vast reach and popularity, marketers have searched for ways to join the phenomenon. At this stage, though, the results have been mixed and point to a dramatic change in the way people will accept or reject advertisements. The strongest indication is that it will be on their own terms, not those dictated by the elites running advertising agencies or television networks. The challenge for public relations professionals is that everyone understands that social media is fundamentally changing the meaning of audience, but no one has figured out the spark that sends a campaign into orbit. More often than not, the high-profile campaigns seem to have gotten lucky.

For example, Unilever launched its Dove "Real Beauty" campaign using real women as models, rather than the typical supermodel or actress that most beauty campaigns employ. As part of the campaign, the company placed a video, "The Evolution of Real Beauty," on its YouTube site in October 2006 that was an instant hit. The short ad became one of the most popular YouTube videos of all time, drawing more than 1.8 million views. However, Unilever's next attempt at creating social media buzz for Dove Cream Oil Body Wash fizzled. Unilever bought space for the video on YouTube's front page, which guarantees a large number of hits, but negative reactions ensued, including rebuttal videos discussing how the company does not understand the concept of user-generated video (Morrissey 10).

The Dove success and failure left marketers shaking their heads and forcing them back to the drawing board in hopes of finding a better way to build brand equity. The challenge is that social media audiences are fickle and have a finely tuned marketing meter. They are quick to label promotional videos "unauthentic" and stand up for the unwritten code that guides such sites. For corporations, viral marketing is a dicey proposition. Companies like Unilever, Coke, or Microsoft spend billions to build their brands. A great deal of equity can vaporize quickly when something like the Dove campaign goes wrong.

A surprising success that points to the breakdown of the wall between marketers and consumers is the user-created commercial. For example, Chipotle Mexican Grill ran a thirty-second commercial contest for college students, offering $40,000 in prize money. The company posted the two winning entries on YouTube and received seventeen million viewers the first month. Since Chipotle targets 18–34-year-olds, the YouTube exposure hit their primary audience.

Ultimately, what high technology has done is further remove marketers from what they most covet—control. Once a message reaches cyberspace, the corporation/agency no longer wields power over it. Web-savvy consumers satirize ads, develop their own competing messages, and discuss its content without the originator having much, if any, recourse. A mocking image of a corporate logo or unintended use of a product sent out over YouTube or MySpace damages the efforts taken to build the brand. The popularity of these social media sites almost ensures an audience. For some videos that get the magical viral marketing bump, the number of viewers can be staggering.

While the available technology gives consumers greater control over how companies market to them, marketers are exploring ways to use social media to develop deeper relationships. One company, Utah-based Blendtec, a maker of high-powered blenders, created David Letterman-like videos of founder Tom Dickson blending a variety of odd items, like marbles and golf balls. Dickson's online grinding of an iPod garnered more than three million views. The media soon picked up on the company, which received press coverage and a feature on NBC's *Today* show. According to author Paul Gillin, "Online video is the most cost-effective tool ever invented to test and refine ideas and messages. If you're lucky, it may be a bonanza of free publicity" (2007).

Gillin believes that public relations practitioners need to concede control if they want to use social media effectively, something that marketers are loath to do. "Once you put your video online, you've lost control of it. People will copy it, modify it, mash it up, and have their way with it," he says. "Accept this, and don't try to control what they do. On the contrary, resolve to learn from the changes they make, because there may be a better product or marketing opportunity hidden there" (2007).

Putting It into Practice

Audience is a difficult concept for public relations majors to fully grasp, since an organization's audience can be as specific as one journalist or as broad as all of a company's current and future customers. For example, consider the many potential audiences for a press release and fact sheet announcing Microsoft's new Vista software, a virtually unlimited number of interested parties. Then, think about the publics addressed in a speech on the War on Terror delivered by a prominent local congressman. In both cases, what the public sees or hears is generated by public relations writers and meant to inform, motivate, influence, and persuade. For students, the link between research and writing is difficult to ascertain. Writing teachers, therefore, must develop methods to force this linkage consciously and subconsciously. I confess that the way I go about teaching this notion to my students is by blatantly tricking them into answering incorrectly on one in-class and one take-home assignment. Then, I spend a significant amount of time leading in-class discussions and thoroughly editing their papers so they understand the best way to approach the assignments.

Since the students in the course are pre-professionals, most of them care deeply about the subject. They understand the benefit of becoming professional-level writers as they search for internships or jobs. Once we have talked through the assignments and they realize the significance of understanding audience that results from the discussions, they do not mind being tricked. As a matter of fact, a "once bitten, twice shy" effect comes into play. The trickery actually solidifies the lesson in their minds. Rarely do students make the same mistake again, though I do attempt to trick them again with a follow-up take-home assignment to make sure the idea really sinks in.

The following are the actual exercises I use to teach audience to students struggling with the idea. Though the work is designed specifically for public relations students, I believe that they could serve other disciplines as well. The first is an in-class assignment, while the second is take-home. In tandem, these exercises force students to spend significant time thinking about storytelling and audience.

In-Class Exercise

Early in the semester, I need students to break themselves of the journalist point of view, which is central to the writing courses they have taken previously. Bursting into class, I begin outlining events surrounding a fictitious fire in the early morning hours at a hotel in Incline Village, Nevada, on the shores of Lake Tahoe. Supposedly started by a bumbling guest, the fire destroys most of the hotel and leaves three people injured, including a local firefighter. The students are to imagine that I am the director of communications for the hotel and we are conducting a conference call to fill them in on the tragedy, since they are writers at the hotel's public relations agency of record. I need them to compose a press release for distribution to the local newspaper/media and to place on the company's website.

In supplying details and answering questions about the fire, I also provide a series of speculative points and inferences, including that I "believe" a guest started the fire in his room while using an indoor grill to make s'mores, a treat available through room service. I also give them completely useless information, such as the nightly cost of rooms. Remember, this is a crisis, so I am supposed to be agitated—half my hotel just went up in flames. After asking a handful of questions, the students get to work. They have about an hour to craft the best draft possible. I do not expect them to finish in that amount of time, but I do expect a solid start.

With great anticipation, I review the releases that evening and similar words jump out of the headlines and leads—"devastating fire," "tragic injuries," "total destruction," and so on. In the heat of the moment and under duress, the student writers fall back on the skills they learned in their journalism-based courses. They write investigative pieces that would make Woodward and Bernstein proud. The students proceed to tell the media story, including that a guest started the fire by mishandling a grill used to make s'mores. My reply: Gotcha!

The next class period, before returning the students' heavily edited papers, we begin another discussion about storytelling and audience. I draw an imaginary line down the center of the room. Jumping over to one side, I announce that I am a journalist and outline how I would approach covering the hotel fire to inform the public about the event. Then, I jump over the invisible line and begin to talk about what the organization needs to tell its audiences and how the two differ.

Almost on cue, I watch the lightbulbs go on as the student writers figure out why telling the journalistic story is not addressing the many audiences the company needs to reach, ranging from employees and current guests to shareholders and the local community. Definitely some information will overlap for the journalist and public relations writer, but their outlooks are fundamentally different. Moreover, that difference is okay. Each side has a story to tell and, more important, every right to tell that story to the best of its ability.

The need to write persuasively has historically come under fire in public relations and broader communications writing. Joseph M. Zappala and Ann R. Carden view persuasion as a central element in public relations writing and quite different from "propaganda," but many people cannot tell the difference and incorrectly believe all persuasive writing is evil and all public relations writing is propaganda. "Public relations professionals are in the persuasion business," Zappala and Carden explain. "They are advocates for their organizations; every conversation, every proposal, every media event, and every piece of writing is intended to influence, build rapport, and win support. But, winning support at any cost is never an option" (8). There is a fundamental difference between public relations and propaganda, particularly when it comes to developing messages. Public relations is a profession built on ethics—truthfulness, authenticity, respect, equity, and social responsibility (Baker and Martinson 15–18)—whereas propagandists deliberately try to manipulate their audiences through misinformation. Persuasive writing provides the information necessary for its audience to make informed decisions and then take action.

Take-Home Assignment

Another press release assignment serves to further ensure that students understand audience. I provide students with a copy of an op-ed by a prominent writing expert that discusses the business value of effective electronic communications. I ask them to imagine that the article is actually a set of notes that they took in talking about the subject with the author, who has hired their agency to write a feature release for potential placement in a local monthly business publication.

Since it is a feature release, the student writers should focus on the larger theme of electronic communications, rather than overtly selling the expert or his services. Given such an assignment, a seasoned practitioner would attempt to interest a reporter based on the value of the topic and its universal nature in the digital age. In turn, the journalist would quote or feature the expert prominently in the published piece. It is a winning situation for both the journalist and the public relations professional.

As an assignment, the feature release forces students to consider a specific audience (the reporter) and why such a story would benefit the magazine's readers (primarily high-income business executives and self-employed owners), who make up the secondary audience. In addition, the nature of a feature release requires student writers to examine the topic more deeply through additional research, as well as investigate the magazine to see what kind of articles it usually publishes.

Narrowing the audience in this assignment further helps students make the connection between writing style and a targeted public. The content of the feature release must follow from a deep understanding of audience—as the idea is represented by an individual reporter and the potential appeal to all the publication's readers. I give the students a week to complete the assignment, so I know that they have had plenty of time to conduct background research, contemplate the topic, and ask additional questions, if necessary.

Once again, however, I am consciously tricking the writing students. Rather than just assign them a straight news release, I give it a feature twist, fully knowing that many of them will again panic under pressure (this is usually their first or second graded assignment) and turn in a release filled with sales language and focusing solely on the author and his company.

Even though the students learned from the hotel fire release, many of them need a second dose to fully drive home the points about storytelling and audience. They need to draw on what they learned in journalism-based writing courses, particularly what kind of news reporters/editors want to receive and how they expect to get it. The real skill, however, is in the way the students internalize the information and present it from a thematic point of view that respects what the reporter and client require.

Conclusion

An approach public relations programs should consider as they retrain students to think about audience as public relations professionals is to break from the traditional journalism-based introductory writing classes and develop courses specifically designed to change the way students strategically approach audience. Currently, undergraduates in most programs are forced to take required journalism classes. This can be likened to English majors being taught to write in sociology or psychology departments and then brought back for one class in their senior year to learn the complexities of their major department. This system is not doing public relations majors justice, particularly in forcing teachers to reinvent student understanding of audience in a short time period. It is an outdated model based on the idea that journalism created public relations in the late nineteenth century, or that public relations is a subdiscipline of journalism. With the proliferation of public relations majors nationwide, I estimate that within a decade most public relations professionals will have a public relations major. As educators we must be willing to transform the writing curriculum to teach this new kind of student the specific skills needed for future success, developing introductory writing classes that teach journalistic writing style without the burden of a view of audience that students will have to switch when they enter the public relations-specific writing course. If students understand audience from a public relations perspective from the beginning, they will be better prepared for roles as near-term tacticians and long-term strategic counselors. These are the skills that students must command in today's marketplace and what sets them apart from other professionals.

Works Cited

Baker, Sherry, and Martinson, David L. "Out of the Red-Light District: Five Principles for Ethically Proactive Public Relations." *Public Relations Quarterly* Fall 2002: 15–18.

Bivins, Thomas H. *Public Relations Writing: The Essentials of Style and Format.* 5th ed. Boston: McGraw-Hill, 2005.

Ede, Lisa. "Audience: An Introduction to Research." *CCC* 35 (1984): 140–54.

Ede, Lisa, and Andrea Lunsford. "Audience Addressed/Audience Invoked: The Role of Audience in Composition Theory and Pedagogy." *CCC* 35 (1984): 155–171.

Gillin, Paul. "The World's Watching: So Why Aren't PR Pros Using Viral Video?" *Bulldog Reporter's Daily Dog.* 29 March 2007 <http://www.bulldogreporter.com/dailydog/issues/1_1/dailydog_barks_bites/ index.html>.

Hagley, Tom. *Writing Winning Proposals: PR Cases.* Boston: Pearson, 2006.

Hardin, Marie C., and Donnalyn Pompper. "Writing in the Public Relations Curriculum: Practitioner Perceptions Versus Pedagogy." *Public Relations Review* 30 (2004): 357–64.

Lunsford, Andrea A., and Lisa Ede. "Among the Audience: On Audience in an Age of New Literacies." *Engaging Audience: Writing in an Age of New Literacies.* Ed. Elizabeth Weiser, Brian Fehler, and Angela González. Urbana, IL: NCTE, 2009. 42–69.

Morrissey, Brian. "Inside the Promise and Peril of YouTube." *ADWEEK* January 29, 2007.

Newsom, Doug, and Jim Haynes. *Public Relations Writing: Form and Style.* 7th ed. Belmont, CA: Thomson Wadsworth, 2005.

Sellers, Patricia. "MySpace Cowboys." *Fortune.* September 4, 2006.

Vandenberg, Peter. "Coming to Terms: Audience." *Literary Festival* 84 (1995): 79–80.

Wilcox, Dennis L. *Public Relations: Writing and Media Techniques.* 5th ed. Boston: Pearson, 2005.

Zappala, Joseph M., and Ann R. Carden. *Public Relations Worktext: A Writing and Planning Resource.* 2nd ed. Mahwah, NJ: Erlbaum, 2004.

CHAPTER EIGHT

I Can Take a Stance

TOM PACE
John Carroll University

R ecently, one of my first-year writers came to see me about some written comments I had made on his draft. Our brief exchange should be familiar to almost anyone who teaches writing. The writer could not understand why I kept asking the following questions in the margins: "How does this idea connect to your reader?" "Why would your audience need to know this now?" When I asked him in conference who his audience was, he looked at me oddly and replied, "Well, whoever would be interested in the topic, I guess. Or, to you, my teacher." Not only did my writer find audience awareness a baffling part of the writing process, he wasn't aware that it was something to consider when writing.

In their landmark essay "Audience Addressed/Audience Invoked," Lisa Ede and Andrea Lunsford ask, "What *is* the best way to help students recognize the significance of this critical element in any rhetorical situation?" (155). Ede and Lunsford go on to answer their question by arguing that writing teachers should attend to two crucial aspects of audience: the audience addressed, or the real audience identified, and the audience invoked, the fictional audience who is a construction of the writer. Their argument has been a useful reminder in my fourteen years of teaching composition that the dual nature of audience awareness they address should lead teachers and writers to consider the whole rhetorical situation.

More recently, though, Lunsford and Ede have revisited this question about audience, arguing in their contribution to this book that the term "audience" may be too restricting in a world dominated by new media and new literacies such as Facebook,

My Space, Wikipedia, and other types of web-based texts. Indeed, Lunsford and Ede suggest that the term "audience" assumes a singular reader and writer and at times fails to consider the collaborative and participatory nature of these new web literacies. While Lunsford and Ede do not completely abandon the term, recognizing the pedagogically enabling power of audience and the rhetorical situation in the writing classroom, they reflect on their own work in collaboration and audience by noting that "we have come to see that what we thought of as two separate strands of our scholarly work—one on collaboration, the other on audience, have in fact become one" (45). In short, Lunsford and Ede's conception of audience now considers the participatory and collaborative nature of web-based texts and how these new literacies impact the way our writing students consider audience in their own writing.

The experiences that most young writers bring with them to their first-year writing classrooms, however, feature little to no audience awareness. These experiences usually revolve around literature-based writing assignments or the writing they are asked to perform for various standardized tests. In these cases, students usually assume they are writing to a teacher, or to a group of teachers, judging their performance for numerous reasons—grammar, usage, adherence to the five-paragraph essay, thesis sentence—typically in noncontextual situations. Or perhaps, as Lunsford and Ede suggest, the writer/audience dichotomy has been thoroughly blended in the "cyberspatial-postindustrial mindset" most of our students inhabit, a space where "the distinction between author and audience is much less clear than in that of the physical-industrial mindset of print literacy" (44). Most students who enter first-year composition rarely have had the opportunity to write to an audience of a real-life public in order to inform, to persuade, to teach, or to perform any other cross-disciplinary rhetorical activity. Rather, most of the public-oriented writing students perform occurs outside the classroom in the form of email, blogs, social networking sites such as Facebook and MySpace, and other web-based rhetorical activity. In the classroom, however, most first-year students come to us having written only to an audience of one—the instructor. In this chapter, I argue that requiring first-year composition students to write for an academic public that reaches beyond the confines of the classroom contributes to a stronger understanding of cross-curricular discourse, as well as a more complex understanding of the interplay between an audience addressed and an audience invoked. This process of writing for an academic public puts into practice not only Ede and Lunsford's 1984 suggestions, but also their current suggestion for reconsidering audience in the light of new literacies.

To do so, I describe a first-year writing course in which student writers collaborated in small groups to develop, to write for, and to produce their own academic journal. By working on their own journals, these writers learned to address and invoke their academic audience in three key areas: one, how audience awareness impacted their decisions in the writing process; two, how sentence-level conventions connected to audience awareness; and, three, how the rhetorical strategies they needed to write successfully in class transferred as well to their courses outside first-year composition. While the project still asks students to produce a relatively traditional print-based project—the academic journal—most of the work is collaborative and is done by relying on the new technologies of email and the Web.

The Setting

In the fall of 2006, I taught a first-year writing course in which my writers worked in small groups throughout the semester developing, planning, writing, editing, and producing their own academic journal. The journal contained essays written by each group member that explored issues of education, online identity, and cultural critique that students and faculty at the university would find relevant and noteworthy. Student writers were charged with determining the main focus of the journal and selecting which essays should be included, as well as with layout and artwork. Writers were required to complete three major assignments that would be used in their group's academic journal: a piece on the aims of education, a piece on the online community Facebook, and a piece on cultural critique. In the process of putting together their academic journals, students collaborated by using email to send back and forth drafts and revisions. The students also wrote in a collective group when they drafted a "Letter from the Editors" that appeared at the beginning of each journal. Students also made use of various Web resources to help them find models and other materials when they assembled their journals. At the end of the semester, the groups' journals were reviewed by an outside team of writing specialists: the university's Writing Center director and two of his consultants—an English department graduate assistant and an undergraduate senior English major. Each specialist represented a member of the university public to whom the journals were addressed. These specialists came to class on the last day of the semester and discussed with the writers the strengths and weaknesses of each journal. Thus, throughout the semester, my writers became cognizant of the notion that they were writing to an audience of academic readers in a way they normally would not if they were just writing for me or for their class colleagues.

For their projects, they read a number of essays from David Bartholomae and Anthony Petrosky's *Ways of Reading* that revolved around each of the three main themes. For the education paper, students wrote in response to Paulo Freire's "The Banking Concept of Education," Richard Rodriguez's "The Achievement of Desire," and selections from "The Education of Henry Adams." These writers wrote essays about Freire's banking concept and its influence on their education, essays that applied Freire's ideas to their reading of Rodriguez, or essays that performed close readings of Adams's autobiography. For the section on online identity, students read Edward Said's "States" as well as a number of supplemental newspaper and magazine articles about the growing phenomenon of Facebook and its impact on student identity. For the cultural critique sequence, they read and discussed John Berger's "Ways of Seeing," Michel Foucault's "Panopticism," and Susan Bordo's "Beauty (Re)discovers the Male Body." They were then asked to apply these theorists' ideas to their own critical analysis of cultural texts.

In addition to *Ways of Reading*, students also read Gerald Graff and Cathy Birkenstein's little book, *They Say/I Say: The Moves that Matter in Academic Writing*, an accessible introduction to the various sentence-level rhetorical moves that academic writers make in argumentative writing. The authors present dozens of model templates that students can incorporate into their own prose in an effort to see how academic writing is often writing done in response to other people's ideas. The book helped my writers unpack the vagaries and mysteries of academic discourse.

In the course, I consciously wanted to address writing to an academic audience that consisted of readers outside the classroom. I conceptualized for my students an understanding of audience in two stages: I wanted my writers to follow Peter Elbow's suggestion to ignore audience consciously during early stages of their writing process and then to shift to audience awareness by following Ede and Lunsford's dictum to negotiate an audience addressed with an audience invoked. These two stages are recursive and were recycled several times during the semester as students wrote, re-wrote, planned, revised, wrote some more, and then submitted their final drafts. Here, I was very overt about for whom these students would eventually revise their drafts: the larger university public. Using the term *public* in addition to *audience* helped my students expand their understanding of who will read their writing, from a single reader to a larger community. As Lunsford and Ede observe in this collection, recent studies in audience note the changing terms scholars use when discussing readership. Terms like *public*, they stress, "gesture toward and evoke differing concerns, traditions, and interests" ("Among" 47). So, my students' task in revision was to move from writing for themselves, and by extension a single reader, to considering the implications for writing to a larger public with various interests and concerns.

Even though the process itself was generally a recursive one, the students' writing did follow two general steps. In the first step, students wrote drafts of each of the three major papers on education, online identity, and cultural critique. After I provided feedback on those drafts, students took the second step and re-read each other's drafts with an eye toward revising them for inclusion in their group's academic journal. During these steps, students moved through the two stages of audience awareness I wanted them to experience: going from ignoring an audience to considering how addressing and invoking an audience led them from producing academic writing that was bland and teacher-oriented to writing that meant something to them and to an audience of actual readers.

Ignoring Audience/Considering Audience

The first half of the course focused primarily on the first stage of audience awareness—ignoring audience. During this section of the course, students completed two drafts of each paper—one for their peer revision group and one for me. I wanted them at this stage to focus more on their summary of and response to the ideas they had just read about and discussed in class without getting bogged down too much in audience. As Elbow reminds us, "When we examine really good student or professional writing, we can often see that its goodness comes from the writer's having gotten sufficiently wrapped up in her meaning and her language as to forget all about audience needs: the writer manages to 'break through'" (97). This sense of getting lost in their writing, of needing to "break through," is what I wanted my writers initially to experience—fully aware that they are ignoring audience on purpose—so that they would then be prepared for the following step. Of course, most of these students had no problem ignoring audience because most of the writing they have done in the past involved almost no audience awareness. Indeed, most assumed they were writing to a teacher to show them how much they knew about a topic, or they wrote with no reader awareness whatsoever. One of my students, John, told me that he "basically just wrote. I never really considered what an audience would think. I just wrote whatever I had on my mind without ever thinking about what kind of audience I was getting to." Another student, Linda, said that while she had written for her hometown newspaper, she never had made the connection between an audience in the rhetorical situation of newspaper writing and the writing she did in school: "I wrote some small things that were published in my town's local paper, so my audience was my town, I guess, but I still wrote for my teachers because I knew that was the grade I was receiving." The difference between their earlier lack of audience awareness and my asking them to ignore audience is that I wanted to make the lack of audience overt for two reasons: one, to get them to focus solely on the topics and ideas they were writing about, and, two, to intentionally ignore audience so that when the time came in class to begin considering an academic reader, they would revisit their writing with fresh eyes and have a purposeful goal for revision. In other words, I wanted them to recognize the overt differences between ignoring audience and considering it.

Considering the academic reader, of course, came later. Once they had written all three drafts, and I had provided my own feedback, my writers reconvened in their small groups and re-read each other's drafts, this time looking for common themes and connections among the drafts to determine a focus for their academic journal. Once students determined what their theme would be and had a working title, each writer then revised their essays with that theme and with their audience very much in mind. We spent time in class discussing the academic audience, who an academic reader would be, and what they would value and look for in an essay. In their essay, Ede and Lunsford argue that "it is the writer who, as writer and reader of his or her own text, one guided by a sense of purpose and by the particularities of a specific rhetorical situation, establishes the range of potential roles an audience may play" ("AA/AI" 166). Here, Ede and Lunsford stress that the writer must be guided by the contingencies of the rhetorical situation and be prepared to consider both addressing and invoking an audience. As they conclude:

> A fully elaborated view of audience, then, must balance the creativity of the writer with the different, but equally important, creativity of the reader. It must account for a wide and shifting range of roles for both addressed and invoked audiences. And, finally it must relate the matrix created by the intricate relationship of writer and audience to all elements in the rhetorical situation. (169)

This sense of adapting to the various elements of the rhetorical triangle is exactly what I wanted my writers to recognize. At the same time, I also wanted them to be aware of when they address an audience, when they invoke the audience, and when they find it necessary to do both. I challenged them to recognize ways to address their academic audience in their revised essays. On the one hand, they began understanding the needs and desires of an academic audience and who those readers were. On the other hand, they still often found themselves imagining an academic audience and thus became aware of the textual signals used to invoke that audience.

These early drafts reflect how the writers struggled with representing often difficult material and articulating clearly how their own examples and ideas related to what they were reading. Here's an example of the kind of writing that ignores audience, an excerpt from an early draft titled "Oppressor vs. Oppressed in My Educational Experiences." In this paper the writer, Cassie, explores Freire's ideas about critical pedagogy and describes an example from a high school chemistry class in which her teachers tended to follow the banking concept:

> To retain all the information, I developed repetitious study methods such as using flashcards and mnemonic devices, which helped me learn the information and commit it to memory. In Freire's view, this is an example of the "banking concept of education, in which the scope of action allowed to the students extends only as far as receiving, filing, and storing deposits." (257)

> I studied and memorized what I was told, but when I was done with chemistry class, I forgot everything I learned. This reflects Freire's argument of a "ready-to-wear approach [that] serves to obviate thinking." (260)

This section appeared at the end of one of her paragraphs, and shows a lack of audience awareness because Cassie does not take the next step and flesh out how the example from her chemistry class reflects Freire's argument. Here's another example from the same paper in which she narrates a story from a high school history class when she corrected a teacher:

> I raised my hand, and commented about the discrepancy. My teacher admitted her error, changed General Grant's correct title and continued with the lecture as if nothing had happened. The fact that my teacher admitted her mistake was a shock to my educational world. In this instance, the formerly oppressed student found a fault with her oppressor.

Now, perhaps Cassie is overstating the oppressor/oppressed relationship a bit too much and as a result oversimplifies Freire's complex ideas about education. But I find two things very interesting about this passage. One, her stilted academic prose—"and commented about the discrepancy"—reflects a student writer unsure of her audience and relying on academic-sounding language and jargon. Indeed, this student later told me that "writing to the teacher meant doing whatever the teacher wanted. That's pretty much all I did." Her stilted prose reflects a student writing for an ideal teacher in her head and not to a real-world academic reader. The second thing that strikes me about this example, as well as the previous one, is that Cassie is still working out her understanding of Freire's ideas in this draft, and that is what is important here. Ignoring her audience gave Cassie the time and freedom to work through, to break through, Freire's complicated ideas about education, ideas that will not be fully clarified in one or two drafts.

By the time Cassie included this piece in the journal, she had revised it significantly, taking into consideration her journal's theme and the academic audience. Her prose grew stronger, more confident. Her new title, "Problem Posing Education and First-Year Seminar," reflects how she refocused her paper by analyzing only one example from her education, a first-year seminar course she was taking that same semester. This alteration reveals how she attempted to connect Freire's ideas to a class that all first-year students were currently taking, a class taught by faculty across the university. In doing so, she both addressed and invoked an audience made up of the university's academic community. Here's a sample from the revised version of the essay, in which she articulates Freire's vision of problem-posing education:

> Problem-posing, on the other hand, demands that both the teacher and the student take a more active approach in education, and the result involves intellectual stimulation. The key to problem-posing education is established communication and the eradication of the negative oppressor-oppressed relationship.

Here, not only does the writer demonstrate a much more mature grasp of Freire's ideas, but she articulates them in eloquent academic prose. She was also able to flesh out Freire's ideas more fully in this draft by clearly showing how her first-year seminar instructor draws on methods of critical pedagogy to teach her students:

> Freire would argue that her willingness to explore uncharted intellectual territory makes her a prime example of the problem-posing educator, because Dr. Orion is not "merely the one-who-teaches," but one who is [herself] taught in dialogue, listens to the classes' arguments and assertions, and takes them into consideration forming her own views around the opinions we present to her.

Again, the writing is clear, eloquent, and, unlike her first draft, deftly articulates how her example reflects Freire's ideas. Later, Cassie told me that "with the journal, I mostly revised and edited my paper around the theme we chose . . . and it just seemed after a while, writing to the audience came naturally. I knew who it was. It wasn't as hard as before to write to that audience."

Here's another student, Bill, who in an early draft tried to paraphrase Foucault's complex idea of panopticism and apply it to his reading of Susan Bordo's "Beauty (re)Discovers the Male Body." Here's how Bill opens his essay:

> Although knowledge and power go hand in hand, people are often unsure which force controls our lives. As a person in society, we are always under some sort of surveillance which effects our actions and reactions. In his chapter "Panopticism," Foucault discusses how the ideals gained from society determine how we act and behave without ever realizing it. Panopticism is the general principle of political change that deals with the relations of discipline.

Here, Bill tries to summarize Foucault's complex argument and, in the process, fails to clarify fully Foucault's definition of panopticism. Bill also shifts unconsciously back and forth between first and third person, signifying that he is unsure of his reader and of his own position toward the audience. As Bill worked on this draft and rethought it in the context of his group's journal, his revision reflects a greater awareness of audience. As an overall theme for their journal, Bill's group focused on how culture shapes and forms student identities. Here's the revised introduction:

> Although knowledge and power go hand in hand, people are often unsure which force controls their lives. As a student, I am generally under some sort of surveillance, which often affects my actions and reactions to society. In his chapter "Panopticism," Michel Foucault discusses how the ideas developed by society determine how individuals act and behave beyond their control. As Susan Bordo points out in her essay, "Beauty (Re) discovers the Male Body," Foucault saw power as a dynamic network of non-centralized forces. Panopticism penetrates its subjects with relations of discipline just as society places rules and pressures for students to conform to.

While there are still problems with parts of this introduction, I find it stronger than the original, in part because Bill is now more cognizant of his own position in relation to Foucault's argument, and he does a better job introducing Foucault's argument and relating it to Bordo's essay, which goes on to form the focus of the rest of the essay.

Later, Bill uses rhetorical questions effectively to leave his audience with something more to think about after reading the piece:

> Panopticism is a general principle of political change that deals with the relations of discipline. But social Darwinists may take issue with the argument that humans can be manipulated and taught to conform unconsciously. Is this the whole reason for our existence? Are we to gain power only to manipulate people to conform easily? Is it possible that we will learn so much about humans that we will reach a point that where there is nothing to learn?

Bill abandons the conventional student conclusion by avoiding set absolutes and posing questions to the reader for further reflection. In doing so, he does a nice job of both addressing and invoking his academic reader, while at the same time implicating himself in these questions. This implication suggests that, unlike many first-year student writers who tend to separate their world from a larger world, Bill is beginning to recognize the constant interplay between the individual and the social. When our university's writing center director read Bill's essay, he was particularly struck by Bill's conclusion and remarked that this type of inquiry forms the heart of what we as compositionists want to see in strong student writing.

Another student, Kelly, also wrote about Bordo's essay, and her revision of the essay from early draft to inclusion in her group's academic journal reinforces the positive effect that going from ignoring audience to considering audience holds on students' understanding of their own writing. In her essay, titled "A Shift in Cultural Values Introduces a New Demographic," Kelly contrasts definitions of masculinity in the 1950s and 1960s with contemporary definitions of masculinity to show how consumerism influences society's understanding of gender roles. Here's a sample from the introduction of her first draft:

> In Susan Bordo's work, "Beauty (Re)discovers the Male Body," she explores the evolution of advertisements, and the (re) discovery of the male body over the past few decades. When Bordo wrote this essay, pictures of naked women in advertisements had been around for a long time; however, when the first advertisement of an almost naked man hit the media, it caused quite a stir. Women of the time were not used to seeing naked men in advertising. Nowadays, it is a norm to see naked men (and women) in advertisements. This proves that the cultural ideal of a real man today is dramatically different from that of Bordo's day. Over the past few decades, cultural values and ideals in American pop-culture have changed dramatically, for the worse.

I find this original introduction fascinating on two significant levels. One, since Kelly is writing without much of an audience in mind, her prose tends to be somewhat muddled, confusing, and simplistic in her assumptions about culture and gender roles. She makes huge leaps in logic by setting up a rigid contrast between Bordo's ideas and how they differ from Kelly's perception of culture. Two, her lack of audience also leads her to use colloquial language as well as hasty generalizations. She uses the word "nowadays" and makes multiple general claims in her thesis: "cultural values and ideals in American pop-culture have changed dramatically, for the worse." When Kelly chose to include this essay in her group's journal, her challenge was to move from ignoring audience to considering how her audience impacts her language use. As she became more aware of her audience—faculty as well as students—she began to contextualize both her arguments and Bordo's ideas in a more sophisticated way that reveals her awareness of academic audience. Here's her revised opening:

> In Susan Bordo's work, "Beauty (Re)discovers the Male Body," she explores the evolution of advertisements and the (re)discovery of the male body over the past few decades. Bordo grew up in the 1950's and 1960's when consumers were not used to seeing semi-pornographic images of men featured in advertisements. For example, she tells us in her essay, "Women—both straight and gay—have always gazed covertly" (168). It was socially unacceptable for women of Bordo's generation to sexually gaze at images of men. However, this all changed when the first advertisement of an almost naked man hit the media, and Bordo tells us it created quite a stir. Consumers were not used to seeing men represented in a way that invited all types of women and men to linger over it, and many thought it was wrong. Bordo disagrees with this cultural reaction by arguing that since it is acceptable for men to look at and enjoy semi-nude images of women, it should also be acceptable for women to enjoy similar images of men. In contrary to advertising standards of Bordo's generation, today it is a norm to see semi-nude men (and women) in advertisements.

Kelly's revised introduction is much stronger, in part, because she is more aware of the conventions of writing for an academic audience. On the one hand, she addresses her audience by offering a clearer summary of Bordo's work and uses her summary to contextualize her own thesis, which is more nuanced and less reductive than her original draft. She also does a nice job of using signal phrases and other markers of academic discourse to guide her readers from sentence to sentence. On the other hand, Kelly invokes her audience when she notes that Bordo "tells us" about men and women in advertising. Ede and Lunsford note that by getting writers to invoke as well as address an audience, they become more fully aware of the whole composing process, in which "unless the writer is composing a diary or journal entry, intended only for the writer's own eyes, the writing process is not complete unless another person, someone other than the writer, reads the text also" ("AA/AI" 169). Here, Kelly's move from ignoring audience to using the academic journal as a method of understanding audience allows her to address and invoke her readers in often sophisticated ways previously unknown to her.

Each of these three writers realized that their initial prose was lacking in idea development and clarification of source texts, in large part due to their initial disregard for audience. By moving from a rhetorical stance that ignored audience to a stance that fully considered real-life academic readers, these writers were able to write stronger, clearer, more engaged prose. These examples of student writing show all three writers making these moves based on their involvement with the academic journal. Once Cassie was able to visualize her audience of university readers, she was able to focus on her experience in a first-year seminar classroom and draw connections between Freire's theories of pedagogy and her professor's practice of that pedagogy. Bill, once he was clear about his group's focus in the journal, was more confident in his handling of Foucault's difficult essay and, subsequently, reimagined the function of a conclusion by posing questions rather than wrapping everything up neatly and unproblematically. And Kelly, once she was able to make the move from ignoring her reader to considering him or her, was able to make the sophisticated move to addressing and invoking her reader at the same time. As a result, all three writers made impressive gains in their understanding of academic audience and the impact it has on rhetorical choices in their writing.

Putting It into Practice

Here, I would like to share my writers' reflections on how developing and writing for their own academic journal led them to greater audience awareness through seeing the overt connections between their writing choices and the audience they were addressing, through considerations of sentence-level features, and through their heightened awareness of audience when they wrote for courses across the curriculum. For instance, Cassie noted how focusing on an academic audience outside the boundaries of the classroom and the writing teacher made overt the audience being addressed.

> With the academic journal, I knew that other people who did not sit in this classroom, who were not teaching me, who I

had never met before were going to read my writing and not just my writing but the writing of my group, and so we helped each other edit our papers so that they could fit together in the journal. During the whole project, we took in mind that it wasn't just [you] and the consultants from the Writing Center. I knew they were going to read our journals, but I didn't know how many would be there.

Notice how Cassie's attitude toward audience awareness was developed through the experience of collaborating with a group on a project written for a real-life academic reader. Notice, too, how she makes the cognizant leap from writing for a teacher to writing for other academic readers and that those two audiences are often very distinct. The implication is clear: it's easier to teach audience awareness when students are asked to write for real-life readers who take genuine interest in what students write. It becomes easier for students to communicate their ideas in real contexts rather than just perform some artificial writing task for a teacher. As a result, Cassie has become an engaged writer, one with a clear sense of how to address audience and purpose in her prose.

Another writer, Linda, made similar connections. "I think that instead of just being assigned a topic and writing what you think your teacher might argue to please that reader, I can write about what I want but still have in mind that people are going to be reading it and to back it up with my personal experience along with other evidence."

Again, the implication is fairly clear: setting up real-life academic readers for students allows them to recognize overtly how audience consideration helps determine the choices they make in their writing and, as Linda pointed out, encourages them to take hold of their writing.

The same students told me later that writing and revising their essays for academic readers made them more aware of numerous sentence-level strategies that, before, seemed dry and lifeless but now appeared to connect overtly to rhetorical communication. We had spent considerable time in class examining issues of clarity, cohesion, transitions, signal phrases, and other sentence-level features necessary for strong academic prose. Cassie was particularly influenced by the guidelines for writing strong academic prose posited by Graff and Birkenstein's book:

> *They Say/I Say* really helped me with transitions, mostly, and got me thinking about my audience. But, what really got me thinking about audience was talking in class about the rhetorical triangle . . . It helped me establish the triangle for each class, and then I can plot the triangle not just for composition class but try it for science, for communication, for political science, etc. It helped me break down the papers in those other classes.

Notice how Cassie was able to take her work on sentence-level concerns such as using transitions—something many students may find dry or akin to rule-bound pedagogy—and draw connections to audience awareness. In other words, sentence-level concerns such as transitions become tools writers use to consider audience in their writing. At the same time, she was also able to see her writing as part of a much wider rhetorical triangle of audience, subject, and author.

Linda also recognized the power of sentence-level rhetoric and its connection to audience awareness, specifically when she was editing her sentences and paragraphs. In her group, Linda was in charge of reading the final drafts for editing and proofreading matters, and this experience helped her be more aware of audience in her own writing: "By editing other people's papers, I realized that it was easier reading my own papers. And, also looking at ways to tie the papers back to the theme of the journal made correcting my papers easier." Here, Linda takes what is normally a dry, lifeless exercise for most students—editing sentences—and turns it into a meaningful experience in learning rhetoric and audience. Writing for their academic journal also led my students to be more audience conscious when they wrote for their other classes. Cassie related to me a story from later in the semester when she wrote a paper for her political science class:

> I think writing and editing for the academic journal really helped me with my own writing. In political science, I wrote one paper on individualism and another paper on participation in a democracy, which we read a book about. And, I remember the first paper I wrote—she gave it back—and there was a lot

of comments that asked, 'So what?' 'Explain what you mean here.' And, it made me consider how I can't be too vague about this. I have to explain further my ideas, because that if someone was reading this, they could completely disagree with this, and they would have a lot of reason to because I don't provide any opposing arguments. So, when I wrote my next essay, I put into consideration not my teacher reading this, but maybe a political science major or someone interested in that field . . . and I can say, "Okay, here's your view and why I think it's wrong because of my interpretation." And that's how I did my essays, and I did much better on my next paper.

Linda tells a similar story about making writerly decisions in her interdisciplinary first-year seminar class and considering her instructor as audience in other classes. Here, Linda recognized how audience consideration led her to take more control of her ideas and of her writing:

By learning how to write for the [university] community in English 111 I learned to elaborate on ideas that assumed students would understand, but when I was writing to my first-year seminar instructor I would elaborate more on things that I understood but that I thought maybe he wouldn't understand. I learned more to take a stance and try to explain it to my audience even if it is just my teacher; I can still take a stance.

Conclusion

Linda's declaration that audience awareness taught her to "take a stance" in her writing seems an appropriate place to wrap up. This awareness of her own rhetorical power stems from the rhetorical situation in which she found herself, the situation of having something worthwhile to say to a public of actual academic readers. Placing these writers in similar rhetorical situations, such as the academic journal assignment I have described here, in which the academic reader becomes a viable audience, allows student writers to take control over their writing process and to recognize that their writing matters to a reader.

Ultimately, the assignment leads students to accomplish a number of writing goals that many of us want out of our first-year writers by making more overt the role a reading public plays in the writing process. First, moving from ignoring audience to addressing and invoking the audience leads to more powerful prose that means something to both reader and audience. Second, writing for an academic journal makes my writers more aware of sentence-level rhetorical strategies that, before, seemed disconnected to larger audience needs. And finally, writing for specific and varied university audiences enables student writers to understand more clearly the competing rhetorical situations they will be asked to negotiate when writing across the curriculum.

Works Cited

Ede, Lisa, and Andrea Lunsford. "Audience Addressed/Audience Invoked: The Role of Audience in Composition Theory and Pedagogy." CCC 35 (1984): 155–171.

Elbow, Peter. "Closing My Eyes as I Speak: An Argument for Ignoring Audience." Everyone Can Write. Oxford: Oxford UP, 2000. 93–112.

Lunsford, Andrea A., and Lisa Ede. "Among the Audience: On Audience in an Age of New Literacies." Engaging Audience: Writing in an Age of New Literacies. Ed. Elizabeth Weiser, Brian Fehler, and Angela González. Urbana, IL: NCTE, 2009. 42–69.

CHAPTER NINE

When the Teacher Is the Audience

MARIE C. PARETTI
Virginia Tech University

Teaching Audience: Defining Rhetorical Knowledge

Discussions of "teaching audience" inevitably begin by describing what we mean: just what is it that we are presuming to teach? As Andrea Lunsford and Lisa Ede point out in their "Among the Audience," this question has been complicated in recent years by the emergence of online communication tools and spaces that offer an array of complex multimodal venues for social networking and collaborative textual production ("Among" 43–44). But while the term remains, as they note, overdetermined, as a writing teacher I believe *audience* continues to provide a useful framework for helping students understand texts not as static artifacts on a shelf (or a computer screen) but as dynamic sites of engagement among real people–blog readers, Facebook friends, clients in a business meeting, and even, as I argue here, teachers in a classroom. New online literacy practices have complicated notions of authorship, agency, ownership, and text. But even as *audience* becomes *co-creator* in a wiki or a Flickr album, even as the text itself is re/overwritten by multiple authors, the concept of individuals encountering, engaging, using, and responding to that text remains a key dimension of the process of composing as it occurs in "precise, concrete situations" ("Among" 47). And it is this dynamic of individual human engagement around a text that is central to teaching students about audience.

Audience is always localized and particular, and in this chapter I focus on helping students think about audiences as concrete components of their professional lives in ways often associated with technical/business writing or communication in the disciplines (CID). While a binary between personal and professional literacies is easily dismantled, it offers a useful heuristic here to distinguish between an emphasis on students' civic, public, or social literacy practices and an emphasis on the literacy practices that typify their future workplaces. Certainly these literacies intersect: as the digital natives move into the workforce they will carry their literacy practices with them, and personal literacies are often an important starting point for and bridge to professional practices. Still, despite the fuzziness of the boundary, it may help my own audience to frame the practices shared in this chapter in terms of helping students engage in the process of constructing and sharing knowledge as professionals, be they historians or geologists or urban planners or chemical engineers. That said, the theoretical framework described in the next section clearly spans the boundary and provides insights useful across all domains of writing instruction.

Given the emphasis on outcomes assessment in education, one starting point for navigating the issue of audience in professional contexts is to consider what students need to do with respect to audience—what, in other words, does "learning audience" look like? Toward that end, the Outcomes Statement for First-Year Composition developed in 2000 by the Council of Writing Program Administrators (WPA) offers a productive starting point. Under the area of rhetorical knowledge, the Outcomes Statement posits that students completing first-year composition should be able to:

- Focus on a purpose

- Respond to the needs of different audiences

- Respond appropriately to different kinds of rhetorical situations

- Use conventions of format and structure appropriate to the rhetorical situation

- Adopt appropriate voice, tone, and level of formality

- Understand how genres shape reading and writing

- Write in several genres (WPA)

To foreground the articulations between first-year composition and writing in the disciplines, the outcomes statement also includes ways upper-level disciplinary faculty can support or enhance students' skills. Under rhetorical knowledge, this support consists of introducing students to the main features and uses of writing in their fields and the expectations of readers in their fields (WPA).

These expectations for both first-year composition and writing in the disciplines make it clear that being able to adapt to different audiences, and specifically to common audiences in one's field, is one key outcome for writing instruction across the university. "Learning audience" thus includes learning to adapt to different needs, expectations, and uses—including those encountered through new media, where audiences can engage in dynamic and immediate ways with authors and texts. This adaptability, in turn, implies learning how to analyze those audiences and how to make choices appropriate to the exigencies of the situation (including, perhaps, choosing not to write at all but rather to communicate via a different modality). Developing such flexibility involves more than simply learning a list of common audience expectations and mastering specific formats appropriate to each audience "type"; indeed, such lists and formats quickly become outdated as the needs and expectations of audiences continually shift in response to new exigencies and new technologies.

At its richest, the phrase "teaching audience" involves teaching writers to understand the complex ways in which the audiences of a given rhetorical situation shape the texts the writer creates to mediate that situation. Such an approach embraces not only the addressed and invoked audiences for print texts described in Ede and Lunsford's original "Audience Addressed/Audience Invoked" article, but also the more digitally engaged, diverse, collaborative audiences for many of the new modes of literacy they outline in "Among the Audience." Moreover, the audience is only one element of the dynamic. The audience has needs and expectations, but the writer also has particular goals for the situation at hand (as implied by the ability to "focus on a purpose"). As Ede and Lunsford argue in AA/AI, writing "is a means of making meaning for writer *and* reader" (Ede and Lunsford "AA/AI" 160). Even as communication environments shift and concepts of author and text are destabilized, an effective writer understands the interplay between her own goals and those of the readers she seeks to engage, as well as the larger system that influences and responds to those goals. In their conclusion to AA/AI, Ede and Lunsford explain:

> A fully elaborated view of audience, then, must balance the creativity of the writer with the different, but equally important, creativity of the reader. It must account for a wide and shifting range of roles for both addressed and invoked audiences. And finally, it must relate the matrix created by the intricate relationship of writer and audience to all elements in the rhetorical situation. (170–171)

A fully elaborated approach to teaching audience in both new and old literacies, by extension, should engage writers in understanding and responding to this "intricate relationship," even as that relationship grows more complex in digital, multimodal, and participatory environments. Such an approach, I would suggest, involves helping students: (1) develop tools and processes they can apply to new rhetorical situations outside the classroom to analyze audience knowledge, attitudes, expectations, and needs, and then (2) use that knowledge to produce texts that simultaneously respond to the specific audiences at hand and further the writer's own goals for the situation.

Theoretical Perspectives: Genre Theory and Activity Systems

In considering approaches in which "teaching audience" means teaching a process of analyzing and critically responding to an infinitely variable array of rhetorical situations, two theoretical frameworks offer a useful foundation. Both genre theory and activity theory can enrich our understanding of what we are teaching, clarify the dynamics of classrooms that impact such teaching, and ultimately inform our design and evaluation of writing assignments.

As Barbara Little Liu points out, the emphasis on "genre" in the WPA Outcomes Statement ("understand how genres shape reading and writing," "write in several genres") implies more than simply teaching students a set of modes or formats for creating different kinds of documents. Drawing on recent scholarship on genre theory, beginning with M. M. Bakhtin and extending through scholarship produced in the 1990s, Liu reminds writing instructors that genres—be they academic or professional, public or personal, and, I would add, print or digital, composed of words or sounds or images—are always socially constructed (Miller; Bakhtin; Bazerman and Paradis; Bazerman; Berkenkotter and Huckin; Liu). As Carolyn Miller explained in her seminal 1984 article, "Genre as Social Action," the term refers not simply to modes or formats of writing, but to a regularized (but dynamic) structure of content and form that responds to a recurrent social situation—one involving writers and readers engaged in some larger activity. That is, genres represent accepted patterns of interaction between writers and readers to mediate common situations—and as her more recent work suggests, genre theory both informs and is informed by emergent genres such as blogs (Miller and Shepherd; Miller). Hence grant proposals arise from the need for researchers to secure funding and the need for foundations or government agencies to ensure that the money they distribute achieves their goals. Similarly, the accepted structure of scholarly articles in various fields emerged from the need for researchers to share their work with one another; these structures reflect shared norms about appropriate research subjects, methods, modes of inquiry, and relevant contexts. More recently, concerns about the gap between the pace of technological changes and the time lag for print journal publication have pushed scholarly communities toward online publication and prepublication of research findings; new genres, new structures for peer review, and new guidelines for tenure are emerging (in contested ways) as the needs and expectations of contemporary digital writers and readers transform print genre structures (Quint; Brown, Correia et al.; Owen; Correia and Teixeira).

The ability to write in a given genre, then, whether online or in print, textual, or multimodal, implies not only accurately replicating a model of that genre, but also understanding the role that genre plays in mediating dialogic relationships between particular writers and readers, and adapting the content, structure, style, and even medium to effectively support those relationships. The shift to digital dissemination of research results is but one example of such adaptations as writer/audience needs have shifted. Within this framework, genres are not fixed forms (a history essay always looks like this, a blog always looks like that), but rather socially situated texts that respond to and shape rhetorical situations; genres thus engage the real audience addressed who reads the text and the imagined audience invoked whom the writer creates through language.

Consequently, teaching students to "write in several genres" and "understand how genres shape reading and writing" means teaching them, on one level, the situations specific genres respond to, the needs of writers and readers that shape the genre, and how that genre may be adapted to changes in the rhetorical situation. But more important, at another level it means teaching them a metacognitive approach that enables them to analyze the rhetorical situation (including the needs, interests, and characteristics of the audience with whom they are in dialogue), assess how the expected genre does and does not respond to the situation, and adapt the received genre to the needs of the individuals involved in this particular social situation. They also need to learn how to apply that analysis to produce a text that not only satisfies the audience but also achieves their own goals. A number of scholars have already described successful approaches to using genre theory and its understanding of audience as the basis for writing instruction (e.g., Artemeva, Logie et al.; Walker). Such approaches, grounded in understanding texts as mediating social relationships, are always instantiated in specific genres and situations, but their larger goal is enabling students to engage as authors, agents, collaborators—even audiences—in new situations, using new technologies and modalities as they emerge. It teaches students to see both texts and audiences not as static and passive but as dynamic and engaged.

Where genre theory provides a framework for understanding the ways in which audience needs shape the form and content of texts, activity theory provides a broader way of understanding the work that texts do and the complex factors that impact their

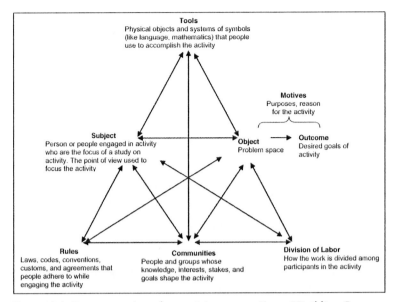

FIGURE **9.1.** *Representation of an activity system. From "Building Context: Using Activity Theory to Teach about Genre in Multi-Major Professional Communication Courses" by Donna Kain and Elizabeth Wardle.* Technical Communication Quarterly 14.2 (2005), *reprinted by permission of the publisher, Taylor & Francis Group, http://www.informaworld.com.*

creation (Spinuzzi; Russell, Kain, and Wardle). Emerging from the work of L. S. Vygotsky and his colleagues, activity theory offers a rich way of analyzing rhetorical situations that considers not only writer and reader but the larger activity in which the individuals and the texts operate (Figure 9.1).

In this formulation, writers and readers are subjects engaged in a larger activity directed toward a specific object (with a desired outcome) and shaped by contextual factors, including not only the problem or activity at hand (object), but also the laws and customs governing the system, the communities to which individuals belong, and the structures used to organize the activity. Texts are one of many tools, or mediating artifacts, shaped by and shaping the entire system. Importantly, as Russell points out in his discussion of genre and activity theory, activity theory provides a way to expand our understanding of genre beyond the dialogic relationship between reader and writer to see texts as parts of a series of tools that operate within the system. Moreover, it provides a way to talk about texts that do not conform to recognized genres (to use Miller's terms, there is no "recurrent situation" that requires a "typified response" [Miller 159]), but instead emerge and dissolve to meet localized, even one-time, needs to exchange information. This framework is useful to writing instruction in a number of ways, particularly in helping students understand the larger dynamic of literacy practices in their professional lives. With respect to audience, it reminds us that, at the very least, audiences cannot be neatly defined solely by job function, community membership, or even individual character traits. A given individual may have one set of needs as a reader in one activity system, and a different set under different circumstances.

Audience in the Classroom: The Problem of Multiple Activity Systems

Both genre theory and activity theory provide ways of understanding what texts do as they mediate the audience/writer relationship, and thus they provide ways to talk to students about how audience can and should shape their creation of those texts. Each emphasizes the transactional nature of writing, its function as a site of information exchange, dialogue, and collaboration between individuals engaged in a larger enterprise. But activity theory, in particular, also provides a useful lens for understanding the problems instructors face when trying to teach writers about audience—a problem characterized by the bifurcation of the activity system within the writing classroom and the external activity systems for which writing teachers seek to prepare students. A number of scholars have articulated this bifurcation, which is particularly apparent in courses designed to prepare students for their professional communication practices. Freedman, Adam, and Smart, though not explicitly invoking activity theory, report a case study of an upper-level finance course that, while it engaged students in the kinds of writing expected of them in the workplace, still retained the social network of the classroom—with the result that students always knew they were writing for the teacher in order to be evaluated, not for a real client who planned to use the information they provided to implement change (Freedman, Adam et al.). Decades earlier, W. Earl Britton made the same observation when he wrote:

> [The student] writes about a subject he is not thoroughly informed upon, in order to exhibit his knowledge rather than explain something the reader does not understand, and he writes to a professor who already knows more than he does about the matter and who evaluates the papers not in terms of what he has derived, but in terms of what he thinks the writer knows. In every respect, this is the converse of what happens in professional life, where the writer is the authority; he writes to transmit new or unfamiliar information to someone who does not know but needs to, and who evaluates the paper in terms of what he derives and understands. (Britton 116)

The problem, in other words, is that the teacher is always the wrong audience with the wrong needs and the wrong goals. Spinuzzi, in his work on technical writing classrooms, describes this problem specifically in terms of conflicting activity systems, and terms the result "pseudotransactional writing—that is, writing that is patently designed by a student to meet teacher expectations rather than perform the 'real' function the teacher has suggested" (295). Hunt makes a similar claim when he argues that "looking at typical classroom and institutional context for writing, it seems clear that there is in more situations in schools and universities virtually no opportunity for written language to serve as the medium for direct and authentic dialogue" (Hunt; see also Russell and Dias, Freedman, et al). Importantly, "authentic" as it is used in this context (and elsewhere in this chapter) does not reflect the way that is most often used in composition theory—that is, as a quality of authorial voice, linked to nuances of tone and style. Rather, "authentic" here refers to the nature of the interaction between the writer and the audience, and the degree to which the stated purpose matches the use to which the text is put. For example, a letter to the editor submitted only to a composition instructor for a grade would be "inauthentic" because the stated purpose (to express one's views to a newspaper audience) and the actual purpose (to have one's writing ability evaluated) do not match. Submitting the letter to the newspaper would be authentic. A more recent study by Dannels on oral communication identified the same kind of activity system split in an engineering capstone design course in which students conducted design projects for real-world clients and presented their results to those clients (Dannels). Dannels's study revealed that while the students attended to the clients to some degree, the needs and expectations of the teacher, and consequently the classroom activity system, remained paramount. The teacher, grading them on academic performance, remained the dominant audience.

Finally, in articulating the differences between school and workplace activity systems, activity theory also offers a useful lens to view Lunsford and Ede's own reexamination of "Audience Addressed/Audience Invoked." The concept of audience as it emerges in more elaborated discussions of classroom activity systems provided by Russell and by Dias, et al., help explain what Lunsford and Ede refer to as "the multiple ways in which the student writer's agency and identity may be shaped and constrained not only by immediate audiences, but also, and even more forcefully, by the ways in which both she and those audiences are positioned within larger institutional and discursive frameworks" ("Representing Audience" 170–171)—a positioning they say they largely omitted from their earlier work, but which can be exposed by an activity system analysis. Similarly, activity theory offers a complementary approach to analyzing the larger contexts Lunsford and Ede describe in the opening chapter of this volume by illuminating various components of context as they operate in both virtual and physical systems. *Communities*, for example, provide a way to analyze the types of cultural, geographical, professional, and online communities in which readers and writers participate. *Rules* offer a lens for examining not only the genres that mediate the reader/writer exchange, but also the tacit practices that govern social interactions within the system. *Division of labor* offers a category for understanding the ways in which writers and readers collaborate in textual production. As I have argued elsewhere (Paretti and McNair), activity theory is a particularly useful framework for understanding the kinds of complex communication challenges associated with virtual collaboration; it enables us to illuminate the context not only for traditional print writing, but also the more complex multimodal, participatory contexts engendered by technological changes.

Designing Assignments When the Teacher Is the Audience

Without dialogue between a reader and a writer, the problem of teaching audience in a meaningful way comes to seem virtually impossible, particularly in technical/business writing courses where research suggests that even client projects often still achieve only simulation status. Given the bifurcation between audience in the classroom, where evaluation of learning is always at stake, and audience in professional contexts, where usefulness of information is critical, how can faculty "teach audience" in ways that enable students to transfer learning from one setting to another? The studies cited earlier, along with others (Anson and Forsberg; Freedman and Medway 1; Freedman and Adam) make it clear that school is not work, and attempts to teach genres—and more specifically, audiences—outside those already present within a classroom are always conflicted. Yet some of this work on school versus workplace activity systems also points toward productive ways forward. Dias et al., for instance, even as they draw sharp divides between school and work, note that "certain habits of mind, certain ways of marshaling data or constructing arguments . . . may very well be transferred from university to workplace and vice-versa—according to the discipline" (Dias, Freedman et al. 12). Lunsford and Ede, even as they acknowledge the constraints of institutional contexts that challenge easy notions of bringing students into academic discourse, argue powerfully that they, and we as writing teachers, can still offer students "a way of being in language and a way of both inhabiting and shaping knowledge structures, ways that strive to be critically self-reflective, multi-perspectival, and complex" ("Representing Audience" 177).

Extending this work, I argue here that if we adopt the notion of "teaching audience" as teaching students the process of analyzing and adapting texts to meet the needs and interests of real audiences and real writers, then we can leverage classroom writing assignments to provide Hunt's "real and authentic dialogue" or

Spinuzzi's true "transactional" writing—even without external audiences. To do so, however, we need to break open the bifurcation and make the needs, characteristics, and functions of the teacher-as-audience explicit, and highlight rather than mask the ways that all genres shift when they appear as course assignments, apart from the social situations they were designed to mediate. That is, as teachers, instead of consistently pretending that we are teaching students to write *exactly* the way they need to for a specific audience outside our classroom— and thus creating the kind of pseudotransactionality Spinuzzi describes—we can make our own role visible within the structure of the assignment and its evaluation. Students already know, as research makes clear, that they are always writing for the teacher, and that the teacher who is grading them has expectations, standards, and preferences that may or may not overlap with those they will find elsewhere (on the job, in courses in a different major, etc.). As writing teachers, we seek to help our students understand in particular the ways in which the needs and expectations of a given audience within a specific activity system require adaptations of genres to the exigency of the situation. One way to do so is to make our own needs and expectations, and the resulting adaptations, explicit to students by entering into the system as participants, not simply external evaluators.

The approach has implications on a number of different levels; here I examine ways to design writing assignments to make the relationships between teachers' uses of information and their expectations for writing assignments accessible to students, focusing on ways writing teachers can explicitly "teach audience" by first considering what they as teachers need from a given assignment, and second, how the genre (form and content) they are asking students to produce meets that need. To illustrate the approach, I describe two assignments that rely on real needs that I, as a course instructor, have for information that students can provide. Both are relatively common assignments in writing courses; in adapting them to this approach, the difference lies in the ability of the instructor to move from pseudotransactionality to authentic dialogue, and to make explicit the ways in which the text is mediating that dialogue.

Putting It into Practice: Field Research on Writing in Specific Settings

First, consider an assignment in which students conduct field research on writing in a particular setting. In first-year writing courses with a focus on academic discourse, such assignments often ask students to explore the kind of writing expected in their majors. In technical or business writing courses, students interview workplace professionals to document the kinds of communication they can expect to encounter on the job. These assignments serve as tools to help students learn what will be expected of them outside this classroom—what genres their majors require, what guidelines they must learn to follow, and what standards and expectations apply in these settings. They are useful for achieving those goals. But, if we consider our own roles as teachers, those assignments can also be useful to us and those uses can inform how we ask students to communicate their findings and how they view us as the audience for their work.

I designed this assignment for a professional development course for sophomore engineering students; students interviewed professionals in the field they hoped to enter. Initially, I taught the course myself, and the following description reflects that framework. More recently, my role has shifted and a colleague teaches the course; the shift in roles, as well as the availability of online tools, have begun to shift the assignment, as I describe at the end of this section. The original assignment resulted in two texts: a memo, written to me as the director of a three-year (sophomore through senior) communications in the disciplines program, and a presentation in which groups of students synthesized their interviews to provide advice to their classmates about how best to prepare themselves for the workplace. A brief version of the memo assignment appears in Figure 9.2.

As Figure 9.2 makes clear, the memo assignment (and our class discussions around the project) foregrounded my need as a program director trying to keep assignments up to date with contemporary workplace practices (similarly, the discussion of the presentation focused on the students making choices about courses and extracurricular activities over the next few years to

The Basic Task
Your goal for this assignment is to develop a picture of what life as an engineer is like on the job, with a particular focus on what "communication in the workplace" involves. To that end, you each need to interview a working professional about his/her job, and particularly job-related communications and other professional issues (e.g. teamwork, ethics, globalization, lifelong learning, impact of contemporary issues). You may interview employers, coworkers, or even family members if they are or have been professionals in your intended field. Do not interview faculty members unless you plan to pursue an academic career. If you do not know a practicing engineer, come talk to me.

Audience and Purpose:
The memo to me is one tool I use as a program administrator to make sure the curriculum for the communications program remains consistent with the needs of the workplace. Although I gather this information in multiple ways, your real-world interviews are very important pieces of information for me. Thus, your memo, though it may include other kinds of information you find out, should focus on communication practices in the workplace.

Writing the Memo
- You only have a page or two to work with in your memo, so obviously you can't include everything you learn. Sift through your data to decide what information to include and what to exclude based on what you know I'm concerned about in coordinating the program. Consider what's most useful or relevant and what is less useful or interesting, bearing in mind that I need to make sure the specific assignments included in the program will be useful to you once you graduate and begin working.
- Organize the memo based on categories that you think will be useful to me as I plan courses and assignments.
- Use formatting techniques such as white space, bulleted lists, and headings to help organize the content so that I can easily read through 50 of these memos, and skim them at a later date to find specific information I can use.
- Write a conclusion that not only sums up your main points, but also discusses their significance to me as I plan courses, assignments, and activities.

FIGURE 9.2. *Sample interview assignment.*

prepare themselves for the workplace). The assignment is, of course, a learning exercise to help students understand the rationale behind the communication assignments embedded throughout their engineering curriculum. But I also designed it explicitly as a tool to help me gather information on the communication trends in the workplaces my students would enter. As a result, the information transaction represented by the memo is real rather than "pseudo." Importantly, when introducing the assignment, I made my uses for the information explicit, talking about findings from prior years and describing resulting curriculum changes I'd made. Additionally, after students submitted the memos and gave the presentations, I asked about choices they might make over the next few years as a result of what they've learned, and I described what I'd learned. We would then talk about what things the curriculum should emphasize based on the information they reported. Such discussions help students see the information they gather as useful—part of a dialogue among us that, because it happens at the beginning of a three-year program, shaped our future interactions as well as my interactions with the classes that followed them. Moreover, because in this case the course is part of a longer sequence and their findings could impact assignments in future courses, they had a stake in the outcome; what they suggested I do in future assignments affected their own lives. The text thus became a functional tool for dialogue within the larger activity system of the curriculum.

While these uses shaped what information they gathered and presented, we also talked about the structure they used to present that information and the ways in which that structure was tied to both how I wanted to use the information in the future and how I needed to respond to it immediately as their writing instructor. In these terms, the constraints and responsibilities of my job played a clear role. For example, the fact that I taught two sections and evaluated fifty or so memos meant that, as in the workplaces these students would enter, being both concise and complete was critical. My need to reference the information again later also meant that I needed documents that were easy to skim in search of key points or specific items. Similarly, the fact that the curriculum addressed workplace writing meant that an essayistic structure was not appropriate. In this instance, there was no specific genre that framed the assignment, though "workplace memo" could be considered a loose formatting structure. Instead, students were learning to gather data and present it concisely to someone who planned to make use of the information but also needed to evaluate their ability to communicate effectively.

In responding to and evaluating the assignment, my comments addressed the usefulness and implications of their findings, the ease of understanding those findings, and the implications of the findings for the curriculum. The rubric attended to specific features (uses of headings and lists to visually organize information), but emphasized the use value of those features in this context.

In short, the goal of the assignment was not to teach students "how to write an interview" or even "how to write for me." Rather, the assignment represented a real site of information exchange, surrounded by a dialogue. The written assignment, class discussions, and evaluation rubrics addressed the project in terms of understanding the needs of the audience (me) and the writers (them), and then creating texts that supported those needs. As noted earlier, in recent years my needs with respect to the assignment have shifted slightly; while the assignment still provides important information about current workplace practices that I use in curriculum planning, the assistant program director now teaches the course and leads the assignment (which now includes globalization and collaboration in the interviews). She summarizes the memos for me and highlights curriculum changes she thinks are necessary. I attend the presentations, which now have a dual audience (the other students and me). We continue to use the assignment to discuss the curriculum with the students and seek their input, so the element of dialogue remains. And in the next set of courses, we'll be incorporating the students' findings into a wiki to provide a dynamic repository available not only to the program staff but to future students so that we can trace new trends and changes; students will then have the opportunity to see textually what happens when their intended audience becomes a collaborative author and the texts are synthesized and translated from one medium to another, and future classes will become digital audiences for the work. Each of these changes represents an important opportunity to continue to foreground for students the ways in which audiences respond to and use texts in meaningful ways.

Progress Reports on Ongoing Projects: Assignments to Monitor Student Learning

The second example, progress reports regarding ongoing projects, I have described in significant detail elsewhere as a means for disciplinary faculty to effectively incorporate writing into project-based courses (Paretti). Unlike the field research assignment, which finds applications in a broad range of writing courses, progress reports are typically confined to technical/business or disciplinary writing courses, and almost every technical/business writing textbook describes the genre and provides a standard structure for content and organization (time period covered, work completed, problems/solutions, future work).

I use progress reports in an engineering design course, in which students complete an open-ended design project over the course of two semesters, but the concept applies to any extended project in which students have intermediate work to report. As with the interview assignment, the description of the progress report emphasizes its use as a tool for mediating activity within the course. These reports become part of a portfolio evaluated by an external advisory board as part of the departmental assessment. In class, then, we talk about the complex nature of the social situation they are trying to mediate: because I want to see their projects succeed and ensure that they have results to present to the department at the end of the year, I need them to be honest about what is and isn't working, and tell me about any challenges or concerns they have. At the same time, because I have to evaluate their performance, it is always in their best interest to describe those challenges and concerns in terms that show their initiative, their attention to detail, their efforts to seek out solutions on their own, and their ability to work together as a team. In emphasizing the kinds of information I gain from the reports, I reference the reports throughout the project in ways that emphasize their use value; for example, when I meet with design teams to discuss their progress, I use their most recent report as the basis for questions. When I see students in class or in the hall, I often ask them about issues identified in the report, or congratulate them on progress made in specific areas. As with the interview assignment, these progress reports become active texts in the class that mediate my interaction with the students about the larger project. Students come to see me not only as "the grader," but as someone who needs information from them in order to do my job of supporting and evaluating their projects.

The structure of the reports also reflects both accepted standards for the genre and specific needs that I have in this particular course. In discussing the reports, I clarify differences between what I need or expect and what an employer using progress reports in a different context might need. I ask students to highlight information about team behavior, for example, because I am responsible for teaching and evaluating collaboration skills. And finally, as with the interview assignment, the evaluation of the report reflects its uses; an "A" report "clearly and effectively provides details on progress to date to support management activities" while a "C" report "provides some detail, but is missing important information or is not clearly organized to support project management." In each case, the criteria are tied to the ways in which these reports are used.

Conclusion

In both theoretical and practical terms, what I have offered here is a way of understanding the teaching and learning of audience not as a set of facts applied to specific settings, but as a process of first analyzing rhetorical situations to understand the complex interplay between writers, readers, and larger contexts, and then creating documents appropriate to those situations. I offer the two assignments described here not necessarily as models that other writing instructors can or should mimic, but rather as examples of ways in which we might uncover the ongoing work of the classroom activity system—including the ways in which it is inflected by new online, multimodal, participatory literacies—to create opportunities for students to engage in truly transactional writing, and, in doing so, to understand the conditions of audience and circumstance that shape the transaction. This approach suggests that, rather than trying to mask the role of the teacher in the classroom as both user and evaluator of information, writing instructors can explicitly design assignments that open up their roles. In doing so, they can help students understand the teacher as audience, make connections between the requirements for a given assignment and the structure of the classroom activity system, and identify ways in which a given text might be different in a different activity system. Such assignments call instructors to consider what information students may provide that does offer an opportunity for authentic dialogue. But it also calls instructors to think about how their own institutional context—the need to evaluate student learning, in particular—shapes the guidelines and standards they create for assignments. The end of such thinking is not a new way to mask the university system; rather, it is a way of making that system and its impact on students' texts apparent, and offering students a process by which they can metacognitively navigate this and other systems using texts as mediating tools to engage their audiences.

Works Cited

Anson, Chris M., and L. Lee Forsberg. "Moving Beyond the Academic Community: Transitional Stages in Professional Writing." *Written Communication* 7.2 (April 1990): 200–231.

Artemeva, N., S. Logie, et al. "From Page to Stage: How Theories of Genre and Situated Learning Help Introduce Engineering Students to Discipline-Specific Communication." *Technical Communication Quarterly* 8.3 (1999): 301–316.

Bakhtin, Mikhail M. "The Problem of Speech Genres." *Speech Genres and Other Late Essays*. Trans. Vern W. McGee. Ed. Caryl Emerson and Michael Holquist. Austin: U of Texas P, 1986. 60–102.

Bazerman, C. "Introduction: Changing Regularities of Genre." *IEEE Transactions on Professional Communication* 42.1 (1999): 1–2.

———. "Systems of Genres and the Enactment of Social Intentions." *Genre and the New Rhetoric*. Ed. A. Freedman and P. Medway. London: Taylor & Francis, 1995. 79–101.

Bazerman, C. and J. Paradis, eds. *Textual Dynamics of the Professions: Historical and Contemporary Studies of Writing in Professional Communities*. Madison: U of Wisconsin P, 1991.

Berkenkotter, C., and T. Huckin. *Genre Knowledge in Disciplinary Communication: Cognition/Culture/Power*. Hillsdale, NJ: Lawrence Erlbaum Associates, 1995.

Britton, W. E. "What Is Technical Writing?" *CCC* 16.2 (1965): 113–116.

Council of Writing Program Administrators. *WPA Outcomes Statement for First-Year Composition*. Council of Writing Program Administrators, 2000. <http://wpacouncil.org/positions/outcomes.html>.

Dannels, D. P. "Teaching and Learning Design Presentations in Engineering: Contradictions between Academic and Workplace Activity Systems." *Journal of Business and Technical Communication* 17.2 (2003): 139–169.

Dias, Patrick, et al. *Worlds Apart: Acting and Writing in Academic and Workplace Contexts.* Mahwah, NJ: Lawrence Erlbaum, 1999.

Ede, Lisa, and Andrea Lunsford. "Audience Addressed/Audience Invoked: The Role of Audience in Composition Theory and Pedagogy." *CCC* 35 (1984): 155–171.

Freedman, Aviva, and Christine Adam. "Learning to Write Professionally: "'Situated Learning' and the Transition from University to Professional Discourse." *Teaching Technical Communication: Critical Issues for the Classroom.* Ed. James M. Dubinsky. Boston: Bedford St. Martin's, 2004. 310–336.

Freedman, A., C. Adam, et al. "Wearing Suits to Class: Simulations as Genre." *Written Communication* 11.2 (1994).

Freedman, A., and P. Medway, eds. *Genre and the New Rhetoric.* London: Taylor & Francis, 1994.

Hunt, R. A. "Traffic in Genres, In Classrooms and Out." *Genre and the New Rhetoric.* Ed. A. Freedman and P. Medway. New York: Taylor & Francis, 1994. 211–230.

Kain, D., and E. Wardle. "Building Context: Using Activity Theory to Teach About Genre in Multi-Major Professional Communication Courses." *Technical Communication Quarterly* 14.2 (2005): 113–139.

Liu, B. L. "More than the Latest PC Buzzword for Modes: What Genre Theory Means to Composition." *The Outcomes Book: Debate and Consensus after the WPA Outcomes Statement.* Ed. S. Harrington, K. Rhodes, R. O. Fischer, and R. Malenczyk. Logan, UT: Utah State UP, 2005. 72–84.

Lunsford, Andrea A., and Lisa Ede. "Among the Audience: On Audience in an Age of New Literacies." *Engaging Audience: Writing in an Age of New Literacies.* Ed. Elizabeth Weiser, Brian Fehler, and Angela González. Urbana, IL: NCTE, 2009. 42–69.

Lunsford, Andrea, and Lisa Ede. "Representing Audience: 'Successful' Discourse and Disciplinary Critique." *CCC* 47:2. (May, 1996): 167–179.

Miller, C. "Genre as Social Action." *Quarterly Journal of Speech* 70 (1984): 151–167.

Paretti, M. C. "Audience Awareness: Leveraging Problem-Based Learning to Teach Workplace Communication Practice." *IEEE Transactions on Professional Communication* 49.6 (2006): 189–198.

Russell, D. R. "Rethinking Genre in School and Society: An Activity Theory Analysis." *Written Communication* 14.4 (1997): 504–554.

———. "Writing and Genre in Higher Education and Workplaces: A Review of Studies that Use Cultural-Historical Activity Theory." *Mind, Culture, and Activity* 4.4 (1997): 224–237.

Spinuzzi, C. "Pseudotransactionality, Activity Theory, and Professional Writing Instruction." *Technical Communication Quarterly* 5.3 (1996): 295–308.

Vygotsky, L. S. *Mind in Society.* Cambridge, MA: Harvard UP, 1978.

———. *Thought and Language.* Cambridge, MA: MIT Press, 1962/1986.

Walker, K. "Using Genre Theory to Teach Students Engineering Lab Report Writing: A Collaborative Approach." *IEEE Transactions on Professional Communication* 42.1 (1999): 12–20.

CHAPTER TEN

The Self-Addressed Stamped Envelope

ALEXANDRIA PEARY
Daniel Webster College

When a writer's notion of audience and purpose is un-encumbered by classroom fictions, the real rhetorical challenges begin.

—Joseph Petraglia

It's striking how few undergraduate writing courses consistently employ publication as part of instruction, despite its significant benefits to students and writing curricula. Most undergraduate publication is confined to an in-house institutional venue such as the campus newspaper, so the efficacy of student writing is not tested beyond its immediate academic context. Few examples of writing-for-publication courses are present in writing studies, and even fewer occur within the undergraduate student's discipline.

The lack of writing-for-publication courses for undergraduates is conspicuous because of the way in which publication can increase the efficacy of audience instruction. Audience instruction is intricately tied to the amount of transactionality and authenticity in a course. Transactionality occurs when writing accomplishes some end beyond its own completion: it gets stuff done in the world (Petraglia). Authenticity refers to students' perception that a task corresponds to the writing done outside of the classroom, such as in the workplace (Blakeslee). In contrast, pseudotransactionality is "the illusion of rhetorical transaction," and pseudotransactional texts carry only the potential of accomplishing or changing something outside their own task completion (Petraglia). A primary cause of pseudotransactionality is the unnatural act of writing only to inform an involuntary audience (the writing instructor) who presumably already knows the relayed information and thus does not need it. Students can get tangled in the pseudotransactional ropes of writing just for teachers, with two consequences: such writing instruction may inadequately prepare students for the complexity of different rhetorical contexts in workplace writing, and it causes students to perceive writing instruction as a meaningless matter of hoop jumping (Blakeslee; Freedman; Petraglia). Publication for venues outside of the academic institution may alleviate many of these pedagogical issues by offering alternative audiences for student texts. As one student, Jason Goodman, reflected on his experience in an undergraduate writing-for-publication course several years afterward, "writing for editors fostered a different writing education. I experimented with writing tools, techniques, and genres that are usually left uncovered in undergraduate education."

Traditional avenues for becoming an author are still popular even with changes in media, as shown in the "robust" numbers of first-time novels in the publication works as well as independent literary journals (Alterman). Yet any discussion of freelance publication these days invariably includes online venues: magazines, newspapers, and literary journals that are strictly virtual as well as those that are complements of standard hard copy magazines. In many ways, the Web has already altered students' relationship to writing, to audience, and to community. Writing on the Web has given students greater experience in transactionality and authenticity: "we can write for real purposes and publish to real audiences more easily and more widely because of the Read/Write Web" (Richardson, "Hyper-Connected Classroom"). Students are the *digital natives*—as Andrea Lunsford and Lisa Ede term them—of the boundless virtual environment in which our classrooms are one-acre plots ("Among" 57). That students are seeking out opportunities to write for people beyond their teachers is evident in the fact that 57 percent of teenagers in the United States have purportedly created content for the Web. As such, students are part of a general trend of participatory literacy in which new media seemingly affords "opportunity for anyone and everyone to become both author and audience" ("Among"

53). Students are aware of the need for transactional writing experiences, and a writing-for-publication course should make use of student digital experience in order to leverage further transactionality. Just as new media challenges the conventional mindset, so teaching students writing-for-publication generates a different mindset concerning audiences and their literacies than conventional writing for a teacher.

While the Web has provided students with writing acts of enhanced transactionality, it can resemble self-publishing and therefore lack the gritty transactionality of workplace or published texts. As self-publication, writing on the Web really isn't any more transactional than in-house publications such as the class magazine an instructor compiles or the service-learning writing done for a university club's brochure. Audience and genuine transactionality are not just a matter of being heard or even responded to; they entail accountability to a particular, influential, and demanding individual (the editor in this scenario). Students benefit from explicitly learning publication, whether they are submitting their work to online or hard copy venues, because attempting publication sets up a special dynamic between audience and writer that can't be duplicated by only blogging, emailing, instant messaging, or even posting a product review at Amazon.com. A rejection is a rejection is a rejection, no matter whether from a new-on-the-scene e-zine or a newsstand magazine with a century-long history of hard copy presence. It means the writer has somehow failed to meet the editor's requirements (and, conversely, an acceptance slip signals their fulfillment). According to Meredith Johnson, a student in the course, "Real world rejection is much more difficult than the rejection of an 'F' in the vacuum of a college class. On the other hand, the way it feels to see your name in print can not compare to the feeling of a red 'A' at the top of a paper only your professor has read and dissected." Another student, Christopher Hilbert, said of rejection letters that they "initially brought frustration" but that he "found them by far the most effective tool to motivate refinements in my writing style and process." Students are savvy; they recognize the differences in experiences of publication, and a significant number of them will be interested in a course on formal publication.

In this chapter, I differentiate between the writing-for-publication course I teach and a first-year composition, professional writing, or creative writing course. I then apply activity theory to writing-for-publication to show how the subject and object categories of the theory help us perceive the changes in interpersonal activities that help ameliorate pseudotransactionality and inauthenticity. Activity theory highlights contradictions inherent in writing instruction (Dias) and thus shows how writing for publication significantly increases the efficacy of audience instruction. Lastly, I discuss the ways in which writing-for-publication establishes a *textsite,* a particular audience zone in which undergraduates communicate with writing professionals in their future field, either in person (through class visits by editors and writers) or in writing (by submitting for publication and corresponding with editors).[1] The results of this more transactional instruction of audience is writing-in-the-profession, or writing which utilizes content from a profession (unlike general writing skills instruction) but is not required (unlike workplace writing) by the employer. While student exposure to a textsite is limited to the writing-for-publication course, student involvement in writing-in-the-profession may continue long after the last day of class.

Description of a Publication Course

The prototype for this discussion is a writing-for-publication course for upper-division students at a four-year private college with an emphasis on professional preparation. Note that this course in publication is designed for students with a fairly developed sense of professional direction and is not intended for students just entering academia who may be discouraged by editorial criticism and rejection. Ideally, students should be two to three years into their major field of study in order to understand their fields' concerns and objectives, as well as previously trained in basic academic writing conventions. In its first offering, the course specifically focused on writing for publication in the field of aviation. This course was team-taught by the writing program director (myself) and a professor whose publications included articles for nonscholarly aviation magazines, a technical textbook , and a memoir. In the second offering, I taught the course alone and provided information about writing and publication, while the students relied on each other for the accuracy of their professional content.

Students in both versions of the course wrote in a variety of genres that were staged to increase in complexity. The genres included humor, participatory features, topical poetry, short fiction, interviews, profiles, and service pieces (informative articles providing contact information for businesses and services and commonly found in magazines and newspapers). Although students were not required to use content from their majors, they were strongly encouraged to do so in order to engage an audience in their profession. As David W. Smit has proposed, writing instruction becomes more effective when students are exposed to a variety of discourse communities, including that of their prospective profession. For instance, students submitted to the humor page of a regional general interest magazine, *New Hampshire Magazine*, and to a professional magazine, *Aviation Digest*. Assignments were staged to help students quickly develop "clips"—the history of publication that establishes a freelancer's credibility with editors. Consequentially, the course began with shorter assignments for venues with quick turn-around times, such as newspapers.

Prior to the semester, I arranged interaction between students and editors of publications in their disciplines, which took the form of writing opportunities for students and guest visits by the editors. Some of the writings done by students were from assignments I had obtained for them from editors, while other writings were submitted to venues with which I had not established contact. These "blind" submissions provide students with an experience of transactionality which is greater than the submissions made through my arrangements with editors, since students need to fully understand and satisfy editorial rhetorical needs on their own, similar to a professional freelance writer. For the more mediated writing tasks, I contacted several regional editors of topical and nontopical publications. In addition to providing class visits, regional editors are likely to provide students with local interview sources and ease students' introduction to the work of freelance writing.[2]

Students' assignments were not evaluated on the basis of success with publication, since publication is difficult, and its time frame does not always coincide with the length of a course. Additionally, student assignments were not assigned a letter grade in order to prevent students from writing to the instructor as a grade-giving audience. The expectations and perceptions of the instructor may not coincide with those of an editor, and the grade-free writing allowed students to concentrate on those editors who were their actual audience. Students who attended and participated in class, completed all writing assignments, participated in the public reading that was in lieu of a final exam, and submitted seven pieces for publication were guaranteed a final grade of an A-minus. Peter Elbow's contract grading system would be viable for the course.

In the first offering, a third of the students were published; in the second, half of the students were published; by the third offering, nine of fourteen students had acceptances by semester's end. Several students saw multiple acceptances. Two years later, several students reported continuing to write for publication.

Theoretical Background: Activity Theory and Writing for Publication

The three components of activity theory provide an effective lens through which post-secondary writing instruction can be evaluated: subject, the people involved; objective, the goal of the writing task; and tools. A writing-for-publication course alters two of the three activity theory components—subject and objective. It may appear that a writing-for-publication course would most alter objective since what distinguishes this course is the intent of publication. Publication arguably constitutes a less ambiguous objective than that which occurs in other types of writing instruction since it seeks a real effect in the world, one of the qualities of transactional texts. However, publication most impacts transactionality through the alterations it causes in the subject category. What is altered is the number of individuals involved in the task environment and the audience roles of these individuals. Furthermore, of the roles altered by publication, that of the instructor is most changed—a positive development, since one complexity in writing instruction is the role of the teacher as primary audience to student writing.

Subject Category: The Instructor and the Editors

Most classroom writing is confounded by the communication act of writing to inform the instructor who presumably already knows the relayed information. Typically, one purpose for normal communication is to inform another person, but when writing for a teacher, the student reverses the stream of normal communication (Elbow). In writing for an instructor, the purpose is to meet instructor expectations (deadline, page limit, number of revisions, content accuracy). The efficacy of the student's text is founded largely on the notion of its potential effect on a different type of audience who would be informed or entertained by the student's content. The objective of student writing is to serve as an adequate demonstration of the student's learning to the instructor; it does not need to "get something done" in the world. What differentiates the publication task environment from other approaches is the way in which the instructor's relation to content has changed both in terms of the knowledge an instructor brings to the reading of a student text and of the instructor's response to the text.

In teaching publication in students' disciplines, the expertise of the instructor resides in knowledge of writing rather than content. The decentered instructor's intent is to help students best meet editorial expectations. Michael Orth described how this new instructor-student dynamic worked in his writing-for-publication course: "When they turn to me for help with a paper it's not because I'm 'the teacher,' who must be pleased with the product, but because I'm another writer who may be able to help them reach the readers they want to reach" (212). The decentered instructor provides information and experience with genre and textual analysis, publication etiquette, and the freelance writing process but is likely to be completely unfamiliar with students' disciplines or profession-specific content. Replacing the traditional instructor, students of the same major provide accuracy and relevancy checks during workshops on drafts in a writing-for-publication course. From this experience of instructor decentering, one student learned "the importance of obtaining outside opinions and heeding the suggestions of peer reviewers . . . I fancied myself rather talented at the academic writing process . . . and as a result, I rarely sought out external critiques. Writing for publication forced me to recognize limitations and shortcomings in my writing" (Hilbert). Thus, this turn to readers other than the instructor for feedback can in itself provide valuable lessons about audience.

Analyzing genres of publication helps students both address and invoke an audience, and knowledge of genre analysis is one of the main jobs of the decentered writing instructor. Textual analysis helps them separate freelance writing from academic discourse, as academic stylistic features such as thesis, topic sentences, and citations would be unwelcome in mainstream publication. Students are taught instead to identify textual features (including paragraph size, article organization, sentence length, diction, amounts of narration and description, and lead styles) for both hard copy and online publications that require distinct analyses. By helping students perceive the needs of a particular magazine or newspaper audience and differentiating online and traditional forms, genre and textual analysis situates writing and prevents the lack of authenticity that David Russell describes as resulting from the teaching of detached writing skills (56–59). When students are taught about the media kits frequently available on publications' websites, they learn the demographics of an audience and thus engage in audience-addressing, similar to the "genealogy of audiences" that Lunsford and Ede urge students to create around social networking sites ("Among" 57). Students also need explicit guidance on "occluded genre," or the genres that are intrinsic to publication but are not visible in the final document (Swales). Occluded genre, in the case of undergraduate writing-for-publication, would include electronic and hard copy cover letters, email correspondence with editors, and requests for interviews.

The reciprocity of the reader and writer relationship on the Web also affords students ways of extending peer feedback beyond the workshop of a conventional class. Not only are social networking sites an invaluable means to obtain sources for articles and verify information, they can also be useful for feedback as students share drafts with these virtual communities. For instance, a student could post an article draft on an iVillage site where the student originally found interviewees for a topic and receive feedback from the interviewees as well as their community. New media devices, such as social bookmarking and RSS (Real Simple Syndication), allow students to conduct research for their articles, allowing what Will Richardson calls "creating your own community of researchers that is gathering relevant information for you" (*Blogs* 91). Writing for more conventional publication on the Web really becomes the "peer production" that Daniel Anderson has attributed to simply writing for new media, and it also resembles recent moves in composition studies to include feedback from research participants in qualitative research.

This alteration in the subject components of the activity network of the class addresses a discrepancy between the writing purposes of educators and students. Most writing instruction is predicated on the idea that students should be both making and gaining knowledge; however, as Cheryl Geisler has argued, students seldom actually engage in the making of knowledge. Knowledge-making has been the purview of faculty, and consequentially, the goal of instruction is never actually fulfilled (Geisler). By teaching writing in the context of students' specializations, this long-standing discrepancy is alleviated, and students are shown how "knowledge-making activities go hand in hand with professional status" (118). No longer does the instructor dispense the heavy dose of both content and writing expertise, an alteration that allows students to create knowledge and engage more authentically with an audience.

The publication task environment also changes teachers' response to student text. A significant factor in pseudotransactionality is the way in which the instructor in a conventional class is an involuntary reader. The involuntary instructor as audience is obligated by academic employment to respond to each composition, presumably reading every page, every paragraph:

> [The teacher] sits at his desk reading student papers. . . . If he is a conscientious teacher he assigns a paper every week to every student he has. But he also kicks himself as he sits there sipping tea because he is acutely aware of how it is *he* who brought this

job down on his own head. Every time he stands up in class and assigns a paper he sees in his mind's eye that stack of papers on the corner of his desk waiting for him to grade. (Elbow 218)

Writing for the involuntary instructor is partially advantageous. Because the instructor is bound to read the entirety, the instructor acts as a dedicated coach, providing practice shots in a dress rehearsal for real-world writing expectations. This involuntary coach also provides personal attention. However, writing consistently for an involuntary reader does not prepare the student for the audience of their writing outside of the academic institution. Writing instructors tend not to give student texts the same reading response that they would for texts written by others (Tobin). The audience of the workplace, for instance, is not obligated to read every page of a final draft, let alone to respond to it. As a result of traditional writing education in which the audience is solely the instructor, students can grow to rely on an involuntary reader and expect that they will always have the attention of their reader, a scenario which is not conducive to transactional writing. Placed in an internship or workplace, the student who has established an effective system for meeting instructors' textual needs may be completely baffled by the implicit and explicit requirements for writing in these new environments.

Unlike the conscripted instructor, the editor is a pick-and-choose reader, one who quickly searches for relevant information and is under no obligation to read irrelevant passages. Positioning the editor as the primary reader of student texts increases textual transactionality because the student has to "fully meet the demands of the participants in events" (Britton 158). The editor as centralized audience must be swayed by the transaction of the student submission. Contrast the earlier image of the beleaguered composition instructor with the voluntary reader embodied in an editor. One magazine editor, asked to give her "top list of things freelancers shouldn't do," displays her grievances as a reader: "Don't query me without ever looking at the magazine. Don't try to convince me that you know what I want better than I do. Don't send a laundry list of ideas. . . . Don't try to palm off a sloppy, casual story" (Bykofsky, Sander, and Romiger 46). Repelled by the unwitting mistakes of a novice, an editor will reject the query of a student freelance writer. Additional irritants of magazine editors are apparent in the "Fourteen Things Not to Do in Your Query Letter" page, a standard component of the *Writer's Market*. The list advises such things as "Keep your opinions to yourself. If you're proposing an article on some public figure, for instance, your personal views are not relevant," and "Don't try any cute attention-getting devices, like marking the envelope 'Personal'" (21). A "Query Letter Clinic" section offers several examples of "bad" and "good" query letters, with comments provided by actual editors. Editorial critique of a query letter can start with its address, well before the first sentence. These bits of advice are like prohibitive warnings—some might say like a no-trespassing sign that reads "attack dog"—and show that the editor's stance is less accommodating than that of an involuntary reader.

Unlike publication, successful transaction in a classroom is typically constructed on interpersonal dynamics. Students find implicit cues about genre expectations from interaction with the instructor: "From the instructor's first words, a rich discursive context was created in the courses—through the lectures, seminars, and readings . . . Students responded 'dialogically' and 'ventriloquistically'" (Freedman and Adam, "Learning" 319–20). Compounding the pseudotransactional nature of the classroom is the fact that a student writing for an instructor does so through multiple explicit occasions with different assignments. The instructor then establishes a context for reading a student's text based on prior assignments from that individual. In terms of activity theory, the subject part of the activity network receives "multiple hits" on several occasions during the course of the semester: more so if one tallies the discursive information gained by both student and instructor through the face-to-face classroom meeting. With writing for publication, the student does not interact with the editorial staff in a face-to-face fashion; the texts carry the sole responsibility for transactionality. The student engages in transactional writing at all stages of the publication attempt, starting with the query letter, then the cover letter accompanying the finished text, and, of course, the text itself. If editorial revisions are required, the student will probably need to submit a second successful cover letter addressing those changes, as well as a revised manuscript. On top of that, if more than one editorial staff member evaluates the submission, the student faces not one evaluator (the case of writing for a teacher) but multiple.

Feedback / Iteration Differences

In a writing class with the instructor as primary audience, students are usually given various types of feedback not guaranteed when attempting publication or, for that matter, when completing most transactional writing. Due to their position as voluntary audience, the new participants in the activity system of the publication course, in contrast, can provide a type of feedback that resembles the workplace. For one, a student writing for publication can't assume that he or she will receive any feedback from editors. Editorial feedback is not guaranteed because it is based upon the transactional success of the text: whether the text has met the needs of a specific rhetorical context and whether the student has sufficiently invoked and addressed the editorial audience. While publication etiquette suggests that the editor return the manuscript in the writer's self-addressed stamped envelope, not every editorial staff does so. As a result, feedback may be altogether absent, unless one translates the lack of assessment as a tacit form of negative evaluation. The editor is under no obligation to supply the significant critical feedback that is assumed of the teacher-audience. Editorial feedback, when it happens, occurs in a variety of ways, each on a spectrum of quantity of feedback: an acceptance slip, notification that acceptance is contingent upon certain revisions, a depersonalized rejection slip, or a rejection slip with a brief amount of feedback. Any feedback provided by an editor will not typically occur in the timely fashion students are accustomed to from teachers. I have had to repeatedly coach students on the issue of waiting, reminding students of the difference in audience types between a teacher and an editor, when they wanted to contact an editor after just two weeks of silence. Chances are that if a student did prematurely contact an editor about the status of the query or submission, the student would shortly find a form rejection in his or her campus mailbox or email inbox.

Secondly, publication teaches students how to deal with a different relation between feedback and a final draft. In the standard classroom, students receive one-way, nonreciprocal feedback from the instructor, and the grade represents a response that is both "evaluative and final" (Freedman and Adam, "Learning" 329). In general, students do not expect to revise a text after its final version has been turned in. Writing for publication can help prepare students for workplace writing because both publication and the workplace often require writers to compose after the "final" version has been submitted. As Freedman and Adam have suggested, the majority of feedback in the workplace actually occurs after the final version has been given to a supervisor and is collaborative rather than purely evaluative. Novice writers may misconstrue workplace feedback because of its dissimilarity to that which is provided in the classroom and consequentially resist the mentor's feedback ("Learning" 329). Likewise, with publication, a student may be initially confounded by the number of requests from an editor for rewrites even after the piece has been accepted.

One indicator of the transactional nature of the audience instruction in writing-for-publication is the affective response of some students to the unprecedented task environment of the textsite, a reaction paralleling that which occurs at internships or worksites. Students who easily succeed in classroom writing can be overwhelmed by interactions with editors or by the instructor's atypical role with their assignments. As Chris Anson and Lee Forsberg suggest, students at internship sites undergo three stages—expectation, disorientation, and transition and resolution—as they negotiate the writing task environment. As with an internship, students in a textsite bring expectations—images of themselves as published authors or, conversely, images of mounds of rejection slips. Students who write for publication may undergo periods of disorientation which can quickly turn to frustration. When an instructor further removes him- or herself from the typical role of involuntary reader by providing feedback only when it is requested or by submitting his or her own writings for publication, students' reliance on the dynamics of the traditional classroom can be loosened. To ameliorate the confusion of the new learning context, the instructor can clearly communicate the challenges of the new audience and be understanding.

Subject Category: Guest Speakers

The writing-for-publication course needs to include several visits by freelance writers who ideally are also professionals in the students' fields and who represent a crucial alteration in the subject category of a writing class. Department chairs often receive CVs from professionals seeking adjunct teaching opportunities; these potential adjuncts are often willing to visit classes to discuss professional writing expectations. By interacting with guests, students gain insight into how writing can fit into and enhance their careers. For instance, an aviation writer told students that she obtained her first position as pilot because of her publication track record—the company was looking for someone to help with their in-house publications as well as fly planes. As Ede and Lunsford note, the guest speaker may read and comment on students' writings, thereby providing students with a chance to "engage a representative of that audience in the writing process" ("AA/AI" 166). Guest authors also afford students informal learning opportunities through meals, other presentations the guest may arrange during his or her stay on campus, and campus tours. The social process of situated learning is broader than just the learning of skills (Lave and Wenger). As such, guests provide students with less obvious professional knowledge and better prepare students for the types of learning which occur in the workplace.

Objective Category

Publication serves as the objective in the activity system of publication and as such constitutes a less ambiguous objective than that which may occur in other types of writing instruction. Unlike some other assignments, writing-for-publication does not simply emphasize the potentiality of a text. Whereas a classroom writing assignment is typically epistemic, focused on individual student learning, the emphasis in writing for publication rests on the satisfaction of the subscribing or browsing audience. We wouldn't pick up a magazine in a dentist's office and muse, "oh, good, author Jane Doe succeeded in learning about the used auto trade, and her learning is evident in this how-to article, 'How to Avoid the Lemon.'" In this way, publication resembles workplace writing, which is instrumental rather than epistemic (Spinuzzi). The objective of the writer may be to add a line to their resume, earn some extra income, or just see his or her name in print, but none of those events will occur unless the text meets the readership's needs in the view of the editor.

Differences in usage between classroom and publication writing also arise after the completion of the text. When writing for a grade, that grade signals the completion of activity, and the text enters a recycling bin/desk drawer dormancy. Graded evaluation plays a strong part in causing pseudotransactionality, "for there is an intimate connection between the criteria on which we gauge a text's success and its function" (Petraglia 24). A grade indicates that the end goal of writing is to satisfy the instructor-audience that student learning has happened.[4] On the other hand, workplace and published writing no longer belongs to the writer upon its completion but may be used for a variety of purposes by the employer or reader, with or without the notification of the writer. That a publication's activity can continue well beyond the ken of its author is similar to what occurs to writing on the Web, say Lunsford and Ede, for "the nature and consequence of any act of communication can never be determined in advance" ("Among" 60). Receiving payment for one's publication is also a signal that a transaction has been completed in the world and increases student perception of the authenticity of the writing assignment. As Ann Blakeslee has suggested, even innovative pedagogies that use case studies can be inauthentic because clients receive the completed project gratis, a situation which does not occur in the marketplace.

Textsites and Writing in the Profession

Teaching undergraduates to write for publication establishes a textsite, a transactional audience zone in which undergraduates communicate with writing professionals in their future field, either in person or in writing. The textsite is a learning environment primarily impacted by audience in which students are able to write from authentic rhetorical exigency, indirectly learn workplace writing skills, and perhaps experience the thrill of seeing their work in print. The textsite is not contained in a classroom; neither is it contained in a workplace. Instead, it operates in a larger, more capacious arena involving classroom and possible future workplace, single and multiple audiences, audiences known and hypothetical. Through textsite interactions, students begin to develop what David Russell described as a history of interactions with the activity system that they will encounter in their future profession (qtd. in Blakeslee 351). Student engagement with writing and the textsite may resume after graduation if they continue to write and publish in their profession apart from an employer's requirement that they do so (writing-in-the-professions).

In sum, the textsite can serve as an exploratory site for students to learn about complex audiences. Students can experience the freedom of writing for invisible, albeit participatory, audiences on the Web. Writing-for-publication, however, allows them to write for an individual who they won't know in person (the editor) and have textual expectations to fulfill (what Richardson calls "connective writing"). Their writing education will not have the problems of one that entails solely writing for a teacher but will become stronger from wrestling with a particular audience's expectations. According to Meredith Johnson, "At the time, I remember thinking that [the course] was a way to use writing in my future. After sixteen years of writing essays for academic success, there was no future in sight for my writing. . . . Writing for editors would give me an outlet for my writing as I moved into the aviation industry where writing isn't part of my everyday workplace." The reward for pulling off this communication is the published, perhaps even compensated for, article or column. A second reward is that the student's writing will be sponsored by a publishing venue and the student will become part of that community. A third reward is the enhancement of their understanding of the complexities of audience in our contemporary media world—which, as Lunsford and Ede remind us, is a worthy pedagogical goal. Teaching writing-for-publication can thus show students engaging complexities of audience.

Putting It into Practice

Having students write for the real audiences involved in publication would mean taking steps toward decentering the instructor and placing editors, other professionals, and students' disciplinary knowledge at center. The first step toward designing a writing-for-publication course would be to identify the disciplinary content for the course from student majors on campus. Locate a potential team-teacher from the students' discipline, sit down together, and spread out mainstream magazines and newspapers in that team-teacher's field. Once students have enrolled in the course, ask them to reflect in a process note on their experiences publishing writing on the Web. Do they see it as publication? What sorts of gratification have they received from writing for the Web or from what Lunsford and Ede term *self-sponsored communication* ("Among" 53)? How do they envision writing for editors to be different from writing for teachers or the Web? What will they be putting inside their S.A.S.E. now that their writing has a new audience?

On a cautionary note, the number of magazine, newspaper, and newsletter editors is finite—particularly with regard to regional venues. A textsite is built upon the interactions of its subjects, and the instructor's working relation with editors is easily and permanently damaged by a single student who fails to complete an assignment. Ideally, students in writing-for-publication are strongly motivated by publication and have a demonstrated record of accountability, writing competence, or willingness to learn writing strategies. At smaller institutions, it may only be possible to offer this course once every year or even two years in order to identify a group of serious and competent students, or more frequently at schools with an honors program. An additional practical matter about the course includes the amount of presemester planning required of the instructor to establish arrangements with editors. Students should also be made to understand that the course is more context-driven and subject to change than other courses due to interaction with individuals operating outside of the academic calendar. Lastly, care must be taken to monitor unhealthy competition and self-expectation among these driven students.

That said, a writing-for-publication course, by teaching undergraduates publication in their disciplines, opens vistas for students as they go on to perform writing-in-the-professions in ways that cannot be predicted during the course. Meredith Johnson, for instance, succeeded in publishing two pieces in her profession during the course. Two years into her first post-college job, Meredith had voluntarily started a company newsletter and was assisting a colleague on an aviation-related book manuscript. She reports using her publication course skills in her correspondence with congressional representatives and in her writing of grievances concerning air traffic control contracts on behalf of her union. In the end, the textsite of the course led her to a more lasting sense of writing-in-the-profession: "My view of writing went from a means to pass a class, to something that I could do as a part-time job, or even as a full-time passion. Although I am not quite sure where my writing will go, I am sure that it will continue beyond the classroom, which is what I think this class was all about."

Notes

1. I want to thank Paul Kei Matsuda who helped create the terms textsite and writing-in-the-profession.

2. Lynée Lewis Gaillet describes a similar decentralization of the instructor in her graduate course in writing for publication that enrolls students from different disciplines: "I serve only as the facilitator in this class, often learning more from my students than they learn from me." In her case, she gains knowledge about discourse conventions in the students' disciplines, whereas with the undergraduate course in publication that I teach, I am a stranger to students' content.

Works Cited

Anson, Chris M., and L. Lee Forsberg. "Moving Beyond the Academic

Community: Transitional Stages in Professional Writing." *Written Communication* 7.2 (April 1990): 200–231.

Blakeslee, Ann M. "Bridging the Workplace and the Academy: Teaching Professional Genres through Classroom-Workplace Collaborations." *Technical Communication Quarterly* 10.2 (2001): 169–192.

Britton, James. "Spectator Roles and the Beginnings of Writing." *Cross-Talk in Comp Theory: A Reader.* Ed. Victor Villanueva. Urbana, IL: NCTE, 2003. 151–76.

Bykofsky, Sheree, Jennifer Basye Sander, and Lynne Romiger. *The Complete Idiot's Guide to Publishing Magazine Articles.* New York: Alpha Books, 2000.

Dias, Patrick. "Writing Classrooms as Activity Systems." *Transitions: Writing in Academic and Workplace Settings.* Ed. Patrick Dias and Anthony Paré. Cresskill, NJ: Hampton Press, 2000. 11–29.

Ede, Lisa, and Andrea Lunsford. "Audience Addressed/Audience Invoked: The Role of Audience in Composition Theory and Pedagogy." *CCC* 35 (1984): 155–171.

Elbow, Peter. *Writing with Power: Techniques for Mastering the Writing Process.* New York: Oxford UP, 1981.

Ferrari, Joseph R., Stephanie Weyers, and Stephen F. Davis. "Publish that Paper—But Where? Faculty Knowledge and Perceptions of Undergraduate Publications." *College Student Journal* 36.3 (2002): 335–344.

Freedman, Aviva. "Show and Tell?: The Role of Explicit Teaching in the Learning of New Genres." *Research in the Teaching of English* 27.3 (October 1993): 222–251.

———. "The What, Where, When, Why, and How of Classroom Genres." *Reconceiving Writing, Rethinking Writing Instruction.* Ed. Joseph Petraglia. Mahwah, NJ: Lawrence Erlbaum Associates, 1995. 121–144.

Freedman, Aviva, and Christine Adam. "Bridging the Gap: University-Based Writing that Is More than Simulation." *Transitions: Writing in Academic and Workplace Settings.* Ed. Patrick Dias and Anthony Paré. Cresskill, NJ: Hampton Press, 2000. 129–144.

———. "Learning to Write Professionally: 'Situated Learning' and the Transition from University to Professional Discourse." *Teaching Technical Communication: Critical Issues for the Classroom.* Ed. James M. Dubinksy. Boston: Bedford St. Martin's, 2004. 310–336.

Geisler, Cheryl. "Writing and Learning at Cross Purposes in the Academy." *Reconceiving Writing, Rethinking Writing Instruction.* Ed. Joseph Petraglia. Mahwah, NJ: Lawrence Erlbaum Associates, 1995. 101–120.

Giltrow, Janet, and Michele Valiquette. "Genres and Knowledge: Students Writing in the Disciplines." *Learning and Teaching Genre.* Ed. Aviva Freedman et al. Portsmouth, NH: Boynton Cook Publishers Heinemann, 1994. 47–62.

Hill, Charles A., and Lauren Resnick. "Creating Opportunities for Apprenticeship in Writing." *Reconceiving Writing, Rethinking Writing Instruction.* Ed. Joseph Petraglia. Mahwah, NJ: Lawrence Erlbaum Associates, 1995. 145–158.

Lave, Jean, and Etienne Wenger. *Situated Learning: Legitimate Peripheral Participation.* New York: Cambridge UP, 2003.

Lunsford, Andrea A., and Lisa Ede. "Among the Audience: On Audience in an Age of New Literacies." *Engaging Audience: Writing in an Age of New Literacies.* Ed. Elizabeth Weiser, Brian Fehler, and Angela González. Urbana, IL: NCTE, 2009. 42–69.

Mansfield, Margaret A. "Real World Writing and the English Curriculum." *CCC* 44.1 (February 1993): 69–83.

Matsuda, Paul. "Coming to Voice: Publishing as a Graduate Student." *Writing for Publication: Behind the Scenes in Language Education.* Ed. C. P. Casanave et al. Mahwah, NJ: Lawrence Erlbaum Associates, 2003. 39–51

McKinney, Don. "Fourteen Things Not to Do in Your Query Letter." *2002 Writer's Market: 8,000 Editors Who Buy What You Write.* Cincinnati, OH: Writer's Digest Books, 2001. 21.

"Newsmakers: Nurse-Writer." *Nursing* 15.11 (November 1985): 8.

Orth, Michael P. "An Advanced Composition Course Aimed at Publication." *CCC* 27.2 (May 1976): 210–212.

Pedersen, N. Alvin. "Writing Themes for Magazines and Newspapers." *Education* 39 (1918): 217–224.

Petraglia, Joseph. "Spinning Like a Kite: A Closer Look at the Pseudotransactional Function of Writing." *Journal of Advanced Composition* 15.1 (1995): 19–33.

Russell, David. "Activity Theory and Its Implications for Writing Instruction." *Reconceiving Writing, Rethinking Writing Instruction.*

Ed. Joseph Petraglia. Mahwah, NJ: Lawrence Erlbaum Associates, 1995. 51–78.

Smit, David W. *The End of Composition Studies.* Carbondale, IL: Southern Illinois UP, 2004.

Spinuzzi, Clay. "Pseudotransactionality, Activity Theory, and Professional Writing Instruction." *Technical Communication Quarterly* 5.3 (1996): 295–308.

Swales, John M. "Occluded Genres in the Academy: The Case of the Submission Letter." *Academic Writing: Intercultural and Textual Issues.* Ed. E. Ventola and A. Mauranen. Amsterdam/Philadelphia: John Benjamins, 1996. 45–58.

CHAPTER ELEVEN

The Stranger Question of Audience: Service Learning and Public Rhetoric

PHYLLIS MENTZELL RYDER

Moving from a private to a public voice can help students turn their self-expression into a form of public participation. Public voice is learnable, a matter of consciously engaging with an active public rather than broadcasting to a passive audience. (Rheingold 5)

At the close of "Among the Audience," Lunsford and Ede call for us to help students, "move from the kinds of personal opinions found ubiquitously online to a truly public opinion they can help to create and sustain" (63). I want to explore what it means to develop "a truly public opinion" and how we might teach students to create such rhetorical moments. The transition from personal to public is a complex task. There's a big difference between posting one's thoughts on Facebook and speaking in a town hall. "Going public" in the more robust sense means gathering people and motivating them to work together. Public writing performs beliefs about agency: what does it take to affect change and who has the capacity to do so? Public writing invokes belief in interdependence; we signal how we need friends, acquaintances, and strangers to create the world we strive for. Each time we enter into and create public venues, we assert anew a vision for what that public is—who should be in it (or not), how people should relate to each other, what kind of knowledge should be valued, what kinds of world we live in.

In the age of new media, it is tempting to dive right into the digital world to find pedagogical sites for teaching students about "public" writing. A composition instructor might post student essays to a webpage to remind students that "audiences are there all the time, browsing, searching, engaging, responding, sometimes accusing" (Lunsford and Ede, "Among" 56). When students imagine who might view their now-public work, they may consider audiences they had otherwise "ignored, rejected, excluded, or denied" (Lunsford and Ede, "Representing Audience" 174). Lunsford and Ede illustrate such a pedagogical moment with a composition instructor who posts her students' essays on a course website and hears back, two years later, from a scholar irate that his work has been unfairly used in a student's text. The student "is completely surprised . . . [H]e certainly had not imagined that one of his sources would go to the trouble of accessing his essay" ("Among" 56). I consider this a worthwhile lesson for the student, but the scenario also suggests that we can do more.

While posting an essay to a course website may serve the pedagogical purpose of forcing the student to imagine lurking strangers, it does little to bring strangers to the essays. People using a search engine will come across the page only if it already has received a lot of traffic. More likely, the people who click to the site will be friends and family of the students (reading to keep in touch with each other), other teachers or students (looking for model student essays to teach or steal), administrators (evaluating the writing program or teachers) or—as in the earlier example—scholars policing how their work has been used. None of these scenarios brings the author and audience together as citizens or activists or potential community members. The instructor has addressed part of the problem of *circulation*, a critical component of what makes something public, but has taken only a few, small steps toward creating a public interaction. How can we help students think critically about other components of public formation: the *exigency* that brings people together; the sense of *agency* people gain through their *interdependence* with each other and with *strangers*; where to enter into (or create) the conversations to sustain these beliefs (*circulation*)?

Though we should prepare students to engage public issues through all kinds of media, new and old, we would do well to start in a local, tangible place: community organizations. By asking our students to work with, and write *for*, *about*, and *with* community organizations (to use Thomas Deans's very helpful taxonomy from *Writing Partnerships*), we can help them analyze the rhetorical moves that are central to building a "public voice." In this chapter, I share an approach to teaching public writing through partnerships with community organizations. First, I illustrate the rhetorical moves of public formation, drawing on specific examples from the community organizations with whom my students have partnered. In the process, I describe several writing and research assignments that help students identify and practice these moves. Finally, I consider recent arguments about the potential for new media to help or harm "the public," and I show how these arguments are part of a larger, ongoing conflict about the nature of the "public sphere." I close with a quick review of how one might design a public writing course using service-learning.

Community Organizations as Publics

Public work is fundamentally rhetorical work. A public is never a fixed thing, but is a social entity invoked and circulated through discourse (Hauser; Warner). A group of people can be a group of friends one moment and part of a public another. What changes is not the physical gathering, but how they constitute themselves, how they orient to each other and to potential strangers. Because it is not a fixed thing, a public is always in some state of crisis: it has to persistently call itself into being. With each iteration, it is constituted in a different way. No two texts invoke the same public, even as each text works to assert its way of seeing things as an inevitable and obvious approach. As Michael Warner notes, public writers and readers are always engaged in this paradoxical dance: we have to act as if the public unquestionably exists, even as we struggle rhetorically to make sure everyone believes that public exists (12). Community organizations are excellent sites to study how publics work through these "metapramatic struggles" (Warner 12).

In general, because publics seek to make their particular worldview seem inevitable, students can find it difficult to observe the rhetorical moves that create that "inevitability." However, community groups keep much of their metapragmatic discourse public—they pronounce their mission statements, create mottos, share genesis stories, highlight their success; they provide concrete and located texts. Because community organizations are organized around specific issues in specific places, it easier to see the exigency that brings them together. Moreover, community organizations are surrounded by groups that take on similar projects or work in the same neighborhoods and offer alternate visions of the issues, the solutions, and neighborhood. By juxtaposing the rhetorics of different community groups, students can see how each group projects a particular public image.

Rhetorical Components of Public Formation

What leads people to speak/write/text each other in any situation is *rhetorical exigency*—a situation that "is capable of positive modification and when positive modification requires discourse or can be assisted by discourse" (Bitzer 6). In *public* exigencies, the rhetor posits that positive modification can be affected by people working together, and the rhetor has some way to reach those change-agents (to extend Bitzer 7). Part of the rhetorical task, then, is to make the audience believe that they are capable of making change. The sense of agency invoked in public texts insists on the *interdependence* of the audience members. The invoked choose to orient toward each other to gain this agency. Moreover, the public understands that their collective power is drawn from not only those who are immediately present or known, but also from *strangers* who share their approach and who are signaled in the discourse. Finally, publics are formed not by any single rhetorical moment, but through the *circulation* of discourse. Sharing one's opinion is not, in and of itself, a public act; it becomes so when it joins or instigates a larger conversation. The work has to find its public.

Invoking Capacity

In democratic theory, public agency is often defined as the power to vote, the power to pressure a government official in the name of public opinion. This definition of agency presumes that the process for social change is through government action. Yet other public work is oriented toward the market forces—labor unions, environmental groups, or feminist groups, for instance. Still other publics target sites of cultural socialization, such as schools, TV, Hollywood. And still others locate the most meaningful work through the more personal, intimate action of creating community with those who have been marginalized.

In all of these examples, a public assumes/asserts a power to create (or fight) change. The work of public-making must simultaneously convince others of the *urgency* of an issue, of a particular *way of viewing* that issue, and of a particular *solution* that requires the participation of others. I find that students can begin to unpack these rhetorical moves in community organizations when they juxtapose the discourse of groups working in the same area on the same issue. Consider three organizations that help homeless individuals in Washington, DC. Miriam's Kitchen serves breakfast and lunch and offers an array of social services as well as "after breakfast programs" in art, poetry, and literature. The Dinner Program for Homeless Women (DPHW) serves breakfast to men and women and then becomes a women-only space offering activities, social services, and dinner for women and children. *Street Sense* is a newspaper focused on issues relating to homelessness that is distributed throughout the city by homeless vendors; some vendors also write articles for the paper. Each of these organizations responds to the District's high costs of housing and unemployment by reaching out to people most directly affected, offering them respite, respect, and an array of services. Yet each organization has a unique approach, developed from unique readings of the "problem" and specific assumptions about what other members of the DC community should do to help. It is these distinctions that we explore in our class.

To unpack the range of ways that people commonly define public agency in community organizations—what should people do to solve social problems?—I turn to Keith Morton's "The Irony of Service: Charity, Project and Social Change in Service-Learning." Morton outlines several paradigms for thinking about "service." First, he sketches a continuum that begins with "charity" (direct services, such as providing shelter and food), moves through "projects" (specific, measurable solutions, such as building houses or teaching literacy), and ends with "social change/advocacy" (lobbying, voter education, boycotts, etc.). Many academics approach community organizations with this hierarchy in mind, devaluing "charity" and holding up "social change/advocacy" as the best approach with the broadest reach. Funders, on the other hand, often value projects, with their explicit, measurable outcomes.

While Morton acknowledges why the charity-project-advocacy continuum has strong appeal, he questions it. Through a series of interviews with men and women who work in community organizations (including students), he revises his thinking about these categories. Morton finds that each of the three approaches—charity, projects, advocacy—can promote "thick" or "thin" relationships, and he argues that a better yardstick for evaluating "good service" is to consider how well each lives up to the internal logic and values in the "thick" version of the paradigm. Thick service builds on mutual respect and involves constituents as integral participants. For example, people who perform "thick" *charity* work do not pressure poor men and women to change; rather, they offer a deep level of respect and a place where they will not be judged or marginalized. Morton insists that such work cannot be dismissed as superficial. Likewise, people who perform thick *projects* provide hands-on strategies for moving people out of homelessness, illiteracy, etc. in a manner that respects the knowledge, values, and experiences that the participants have to offer. On the flip side, "thin" social advocacy occurs when organizations design legislation or petitions "for" a community, without consulting citizens or including them meaningfully in the process. Rather than judge each paradigm as part of a continuum, Morton suggests that we evaluate each according to its thickness (28).

I use Morton's essay to help students see the inherent logic within different approaches to public agency. The three homeless organizations are good examples. As low-barrier organizations (people are not required to give up drinking or drugs to enter), DPHW and Miriam's Kitchen profess a "thick charity" approach, highlighting their respect for the worth and dignity of the people who come to them. Miriam's Kitchen calls these people "guests";

DPHW refers to them as "clients." While the programs offer classes and services to help people fight their addictions or gain skills to find jobs or housing, they stress that such opportunities are never imposed. "Guests" at Miriam's Kitchen "are *invited to receive* a wide range of social services," the website explains. "By creating an atmosphere of hospitality *where guests can choose how they receive support*, Miriam's Kitchen is able to build relationships with many vulnerable individuals" (Miriam's Kitchen, italics mine). The language of the DPHW website focuses similarly on the "clients'" ability to choose their interactions. In contrast, while Street Sense also treats homeless men and women with respect, for them respect goes beyond witnessing. They offer men and women opportunities to write for the paper, to make money by selling the paper, and to serve as spokespeople as vendors. Their vision of agency as a combination of advocacy and project is evident in their mission statement: "Street Sense aims to *increase public awareness* of poverty and homelessness in Washington, DC, and to provide homeless people with an *economic opportunity* and *a forum* to be published" (Street Sense, italics mine).

The analysis of "public agency" is useful pedagogically in a service-learning course, because it brings out students' own assumptions about the best ways to affect social change and allows us to talk about how to build respectful relationships with community partners. It's useful in a *writing* class because it helps us identify how publics invoke exigency and agency. As we read Morton's essay, I ask students to summarize the argument and identify its key terms, and we chart the thin and thick versions of each paradigm, looking for indications of how each component might manifest rhetorically in how people talk about the exigency of the organization and its vision of social change. This close work with Morton sets students up to use his framework to analyze the community organizations they have chosen to partner with. They review primary materials they've collected—Web pages, brochures, orientation materials, and media coverage—and write short analyses of which kind of "service" their organization advocates. Students working with the same organization often arrive at different conclusions, which can lead to productive discussions about the ongoing tensions within publics. Both Miriam's Kitchen and DPHW, for example, have to negotiate the more project-oriented ideals of service that their funders demand against the less tangible but equally valuable goals of creating hope and spaces of integrity. (Paula Mathieu explores this tension well in *Tactics of Hope*.)

Invoking Capacity through Interdependence and Stranger-Relationality

A critical component of public agency is not just the power to create change but power built on *interdependence*. Most obviously, leaders create this power of interdependence when they repeatedly and deliberately associate their own power with that of the group. As Michael Gecan, an IAF organizer trained by Saul Alinsky, writes, "Even when I am alone in the public arena, I am not an individual" (39). Interdependence is also developed by staging interactions among participants that allow them to feel the capacity of a larger group. Charles Payne, in his extensive analysis of the Civil Rights Movements in Mississippi, observes that SNCC organizers orchestrated their mass church meetings by inviting movement leaders from across the state. People felt their own power connected with strangers working for their cause elsewhere. Church ministers, business owners, sharecroppers, and others found themselves so bolstered by the sense of power and capacity in the room that they committed publicly to the work of the movement.

If part of a public bond is feeling oneself in a gathering of strangers, then people who are addressed as a public *expect* the address not to match directly with themselves; they want signs that the group is larger than their own identity. One obvious rhetorical move is a shift in diction, as handbooks regularly advise: "More formal language is appropriate, [when] you are addressing people you do not know well" (Lunsford *Easywriter* 146). Such moves invite in the stranger, and equally important, they signal intimates to orient themselves toward the open door. "Our partial nonidentity with objects of address in public speech seems to be part of what it means to regard something as public speech" (Warner 78). The implication here is rather liberating. When I ask students to write to a "public audience," they often insist on writing with bland generality. "If I say anything too specific," they explain, "the general reader will feel left out." However, when we realize that stranger-relationality can solidify the audience as a *public*, we are free to draw on personal narratives, describe places, refer to specific people, and use a variety of rhetorical moves that heighten pathos and urgency. To a great extent, the discourse *succeeds* when each participant recognizes moments when he or she is *not* identified as the only (kind of) recipient.

Because of its commitment to multiculturalism, CentroNía is a good place to find explicit rhetorics of stranger-relationality. Headquartered in DC's Columbia Heights neighborhood, CentroNía's mission is "to educate children and strengthen families in a bilingual, multicultural community" ("Our Organization"). CentroNía has a multilingual daycare, a Bilingual Public Charter School, professional and vocational training for adults, and a center for family and community development. In Columbia Heights, the population in 2000 was 31.7 percent white, 45.7 percent African American, and 24.7 percent Hispanic/Latino (DC Office of Planning). As a Spanish-English bilingual center, CentroNía's most obvious relationship is with those community members who speak these home languages. However, they work to reinforce their orientation toward those with other linguistic and cultural identities. One way these members are made present is through the organization's name. "'CentroNía' is derived from Spanish, Swahili, and Esperanto, a universal language created in the late nineteenth century to help bridge cultures. *Centro* means 'center' in Spanish. *Nía* means 'our' in Esperanto and 'purpose' in Swahili" ("About Us"). The prominence of Esperanto and Swahili within the name highlights their orientation toward people of African descent and invokes Esperanto's desire for a "universal" means of "bridging cultures."

The rhetorical challenge of how to invoke the powerful interdependence of stranger-relationality is one my students often choose to investigate. Students who tutored with CentroNía, for example, analyzed whether the organization does enough to draw in its non-Hispanic students and community members. The organization is bilingual, rather than multilingual; it uses standard English as a primary language but does not explicitly acknowledge Black English, though close to half of Columbia

Heights is African American. In students' investigations, they have considered how the target populations relate to these various languages: would honoring more heritage languages bring those groups in, or would it alienate them, as was true in Oakland when schools sought to incorporate Ebonics as part of Students' Right to Their Own Language (see Smitherman).

Another example of how interdependent stranger-relationality manifests are seen with Washington Parks and People (WPP), a nonprofit that uses the concrete project of cleaning up city parks as a part of a larger strategy: mobilizing community members to revitalize the inner-city neighborhoods around those parks. WPP consistently invokes the power that comes from working together. The mission statement affirms the capacity of neighborhood organizations and leaders: "Washington Parks & People is the capital area's *network* of *community* park *partnerships* . . . working to revitalize Washington by *reconnecting* two of its greatest but most forgotten *assets*: its vast network of public lands and waterways . . . and its *core of dedicated community leaders* and *organizations*" (my italics). WPP professes its belief in building capacity across cultures as one of its operating principles: "Travel and work in multiracial groups" (Hines 124). Moreover, the organization shares two different genesis stories. In one, the group's beginnings lie with a white man, Steve Coleman, then president of the Adams Morgan neighborhood association, who with a group of residents drew on the wisdom of neighborhood elders to reclaim a crime-ridden park. In the other, the origins lie farther back, with the late African American resident Josephine Butler, who also worked to bring the community together. Coleman and Butler, who have each headed WPP, regularly referred to their collaboration as essential to the capacity of their group.

When considering the power of this rhetoric of multicultural interdependence, students who work with WPP have to account for the organization's move from a predominantly multicultural neighborhood (when their focus was Meridian Hill Park) into a predominantly African American neighborhood in Ward 7 (now that its focus is Marvin Gaye Park.) Historically in DC, white citizens (with the help of the federal government) have more often than not displaced African American residents in the name of "revitalization." How can WPP—currently under the leadership of Coleman—build stranger-relationality when this historical memory looks critically at "outsider" participation? My students have experienced this question personally. As they work in Ward 7, WPP volunteers are often the only white people around. An African American student who picked up on this sentiment wrote an essay admonishing WPP to make multicultural strangers feel more welcome, but I pushed him to weigh the competing needs of capacity-building *within* the community and capacity-building through stranger-relationality. Here, public-building demands a stranger-relationality that explicitly affirms local visions of "revitalization."

Circulation of Discourse

When we consider historical events such as Dr. King's address at the National Mall, we might assume that individuals can create publics. But Warner warns us that "no single text can create a public. Nor can a single voice, a single genre, even a single medium. All are insufficient to enable the kind of reflexivity that we call a public, since a public is understood to be an ongoing space of encounter for discourse" (90). A public's capacity is affirmed when others talk *about* it. Other texts must carry forward its unique sense of power and motivation, its unique worldview. Part of the rhetorical work of a public is to make sure that the group is recognized on its own terms.

Such circulation might happen by having a newspaper print the material in your press release or by staging strategic meetings with people in power. Michael Gecan describes a time when the Eastern Brooklyn Congregations (ECB), an IAF organization that fought for affordable housing in the early 1980s, forced Mayor Koch to say their name. The mayor had referred to the group only as "'those churches' or 'the religious people' or some other half-descriptive, half-dismissive term" (Gecan 62). EBC invited Koch to a public groundbreaking ceremony and asked him to lead the countdown. As the event began, they explained that the countdown would be "ten-EBC, nine-EBC . . . " Koch was caught off-guard, but he repeated the words as instructed. "From that day on," Gecan writes, "the mayor used our name . . . when he referred to us" (63). The organization succeeded in getting the mayor to acknowledge them on their terms, to circulate their name in the press coverage of the ceremony, and to signal the capacity of their organization through their accomplishments on the housing project.

A public initially may take advantage of a method of circulation already in place. For WPP, the Adams Morgan neighborhood association provided the initial means for spreading the word about a new concern about the local park. As the organization evolved, it drew on and extended the modes of circulation, such as letters to the editor in the *Washington Post* and articles in local and national magazines and publications of other NGOs. Like many community organizations, WPP archives such documents on their website, which not only provides an easy way to identify some of their venues of circulation but can also serve as an interesting site for comparing which stories WPP wants to forward, and which they do not.

In my course, students explore issues of circulation during a library session in which they search for media references to their organizations as well as for local, public discussion of the related social issue. We search in Lexis Nexis, the historical *Washington Post*, local area papers (such as *East of the River* or *Washington Hispanic*), and civic documents (such as minutes of neighborhood meetings or council members' reports). I invite a government documents librarian to teach the students how to look up demographic information from the Census (using American Fact Finder), and we consider what the data from these reports might teach us about the possibilities and constraints on circulation as well as how the Census itself, as a political document, shapes what data is gathered and how neighborhoods are read.

Issues of circulation become even more apparent to students when they develop projects *for* their organizations. For example, one student developed an information postcard for DPHW on resources for homeless women who had experienced sexual violence. Some of her rhetorical choices had to do with urgency (how explicit should the document be about its purpose? It had to attract the appropriate women without making them feel too self-conscious to pick it up); others with capacity-building (she struggled to find language that would affirm the women's agency—were they "victims"?). But many decisions were firmly rooted in questions of circulation: DPHW planned to distribute the card through its display case, which constrained the size; the student also had to determine what would be easiest for women to carry. She had to consider costs: at DPHW's request, she made the two-color postcard in a form that could also work as black and white. She even considered copyright issues surrounding the blue ribbon, a symbol of support for those who have experienced sexual assault. Finally, DPHW wanted their logo on the flyer; in addition to informing their clients about sexual violence support centers, it could alert other abused women about DPHW. Moreover, with the logo, the card could circulate to funders as an example of DPHW services and outreach.

Public Formation in the Age of New Media

While my students and I regularly analyze organizations' websites and communicate with our partners through email, by October 2008, none of these organizations used Web 2.0 media for their public building. We might attribute this to a deficit of resources (the cost of developing and monitoring spaces for ongoing dialog is high) or to their orientation toward low-income populations. But another explanation may be that Web 2.0 is not a particularly effective tool for invoking this kind of a public. The Internet provides a potential mode of circulation yet it is not a neutral one. Do the newer elements of information communication technology facilitate or hamper public formation?

Much response to the Internet includes optimistic assertions of its democratic power. Lunsford and Ede note that "speakers and audiences communicate in multiple ways and across multiple channels, often reciprocally. And this momentous shift has challenged not only traditional models of communication but also the relationship between 'creators' of messages and those who receive them. Today, as we have pointed out, the roles of writers and audiences often conflate, merge, and shift" ("Among" 48). Gilbert Rodham characterizes this conflation as democratic: "And if a crucial facet of a healthy democracy is the ability of ordinary people to participate actively in the public sphere as both 'speakers' and 'listeners,' then the Net may be the only form of mass media that has the potential to be genuinely democratic" (29).

This vision of public interaction highlights the new possibilities for circulation, but as we know, circulation is only part of public work. Scholars voice concern about how new media shape agency, distress at how they may undermine interdependence among strangers, and caution about how information technology infrastructures control circulation.

Agency and New Media

The Internet can be put in the service of public action by motivating voters to contact their representatives, bringing individuals information that may affect their individual choices (to protect the environment, choose schools, or the like). In much online communication, such as email alerts, we are addressed as *individuals* whose actions, added to others' action, will make a difference. In this sense, we are part of a public that has *some* interdependence—we all have to change our behaviors to make a difference—but we aren't required to engage with each other discursively about the action. In these scenarios, the "public" we join is along the lines of what Robert Putnam has called "tertiary organizations," in which "[f]or the vast majority of their members, the only act of membership consists in writing a check for dues or perhaps occasionally reading a newsletter.... [The ties between members] in short, are to common symbols, common leaders, and perhaps common ideals, but not to one another" (Putnam 71).

For tertiary associations, public agency is tied to donating and circulating roles that are built into the infrastructure of many sites. "Donate now" buttons collect our credit card information easily; "send this letter" buttons generate letters to our government representatives; "tell your friends" buttons send pre-scripted invitations to all the addresses in our mailboxes. Most of these features rely, not coincidentally, on the same infrastructure that makes the Internet work as a tool of the market. Thus, audiences are invoked into a kind of hybrid "consumer-citizen," a role that reinforces our individual roles rather than collective, deliberative interactions.

Interdependence, Strangerhood, and New Media

Other lines of discussion about emerging information communication technologies focus on the scope of the public that is invoked. Some of the mostly widely expressed concerns center rightly on issues of access, noting that when a forum for public discussion shifts online and then professes to yield "public opinion," the move elides the exclusion of many who don't have computer access or computer literacy. Since those perspectives have been well articulated elsewhere (see Peter Levine), I will focus instead on the hyperspecialization of the Web and the quality of online conversations in public discussion arenas. Rather than see these as threats to "public life," I see them as moments where, yet again, different publics struggle to gain the rhetorical power of being seen as "the" public.

The discussion about hyperspecialization and fragmentation is a response to technologies that allow Web users to identify their interests and receive specialized content. Users can narrow their online interactions to feeds from specific websites, blogs, and community forums that match their own perspectives. The fear is that by locating themselves in such tightly subscribed networks, these Web users may lose touch with the larger array of perspectives out there. Moreover, when they do enter discussions outside their specialized domain, such users may act as if the beliefs and discursive practices of the narrow group apply in the new space as well. Their absence from the larger forums keeps them sheltered; their presence in the larger forums disrupts the conversations there. While Lunsford and Ede suggest that the Internet will make writers more aware of broader views, narrowly focused Web 2.0 feeds can also produce citizens who don't distinguish between their specialized public and the larger "public."

I wonder if this fear is as new or as bad as it is often made out to be. If we understand public interactions as the struggles of multiple publics to invoke theirs as the "inevitable" and "obvious" way that things should be, then the "fragmentation" of the Web is not new. "The public" has always been multiple. As I have written elsewhere, publics have always dismissed each other by critiquing their discursive styles as "nonpublic." And as many who write about marginalized groups acknowledge, having a place to feel in community with like-minded individuals is a powerful thing. When those publics choose to intervene in other spheres, they will likely do so in ways that run counter to those publics' expectations; this is part of the ongoing struggle of public life. (See Mary Louise Pratt's analysis of contact zones and safe houses.) We can't assume that those who choose *not* to shift discourse while entering the "broader" public are merely ignorant; the move may be a deliberate challenge to the rhetoric the broader group presumes to be ideal.

Rather than focus on the danger of fragmentation, we might consider the flipside. What happens if publics no longer have a place to work out their beliefs—to deliberate about agency and strategy—without being infiltrated, taken over, and disrupted by those who are admittedly not in that public? This is the challenge of providing open discussion forums, and groups have responded in different ways. Some limit access to people who have demonstrated a commitment through other, nonvirtual channels. Some try to preempt "unproductive" discussions, as we can see in this preface to the wall in the Stop Global Warming Facebook page: "Forum policy: please note that the discussion forum is focused on solving the climate crisis. If you wish to debate whether global warming is a problem, the existence of gravity, or the roundness of the Earth, there are other forums for those discussions" (WeCampaign).

Open online discussion forums are rich sites for evaluating the possibilities and challenges of public formation on the Web. Many groups build their sense of *capacity* using social networking sites. For example, Barack Obama's Facebook page, which began in 2006, listed 2,224,417 "supporters" in October 2008; a sense of capacity grew along with the numbers. Yet the nature of that capacity is somewhat ambiguous. The numbers might be equated with voter-power, but it is not only that, since supporters hail from all over the world, and that worldwide presence signals a different kind of power. Stranger-relationality is integrated in the display of all Facebook groups: under the declaration of the number of supporters, the page displays three people from among the viewer's own Facebook friends who are also in this group, along with three "strangers." A quick survey of the 299,099 wall posts suggests that while public discussion begins with posts directed to Obama ("You are a gentleman, sir"), the members soon begin talking to each other about questions of agency (Can *he* win this year? Can *we* elect him?), and later seek to learn from each other (one thread among people in different states explores the degree of racism in America; in another supporters in different countries sort out international attitudes toward Obama's policies). The site seems to become a place where participants deliberate together about some of the conditions that shape their beliefs and how they may enact those beliefs in their own lives.

In contrast, an ethnographic study of the Blacksburg Electronic Village, an online site linked to the geographic area of Blacksburg, VA, suggests that those participants developed only a vague sense of exigency, agency, or interdependence. David Silver observes that participants use the site primarily to collect consumer information about local businesses and services. Their relationship is proximate and temporary; there is little cost to joining or leaving discussions. One man acts as the community "gadfly," igniting regular flame-wars. Silver argues that the listserv reveals the community working out some of their concerns discursively, but his interviews with participants suggest that they don't feel particularly committed to the online community. In this case, it seems, the online village has not lived up to its (alleged) promise.

As Lunsford and Ede note, more analysis of the ever-changing landscape of information communication technology is needed to understand how it perpetuates or undermines public formations, how online publics may differ from those invoked through other media, and how the relationships between online forums and their on-the-ground counterparts interact. At the same time, as we encounter the literature about the Internet and public life, we need to remain attentive to the ways that "publics" are defined, noting those occasions when the optimism about circulation is unhinged from the other components of public-making: exigency, agency, interdependence.

Putting It into Practice

To teach students to write for public audiences, students must see that, no matter the content of their work, public rhetors always offer up a vision of who can come together and how people create change. In my writing course, students partner with community organizations, and through reflection and practice, experience the struggle that is public writing. I recommend assignment sequences that first ask students to analyze the rhetoric of their organizations and end with projects they write with and for the organization. Students' on-site work at community organizations gives them firsthand experience and a relationship with a public that allows them to think critically about public writing.

I work closely with my university's Office of Community Service to identify potential community organizations within a set range of issues and in the same physical neighborhoods; this way, students can compare how organizations define their issues and their communities (as I showed in my earlier comparison of the three organizations that work with homeless men and women). Before the semester begins, I meet with each organization to identify activities students can perform onsite each week; we also brainstorm writing tasks the students can compose with or for the organization. During the semester, students spend at least twenty hours at the organization; I offset this by cancelling one of our four hours of weekly meeting time.

To prepare students to analyze an organization's public-building rhetoric, I have found a collection of readings that productively introduce these concepts. For rhetorical *exigency*, I ask students to read Lloyd Bitzer's "The Rhetorical Situation." We discuss how publics define *capacity* using Keith Morton's "Ironies of Service" in the manner I described earlier in the essay. I often pair this with John McKnight's "Why Servanthood Is Bad" and "John Deere and the Bereavement Council," two irreverent attacks on thin versions of service. To introduce concepts of *circulation* and *stranger-relationality*, I create handouts and mini-lectures drawing on Michael Warner's *Publics and Counterpublics*.

As students visit their organizations, they collect primary documents, which we examine together in class. We use students' own observations, combined with library research, to identify the potential challenges to the organizations' public-building. We seek evidence of common attitudes about social issues as well as the historical and material conditions in which an organization is located. I work with university librarians to introduce the U.S. Census data, DC government documents, public talk shows, newspapers, and other media where the organization, its leaders, or its constituents are mentioned. Gabrielle Modan's *Turfwars* provides background on the historical tension between local DC and federal Washington. More important, her insightful discourse analysis of Mt. Pleasant, a multicultural DC community, provides a professional model of how to look critically at primary sources to see what publics they invoke. In their first writing assignments, students use theories of public rhetoric to examine primary documents and analyze how their partner organization invokes its public.

The final assignment is to compose a document that has been commissioned by the organization, such as a brochure, a volunteer manual, a PowerPoint introducing the organization to a particular local group, or other assignments that are appropriate for their writing abilities. Within this assignment, students must negotiate with their contact at the community organization to flesh out the requirements. Dean's *Writing and Community Action* includes sage advice and useful model memos for students as they work through this negotiation. In composing their commissioned tasks, students are confronted with the challenge of shedding their sense of writing as individual authors. Depending on the size and scope of the task, students may work collaboratively or individually, but even those who do not work in collaborative groups must adjust their voice and language to fit within the ethos of their organization. Students start to negotiate the rhetorical challenges of public-building that they analyzed earlier in the course, as they consider what terminology to use and what examples will best evoke both the future goals and the current assets of their organization and its constituents. Moreover, the commissioned task forces students to consider the constraints of circulation, as we saw in the earlier example of the student who created an informational brochure on resources for abused homeless women.

Public writing is always a site of struggle, a push and pull that highlights differing views of who can act, what kinds of actions create change, and what ideals we should act toward. If we wish to help students invoke public audiences, we need to create the space where they can investigate these rhetorical components of public-building, and we need to create opportunities for them to practice this important work. Well-designed service-learning courses can provide students with this rich intellectual, powerful work.

Works Cited

Bitzer, Lloyd F. "The Rhetorical Situation." *Philosophy & Rhetoric* 1.1 (1968): 1–14.

CentroNía. "About Us: History." *CentroNía*. 3 Feb 2007 <http://www. centronia.org/html/history.html>.

———. "Our Organization: Mission, Principles, and Structure." *CentroNía.org*. 30 Jul 2008 <http://centronia.org/html/organization. html>.

DC Office of Planning. "2000 Population by Single Race and Hispanic Origin by Ward." 23 May 2007. <http://planning.dc.gov/planning/ cwp/view,a,1282,q,569460.asp>.

Dean, Jodi. "Why the Net is not a Public Sphere." *Constellations: An International Journal of Critical & Democratic Theory* 10.1 (2003): 95–112.

Deans, Thomas. *Writing and Community Action: A Service-Learning Rhetoric and Reader.* New York: Longman, 2003.

———. *Writing Partnerships: Service-Learning in Composition.* Urbana, IL: National Council of Teachers of English, 2000.

Dinner Program for Homeless Women. "About Us: Our Mission." *Dinner Program for Homeless Women.* 29 Jul 2008 <http://www. dphw.org>.

Gecan, Michael. *Going Public: An Organizer's Guide to Citizen Action.* Boston: Beacon Press, 2002.

Grabill, Jeffrey T. *Writing Community Change: Designing Technologies for Citizen Action.* Cresskill, N.J: Hampton Press, 2007.

Harris, Joseph. *Rewriting: How to Do Things with Texts.* Utah State U P, 2006.

Hauser, Gerard A. *Vernacular Voices: The Rhetoric of Publics and Public Spheres*. Columbia, SC: U of South Carolina P, 1999.

Levine, Peter. "The Internet and Civil Society." *The Internet and Civil Society*. Lanham, MD: Rowman & Littlefield, 2004. 79–99.

Lunsford, Andrea A. *Easy Writer 3e + Exercises*. Bedford/St. Martin's, 2005.

Lunsford, Andrea A., and Lisa Ede. "Among the Audience: On Audience in an Age of New Literacies." *Engaging Audience: Writing in an Age of New Literacies*. Ed. Elizabeth Weiser, Brian Fehler, and Angela González. Urbana, IL: NCTE, 2009. 42–69.

Mathieu, Paula. *Tactics of Hope: Street Life and the Public Turn in English Composition*. Portsmouth, NH: Boynton/Cook Publishers, 2005.

Miriam's Kitchen. "Welcome to Miriam's Kitchen." *Miriam's Kitchen* 2006. 29 Jul 2008 <http://miriamskitchen.org/>.

Modan, Gabriella Gahlia. *Turf Wars: Discourse, Diversity, and the Politics of Place*. Wiley-Blackwell, 2007.

Morton, Keith. "The Irony of Service: Charity, Project, and Social Change in Service-Learning." *Michigan Journal of Community Service Learning* 2 (1995): 19–32.

Nieto, Sonia, and Patricia Bode. *Affirming Diversity: The Sociopolitical Context of Multicultural Education*. Allyn & Bacon, 2007.

Payne, Charles M. *I've Got the Light of Freedom: The Organizing Tradition and the Mississippi Freedom Struggle*. Berkeley, CA: U of California P, 1996.

Putnam, Robert. "Bowling Alone: America's Declining Social Capital." *Journal of Democracy* 6.1: 65–78.

Rheingold, Howard. "Vision of the Future." Melbourne, Australia, 1007. 28 Jul 2008 <http://www.educationau.edu.au/jahia/webdav/site/myjahiasite/shared/seminars/Rheingold_Melbourne_Speech.pdf>.

Rimmerman, Craig A. *The New Citizenship: Unconventional Politics, Activism, and Service*. Boulder, CO: Westview P, 1997.

Rodman, Gilbert. "The Net Effect: The Public's Fear and the Public Sphere." *Virtual Publics: Policy and Community in an Electronic Age*. Ed. Beth E. Kolko. New York: Columbia U P, 2003. 9–48.

Ryder, Phyllis Mentzell. "Multicultural Public Spheres and the Rhetorics of Democracy." *JAC: Rhetoric, Writing, Culture, Politics* 27.1 (2008). <http://www.jacweb.org>.

Silver, David. "Communication, Community, Consumption: An Ethnographic Exploration of an Online City." *Virtual Publics: Policy and Community in an Electronic Age.* Ed. Beth E Kolko. New York: Columbia University Press, 2003. 327–353.

Street Sense. "About Us: More About Street Sense." *Street Sense* 2008. 29 Jul 2008 <http://www.streetsense.org/>.

Warner, Michael. *Publics and Counterpublics.* New York: Zone Books, 2002.

Washington Parks and People. "What We Do." *Washington Parks and People* 2004. 29 Jul 2008 <http://www.washingtonparks.net/whatwedo.html>.

WeCampaign. "Stop Global Warming." *Facebook.* 30 Jul 2009 <http://apps.new.facebook.com/causes/24?facebook_url=true&m=f6375&recruiter_id=8411915>.

CHAPTER TWELVE

Moving Audiences, Translating Writers, and Negotiating Difference

SHARON MCKENZIE STEVENS

In many pedagogical applications of Bitzer's "rhetorical situation," one defining component of a situation, *audience*, quickly
becomes a subcategory of another, *constraint*. Teachers and
textbooks invoke imagined audiences to justify genre, topic, style,
vocabulary, grammar, mechanics, and more. By outlining how
expectations shape responses, this approach replaces formalist
emphases on decontextualized rules, offering students a social
context for adapting rhetorical strategies to multiple academic
disciplines, multiple workplaces, and other situations that call
for writing.

This approach to audience is common because it is effective.
While I will use most of this chapter to discuss my concern with
how this can become overly limiting, I wish to acknowledge first
that I believe this typical approach has a place, and I, like so many
other teachers, do at times rely on it. For example, I'm currently
teaching a technical writing course linked to collaborative experimental work in food technologies. Students, working within
a fairly typical scenario, are assigned the role of researchers in a
food products company. Some of their assignments require them
to present findings to a "business manager" who needs to make
decisions about whether, and how, to develop particular food

For her comments on an earlier version of this chapter, I thank Sarah Ross. I
am also grateful to Julie Goldingham and her instructor, Douglas Crane, for
allowing me to use my notes from a classroom peer review of Julie's writing.

products. The manager is presumed to be technically savvy, but without specialist knowledge in the students' research subject.

As a whole, this scenario is easily understood as a collaboration, in which the business manager (the appointed audience) and researchers (students) combine skills, knowledge, and responsibilities to increase profits. This project's success depends on the differentiated roles of students within each team (each student specializes in a different sub-topic) and on the difference between manager and students. Such differences give ample opportunity to teach communication rhetorically as students learn to address their imagined manager's goals and understanding. In short, this audience-oriented approach helps students learn to communicate in an uneven situation in which, rather than writing for peers, students write for a supervisor with a different knowledge base. I appreciate the pedagogical opportunities created through this scenario.

This pedagogy, however, places some limits around writing by shifting the justification for constraints from formalist rules to reified audiences. Assigning audiences too much power leaves students with a reduced set of rhetorical choices, a reduced set of acceptable rhetorically constituted subject positions they are invited to inhabit. Audience-oriented pedagogies can thereby readily understate the *dynamics* of the rhetorical situation,[1] and they can all too easily gloss complicated relationships that throw into question what writer-reader collaboration entails when, for example, purposes or value systems diverge (as might happen if a food tech student questioned a project aimed at developing commercial, value-added technologies for global niche markets, technologies that are often disconnected from more mundane but no less pressing questions arising out of New Zealand's rural base). In this chapter, I raise several questions aimed at unsettling the easy collaborations implied by a constrained interpretation of any given rhetorical situation. Is there space within some situations to defer—to risk indefinite deferral of—the consensus of purpose or meaning that is sometimes assumed to develop through collaboration? Is there space to deliberately challenge audiences in ways that might not lead to timely resolution? If so, how might we create this space in pedagogy? How might we respond to the ways in which different forms of communication, including new forms of web-based communication, impact how readers and writers occupy the relational space between them?

These questions have an ethical component. In complex situations, situations that incorporate substantive diversity, thinking of audience as a constraint contributes to what Donna LeCourt ("WAC"), Victor Villanueva ("The Politics"), and others have called an "accommodationist" or "assimilationist" approach to teaching writing, as when students are asked to join academic discourse communities without regard for the experiences, values, and language practices they bring to those communities. Assimilation is most notable when relatively stable discourses use differences between writers and readers to structure unequal relationships. Students entering the university find themselves writing for an assessing teacher who represents an unfamiliar discourse community, and, as a result, students face pressures driven by the institutionally situated inequality between student and teacher. The pressure to assimilate becomes more pronounced where there is class or cultural difference. While writers might find that subject positions offered within new discourses enable new ways of acting, assimilation might instead (or also) lead to experiences of relative powerlessness, and/or to alienation, the felt loss of prior subjectivities. Even when *individuals* feel enabled as they learn to perform within a new discourse (LeCourt "Performing"), such performances cannot challenge discursive inequality (Stevens 56).

Given that constraining understandings of audiences and rhetorical situations play into this inequality, many instructors seek to teach students that writing might change discourse communities, might change rhetorical situations—and might even change audiences. Rhetorically engaging difference is becoming increasingly important in current communicative contexts, in which the Web and other globalizing systems give readers the opportunity to view—or avoid altogether—the work of writers whose differences underscore the limits of understanding. Online technologies such as newsgroups and blogs readily turn readers into writers, as Andrea Lunsford and Lisa Ede point out in "Among the Audience," but they do not in themselves create ethical habits for engaging difference (as I am reminded irregularly through flame wars in my asynchronous class forums). Confronted, as we are, by the problems difference creates for communication, how can we work to avoid two extremes: (1) the possibility that difference might fragment us into like-minded communities; or (2) the possibility that hegemonic forms of articulating readers to writers might instead assimilate difference into publics that suppress and ignore dissensus?

Perhaps now more than ever, we need pedagogies that help students address different, and more powerful, audiences— without assimilating to audience expectations. When do writers assume authority to challenge expectations? What are the consequences of challenges? How can writers effectively invite audiences to change, reversing the typical burden on student writers to adapt to audiences?

In this chapter, I consider potential changes within audience-writer relations by analogy with linguistic translation and, by extension, cultural translation. Such translations are ethically fraught, and while translation assists cross-cultural communication, it carries a cost. By thinking of writers as sometimes acting like translators, teachers can develop a range of new rhetorical strategies for marking difference, strategies whose consequences have been thoughtfully explored within translation studies. This idea of translation works well with an understanding of the rhetorical situation that does *not* assume the audience is a static constraint, one that instead assumes persuasion sometimes involves inviting audiences to adopt new subject positions offered within deliberately marked discourses. Because translation studies is finely attuned to differences in power, using translation to understand the process of addressing an audience does not gloss over inequality, historically stable discourses, or their consequences for writers who wish to introduce difference to a new audience. Nonetheless, translation offers up the hope that individual acts can participate effectively in the collective transformation of these inequalities.

Translation, Power, and Disruptive Rhetoric

I owe my interest in translation to Julie Goldingham, a student enrolled in a first-year writing course I supervise. During a routine class observation, I listened to Julie as she negotiated revision possibilities with peer reviewers.

"This is a bilingual country," Julie reminded her fellow New Zealanders, arguing that she need not translate words that belonged to one of the two languages of the land. Her classmates invoked their need for basic comprehension. "Like, your audience might not know," one student began, and then started to sound out *tangata whenua*. Apparently recognizing this relatively common phrase, the reviewer interrupted herself, "Or maybe they would!"

Julie didn't let the discussion end. She might use other words, she said, like *wairua*: she wanted to consider the spiritual path to health. She wanted to write from the perspective of Māori cultural concepts that would be misunderstood if translated into English. Uncharacteristically, Julie's peers did not respond. Judging by how infrequently I hear *wairua*, I guessed Julie's classmates were now not only *imagining* an uncomprehending audience; they were also experiencing their lack of understanding of Aotearoa, New Zealand's "second" (temporally first) language.

Peers' incomprehension made clear the gap between their desire to understand and Julie's investment in our country's bilingualism. Nonetheless, Julie's comments revealed that she cared about her audience, but, she explained, even if she translated words, she could not translate concepts, and she did not wish to create false understanding. After exploring several options, she and her classmates agreed a glossary at the very end of the essay might be okay, a choice that marginalized translation while acknowledging potential audience needs.

Whether or not Julie knew translators are commonly associated with treason,[2] her rhetorical choices recognized the potential for cultural harm. This concern is shared by translation scholars. Naoki Sakai, for example, argues that translation can essentialize difference and reinforce language-based nationalism by marking the boundary between languages. Couze Venn argues that translation often serves colonization, especially in contexts where a dominant global language (English) is associated with a hegemonic discourse (neoliberalism) (82). Lawrence Venuti argues that the audience of a translation is privileged over the source of a text because translation marks the desire for an expanded community of readers, signaling some inadequacy on the part of the foreign text.[3] Through these effects, translation domesticates, serving hegemony.

Yet these scholars, all translators themselves, do not condemn translation. Despite the "sharpness" of translation problems, especially "when located in the context of unequal authority to speak and to name," Venn argues that translation is ethically valid: there is a "necessity to translate if one is to speak to the other at all" (82). Translation offers potential changes in power relations that a source text, incapable of addressing its foreign audience, cannot offer alone (Venn). What inequality requires, then, are translations that signal difference and resist homogenization, making manifest tensions between the desire to expand communities and the desire to respect differences (Venn 84; Venuti 483). Translators can shift inequalities by using "discursive strategies where the hierarchies that rank the values in the domestic culture are disarranged to set going processes of defamiliarization, canon reformation, ideological critique, and institutional change" (Venuti 483). This requires knowing the audience's culture and expectations well enough to disrupt typical discourse. Defamiliarization, Venuti explains, places the burden of learning about the other on the translator's shoulders, but this burden becomes the source of the translator's authority to disrupt the audience and invite it to change.

Linguistic and discursive issues overlap, and translators' ethical quandaries are analogous to those experienced by writing instructors facing the assimilative potential of teaching. The translator's dilemma over whether to speak to the audience at all (at the risk of participating in the construction of inequalities) is parallel to the instructor's dilemma about whether to teach academic and other contextually powerful discourses (at the risk of suggesting students' various "home" discourses are worthless). Like translators, compositionists can respond to this dilemma by teaching students how to use dominant discourses while marking difference within them.

Accommodation poses an even more significant risk than individual low self-esteem, however; it misses an opportunity to participate in the collective project of transforming oppressive discursive relations. Strategically marking difference—as did

Julie Goldingham—offers a route to addressing a "foreign" and likely more powerful audience to challenge power relations while signaling the existence of difference and inequality.[4] This strategy does not evade composition instructors' responsibility to teach students how to use discourses associated with power; instead, it requires students to learn those discourses to challenge them more effectively.

Audience and Change (Potential)

How might marking strategies work in practice? How might they transform writer-audience relationships? These questions are answered more readily when rhetorical situations are understood in ways that destabilize the pedagogical practice of invoking audiences to tightly constrain the writing process. The basic features of a revised understanding are offered by Barbara Biesecker, who opens up "radical possibility" (127) by noting that rhetoric calls both writers and audiences to change over time. Rather than taking the identity of either as fixed, Biesecker argues both are subjects-in-process, and persuasion implies they might change.

The subjectivities of writers and audiences shift in relationship, but it is still useful to analyze these roles separately. One way to think about audiences as subjects who are (potentially) in the process of change is to measure the distance between what Ede and Lunsford call the "audience addressed" and "audience invoked," concluding that "a fully elaborated view of audience . . . must account for a wide and shifting range of roles for both addressed and invoked audiences" ("Audience Addressed" 169). When reconsidered in the context of unequal power, these conclusions suggest that while persuasion risks the prior identifications of both writers and audiences, these risks are shared unequally; the less powerful, therefore, require resistant textual strategies.

Turning attention to the writer similarly shows that shifting subjectivity is a potential only, not a given. In this discussion, I consider the potential shift in the writer's subjectivity as the difference between an inventor and a translator, a move that heuristically separates roles that, in literal translation, are fulfilled by different persons. To suggest that writers-as-inventors serve as analogues to translators' source texts does not require viewing the inventor's role as an original or more authentic expression of the writer. Instead, it deliberately creates a role for invention that strives to be temporally prior to orientation to a *particular* addressed audience. Despite the addressivity of all language (Bakhtin 95), complex subjects can nonetheless invent using familiar discourses before seeking to address the unfamiliar. Creating a space to talk about invention outside of a specific address provides a way to accord greater respect to discourses, values, and communities other than those represented by the (often powerful) addressed audience.

The translator, then, must find ways to honor and respect the process of invention while also addressing an audience. To preserve heterogeneity, the translator's goal is not to accommodate the addressed audience, but rather to analyze that audience's discourse fully and to strategically disrupt it by inscribing difference, thereby invoking an audience more fully oriented toward the inventor. Or course the translator is not "pure" of invention; the inventor is not "pure" of addressivity. That is, thinking about the audience can assist invention, and translation creates something new.[5] Applying the translator metaphor therefore complicates rather than simplifies writing for an audience, but by heuristically constructing a second role for the writer as translator, this approach offers instructional space for explicitly discussing difference, inequality, and strategies for change. The process of writing thereby becomes a process of gradual transformation.

Crucially, because subjects form in relationships, the audience's transformation is enabled potentially by the writer's potential to shift subjectivities, to move from "inventor" to "translator," writing new discourses in the process. For this reason, Sakai considers the translator, who is at once addressee of the source text and addresser of the translated text, to be a "*subject in transit*" between two languages. Translation, Sakai argues, "introduces an instability into the putatively *personal* relations among the agents of speech, writing, listening, and reading. The translator is internally split and multiple, devoid of a stable position" (75).

Writers who strategically mark discursive difference illustrate the transformative potential of their writing processes. For example, anthropologist and Cubana Ruth Behar follows her feminist ethnography of an exceptional Mexican India with a "biography in the shadows" that focuses on her own experiences in becoming an academic out of a working-class, Puerto Rican, immigrant background. Through her story, Behar illustrates several possible relationships to academic discourse, and as she moves between them, she illustrates what being a subject-in-process feels like. Yet two of her subject positions, one which she calls a failure to translate herself, and one which she calls translating herself too well, are deeply unsatisfying to her (335). Read in the context of her ethnography, Behar's biography suggests that she prefers something in between these two extremes, a translation that preserves a sense of difference in spite of the way the academic community she wants to join defines success.

Near the beginning of her personal biography, Behar narrates her experiences as an undergraduate studying philosophy. After a devastating interaction with her father, who tears up her letters to him in response to her increasing alienation from the family, Behar refuses to study for her comprehensive exams and does quite poorly on them. At first she assumes this is because she is a failure, unsuited for academic work, and her admired professors confirm this judgment. Much later, Behar interprets her choice as self-sabotage in response to her family's sacrifice and her own. In this case, an unreflective reaction to the difference between home and university leads Behar to refuse to further learn academic discourse, reinscribing the difference between herself and the community she has sought to join.

When Behar attends graduate school in anthropology, however, she recommits to learning academic discourse, and does so with distinction. She writes:

> I forced myself to learn to write cold-blooded logical essays
> . . . I forced myself to keep my flights of imagination in check,
> to learn to muzzle them to facts. I worked very hard and . . .
> [w]hen it came time to write my dissertation . . . , I wrote . . .
> a pure intellectual exercise. My teachers liked my dissertation
> enough to recommend it for publication, so . . . I already had
> a book. (331)

Behar became a graduate program star, she received a prestigious

MacArthur fellowship, and she was sought after by multiple academic departments, eventually accepting early tenure at the University of Michigan. She attributes her academic success to learning to write the safest, most easily recognized form of academic discourse. The process of vacating herself, however, left her feeling empty, lost, so that she lay awake, miserable, at night (335). This perfect translation, this full accommodation of audience expectations, this writing that marked no difference, left her as or more alienated than her earlier failure.

Behar's story makes clear why contemporary translators such as Venuti, Venn, and Simon argue so forcefully that marking difference is critical for ethical reasons. Only through marking difference is the audience called on to acknowledge that more exists than its own worldview and culture; only marking difference can challenge the hegemony of a discourse. Noting that a writer can be a subject-in-process is not enough, for it is not enough to ask writers to travel the whole distance to the audience by themselves, as Behar's carefully theorized experience makes clear. Even pedagogies that directly confront issues of subjectivity and difference in writing, such as the pedagogy described by Donna LeCourt in "Performing Working Class Identities," which celebrates the possibility for writers to perform multiple subjectivities, can too easily place the major burden for change and performance on students who come from historically marginalized social locations. Audiences, then, must also be potential subjects-in-process, and translators should resist accommodating overmuch. Sakai argues this as well, claiming that translators' subjectivity must be ambiguously positioned between what I am calling inventors and audiences. Translators, Sakai argues, cannot say "I," cannot speak for themselves, but only on behalf of inventors.

Sakai's "must" and "cannot" are normative, as a fictional counter-example from Michael Mann's film adaptation of James Fenimore Cooper's *Last of the Mohicans* illustrates. In the film, when the hero Hawkeye offers himself, through a translator, as a sacrifice in exchange for his love interest, the translator makes a crucial decision to translate too perfectly, literally, and therefore speaks in the place of Hawkeye, offering Hawkeye's "I" as his own. The translator's audience is unaware of the nature of the translation. The consequence is the translator's death, and while this act gives an important subjectivity to the translator, who previously had only a marginal role in the scene, the subjectivity is self-destructive, immolated. By analogy, when a writer-as-translator attempts to substitute for a writer-as-inventor, the refusal to acknowledge the inventor's subjectivity leaves the translator's empty as well. This was Behar's experience when she effectively disowned subject positions she identified with prior to her successful assimilation to academic discourse.

Behar offers a third way, one she enacts within her writing of *Translated Woman,* a text markedly different than her described dissertation. Behar considers the life of her informant, Esperanza, within a feminist framework, which seems suitable because of Esperanza's independence and her difficult but eventually successful refusal of male domination. Yet aspects of this Mexican India's life story cannot be readily assimilated to U.S. feminism, such as her reproduction of a culture of child abuse. In response, Behar addresses her U.S. audience with textual strategies that indicate how the lives she is narrating—her own and Esperanza's—cannot be adequately represented, and certainly not in received textual forms. For her disruptive textual innovations, Behar has received significant criticism as well as significant recognition. By making her audience experience difference through the challenge of reading a book that is sometimes imaginative, sometimes nonlinear, never muzzled by checking Esperanza's story against too many extra-narrative facts, Behar clearly argues that *lives cannot be translated* into another worldview, even as she *does translate* Esperanza's *story,* even as she takes it across the border to an academic audience.

The purpose of marking difference is to challenge the audience to change, rather than putting the individual writer in a position of needing to assimilate to become an equal. This transformation of power relations is one of the major themes in Chicana Gloria Anzaldúa's critical autobiography, *Borderlands/La Frontera: The New Mestiza.* Even more than Behar, Anzaldúa uses Spanish (sometimes translated but often not) to mark difference to an audience that is primarily English-speaking.[6] Equally with Behar, Anzaldúa points out the power imbalance between the English and the Spanish speaker, and even more explicitly, Anzaldúa argues for a transformation of oppressive relations, whether between men and women, hetero- and homosexuals, Anglos and Chicanos, landowners and workers, or Americans and Mexicans. For Anzaldúa, the writing process is a process of transforming her own consciousness by exploring difference:

> My "awakened dreams" are about shifts. Thought shifts, reality shifts, gender shifts: one person metamorphoses into another in a world where people fly through the air, heal from mortal wounds. I am playing with my Self, I am playing with the world's soul, I am the dialogue between my Self and *el espíritu del mundo*. I change myself, I change the world. (92)

In this passage, Anzaldúa argues she writes to shift her subjectivity and those of her readers in the way Biesecker's subject-in-process approach would anticipate. As is evident earlier, her writing does not assimilate to reader expectations. Instead, it invites an audience. Though Anzaldúa is quite critical of sexism and racism, for example, she provides points of positive identification for both males and Anglos, opportunities for readers from markedly different backgrounds to share in her vision of a world free of oppressor/oppressed. In fact, she explicitly rejects, at least for herself, the argument that minorities should not address a white audience (107). She believes that Anglos and Chicano/Chicanas, women and men need something from each other, and by speaking to an audience that is other than her while maintaining her difference from them, Anzaldúa believes she can mediate a process of transformation (107–108). Calling her words a "bridge," Anzaldúa suggests marked languages enable writers and audiences to move toward the other.

Putting It into Practice, Teaching Processes

Within composition and rhetoric, Victor Villanueva has called for a change of oppressive relationships through admitting difference into the academy, and his own writing strategies mark these differences within academic discourse. Villanueva recognizes his success might be used in tokenistic ways, but, he explains in *Bootstraps*, he has nonetheless agreed to an academic career to engage and to try to change the system through participation.

One of Villanueva's strategies, overparticipation on committees that seek minority representation, burdens him, but it also offers him the opportunity to address others and to seek to change conditions for those who will come after him. This requires an ethical commitment to a collective. In short, Villanueva opts to directly address an audience in spite of inequality, and he attempts to persuade that audience to change, over time, how it relates to the minorities he represents.

In a review, Raul Sanchez hopefully calls Villanueva's strategy rhetorical. Rhetoric, Villanueva and Sanchez note, can fit somewhere between two approaches to change: the revolution that instates new forms of oppression; the reform that fails to address a truly flawed system. Rhetoric can instead, Sanchez notes, "offer alternative visions of what is good and what is possible," taking hegemony's primary power, the ability to persuade the oppressed to comply, and using it to counter hegemony (167). By "slowly, rhetorically, methodically" incorporating difference within a hegemonic discourse, Sanchez notes, rhetoric can transform the oppressive status quo (168).

By reaching rhetorically to transform, process-oriented teaching offers opportune moments to imagine with students future situations that might value cultural, class, and other differences more than normalized academic discourse does currently. By returning pedagogical and scholarly attention to the central role of the writing process, pedagogy can heuristically separate the writer's role as inventor from the writer's role as translator, valuing forms of invention that arise less from audience subjectivities than from student subjectivities. Like many (perhaps most) writing instructors, I have for years relied on informal writing to lead students through staged steps in a writing process. Increasingly, however, I am turning to informal writing as a way to value student subjectivities that exceed what can be accommodated within a product-oriented, audience-oriented process. My informal prompts increasingly ask students to step away from the process of addressing the putative audience for their work, to explore how their ideas might relate to multiple audiences, to reflect on the values, experiential knowledge, and concerns that inform their research in ways that are not invited by the discursive communities students are trying (presumably) to join. Where I teach, often my least-prepared students (on a discursive level) are nontraditional and have prior work experience related to their subject of study. When these students step away from the process of writing a good essay to write with less extrinsic pressure, they sometimes find forms of authority for critique, engagement, and understanding that are not readily authorized by their readings of daunting academic writing. By privileging spaces for invention that minimize and defer addressivity as much as possible, this type of informal writing provides a freedom not found in invention heuristics that directly pursue a final product.

As important as is protected space for invention, however, is the way readers and writers experience their relationship in the classroom. As student writers address teachers, peers, and respondents to online writing assignments, classrooms can provide a space to step back from direct exchanges and consider the relationships those exchanges imply. When I offer teacher comments, I work to help students think about their continuing ownership of their writing, though I recognize with them our unequal role in assessment. I become in this context a representative of the academic discourse community *who might change*, but this itself requires students to risk themselves in an unequal relationship. In some cases, supporting students through this process means making marginal comments on essays that provide multiple suggestions, requiring writer choice and suggesting the possibility of choices not imagined by me. It means conducting in-class workshops of student writing where I respond to class suggestions with "I don't know, it depends on . . . ," turning to the writer to speak to the class as the authority on whether a suggestion might work. It means developing a conversation with students about what they are hoping to achieve throughout their writing process, so that my assessments reflect the dialogue between students' intentions and my understanding of academic expectations rather than an un-reconstituted version of the latter. Throughout, I acknowledge tensions between writers and readers, and, explicitly against my own authority, I valorize writers.

Similar reflection can valuably accompany peer review. In some classes, I do peer review face-to-face; in others, I do this online. One way or another I encourage writers and readers to enter dialogue with openness to the possibility that discussing a text might change initial responses to that text. A couple years ago, persuaded by Wei Zhu's research indicating how training can make peer review more interactive, I restructured my peer review process. Previously, I typically had given students some instruction on how to do peer review together with a set of written guidelines that directed students to issues embedded within the assignment criteria. With the exception of some open-ended questions aimed at content development, these guidelines typically reinforced generic values, implicitly asking student readers to position themselves as commentators working from the standpoint of academic discourses.

When I reconstructed peer review, I used training to support students in a more complex exchange, one in which they developed their understanding of academic discursive conventions while simultaneously privileging writers' ownership of their writing. This required students to negotiate tensions between invention and translation, though I did not yet think in those terms. I began the semester by having one volunteer peer review group follow standard guidelines in front of the class, but in a follow-up discussion, we considered how and why writers might speak back to readers, not only for clarifications or to request more concrete suggestions, but also to negotiate where readers pointed in directions writers did not want to go. In my asynchronous online classes, I introduced reflective work that supplemented peer review to provide a similar speak-back function by asking students to consider where they might wish to resist agreement with their readers, peers, and instructors alike.

Julie Goldingham, with her essay on *wairua,* was one of the first students who participated in this reconstructed peer review. Her response required risk-taking, and it required hope in a collaboration less with her addressed audience than with an audience from an imagined future. It required hope that by challenging her readers, she might participate in a long-term and necessarily collective process of reshaping cultural relations. It is only through the accretion of multiple attempts to address non-Māori speakers using select *Te Reo* phrases, for example, that the value of *tangata whenua,* "the people of the land," is now better understood by mainstream Pākehā. It is only through continued uses of untranslated *Te Reo* that *wairua* will someday seem more apt to the broader New Zealand culture than any possible translations. Such moves reverse processes of colonization and hegemony, and such moves, which simultaneously address and challenge audiences, are becoming increasingly important as globalizing processes pick up the pace by moving online. Those individuals who mark difference in their writing may meet incomprehension and censure; only if they have a vision of improved future relations will it be worthwhile to challenge the status quo and invite the audience into new subjectivities.

Notes

1. See Lunsford and Ede's introductory questions in "Audience Addressed/Audience Invoked," page 155.

2. Both Gloria Anzaldúa and Gregory Rabassa discuss the association of translators with treason but offer positive alternatives to this association.

3. As discussed in the main chapter, Venuti claims that translation always privileges receiving audiences. New Zealand history suggests that Venuti may be wrong in this particular claim but still correct in his warrant that translation signals the inadequacy of an untranslated source text.

   In New Zealand, translation issues are most apparent in an ongoing debate over the 1840 Treaty of Waitangi between the British crown and many indigenous *iwi* (tribes). There are key discrepancies between the original English and the translated Māori versions of this treaty. In this case, the translator almost certainly mistranslated to make the British text seem more familiar within a Māori cultural context, thereby minimizing the treaty's consequence for Māori. Translation scholars Sabine Fenton and Paul Moon explain that the British entered into the treaty during a relatively humanitarian phase of expansionism, and the colonizers paternalistically believed the treaty was a legitimate way to respond to private land sales that also disfavored Māori. Despite what appear to have been good intentions, through the treaty uncertain politics turned decisively toward colonial power.

   Fenton and Moon argue that a more literal translation would have responded more ethically to the problems motivating the treaty, since literalism probably would have underscored to Māori that the British requested a foreign form of social relations. Even though the New Zealand case otherwise contradicts Venuti's claims about the direction of privilege in translation, Fenton and Moon's recommended literalism converges with Venuti's more generic recommendation to translate in ways that signal texts are foreign. This convergence of recommendations reinforces the argument that translators should make difference apparent. The primary ethical problem in New Zealand (with respect to translation, not colonization) is that translator manipulations left *iwi* without clear understanding of what they were putatively choosing.

In the 1970s, the Māori version of the treaty was recognized as legitimate alongside the English version, giving Māori some leverage to negotiate changing race relations.

4. It is not clear to me whether Julie is Pākehā (i.e. descended from European immigrants) or Māori. Whatever her ethnicity, I do not wish to essentialize difference. Though Julie writes, for the most part, in English, wherever she resists the translation of select *Te Reo* words into the language best understood by her audience, she writes with a perspective created by the Māori language and culture.

5. Translator Sherry Simon argues that translation is more accurately described as "supplement" than as "replacement." While translations may serve as replacements in a legal process, translating supplements a source text, writing new discourses, though such discourses are, Simon explains, authorized by their source (161).

6. Though Anzaldúa's book is bilingual, it would be easier to read as a monolingual English than Spanish speaker, though much would nonetheless be lost.

Works Cited

LeCourt, Donna. "Performing Working-Class Identity in Composition: Toward a Pedagogy of Textual Practice." *College English* 69.1 (2006): 30–51.

Lunsford, Andrea A., and Lisa Ede. "Among the Audience: On Audience in an Age of New Literacies." *Engaging Audience: Writing in an Age of New Literacies*. Ed. Elizabeth Weiser, Brian Fehler, and Angela González. Urbana, IL: NCTE, 2009. 42–69.

Stevens, Sharon McKenzie. "Dreaming to Change Our Situation: Reconfiguring the Exigence for Student Writing." *Active Voices: Composing a Rhetoric for Social Movements*. Eds. Sharon McKenzie Stevens and Patricia Malesh. Albany, NY: SUNY Press, 2009. 47–65.

Villanueva, Victor. *Bootstraps: From an American Academic of Color*. Urbana, IL: NCTE, 1993.

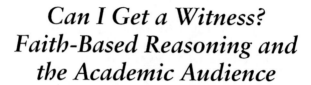

CHAPTER THIRTEEN

Can I Get a Witness?
Faith-Based Reasoning and
the Academic Audience

TRACI FREEMAN
University of Colorado at Colorado Springs

In "Among the Audience," Andrea Lunsford and Lisa Ede ask, "What are the consequences for civic discourse in a world where those interested in a specific topic or audience can easily find sites where they can communicate with like-minded individuals?" (63). While the Web has certainly made such sites more accessible, the challenges to civic discourse posed by online communities are in many ways similar to those posed by the communities in which we live. Those of us who find ourselves teaching writing in relatively homogenous communities have always struggled with students who have limited experience communicating with audiences who may not share their points of view. Of the many students that teachers of writing encounter, no population poses greater challenges than students who come from communities of faith.

Many religious students, especially those who have been raised in communities in which their religious beliefs are dominant, struggle when moving beyond religious discourse conventions to write for an academic audience. As professors of writing, we are often the first ones to question such students' religious appeals and to define what it means to write for the university community. Kristine Hansen characterizes the reactions of many writing professors who find themselves the audience for students' religious papers:

> I have often heard writing teachers express dismay—I have done so myself—when students' papers for or against a particular issue are grounded mainly in their religious beliefs and are more in the genre of sermonizing or witnessing than of political argument. "Don't these kids know," we lament, "that you just can't do that? You're not going to persuade any audience that doesn't already share your beliefs." At the same time, we feel a twinge of guilt because it seems wrong to tell students they can't use as reasons for their position the very beliefs to which they feel most deeply committed. (24)

Like Hansen, when confronted with student writing that employs faith-based reasoning and religious rhetoric, many writing professors frame their comments in terms of audience, suggesting that students who employ such reasoning will not be persuasive to readers who do not share their faith commitments. Jan Worth, for example, advocates discussing concepts of audience with students in order to address the ways that religious writing is differentiated from academic writing "not only by rhetorical and evidentiary protocols but also by the sense of the audience and the writer's relationship to that audience" (7). Chris Anderson encourages students to think about writing for "an audience of outsiders, confronting the rhetorical problems that the task creates or reflecting on the difficulty of expressing religious belief in contemporary America." Douglas Downs argues that writing professors can function as "guides," "translators," and "coaches" for their religious students, explaining how academics think and why "the Bible tells me so" argument is ineffective for an academic audience (50). Similarly, Bronwyn T. Williams advises professors to describe the academic audience for their students and explain "how and why education privileges and relies on the kinds of evidence it does" (516).

While professors of writing largely agree that faith-based reasoning and religious rhetoric are inappropriate in academic writing, few feel completely comfortable telling students that their personal beliefs are not relevant for or persuasive to an academic audience. Like Hansen, we may feel guilt in dismissing students' deeply held convictions. Or we may be disappointed with papers that lack "passion and enthusiasm," which students turn in after our conversations about audience (Williams 518). Or we may feel discomfort excluding religious reasoning and rhetoric out of hand because students of faith comprise a portion of our multicultural campus (Hairston 672; Vander Lei 8; Swearingen 150).

The unease that we may feel when we are confronted by students' writing that employs faith-based reasoning and religious rhetoric, I argue, has a great deal to teach us about how we define the concept of audience in our teaching practices. We agree that we have an obligation to explain to our students how academics make meaning and what we value—to define ourselves as an audience—but we do so primarily by constructing an academic audience as one which is not persuaded by faith-based reasoning and religious rhetoric.

While we may define ourselves against audiences that accept faith-based appeals, our own disciplinary discourse is saturated with religious language and faith-based premises. As Lizabeth Rand observes, "religious metaphors" pervade discussions in rhetoric and composition, frequently as part of negative critique of current traditional and expressivist approaches to teaching writing (356); and Elizabeth Vander Lei notes how frequently composition scholars seek to substitute their own faith in a particular theoretical position for their students' religious faiths (8). The distinctions between academic and religious rhetoric are not as clear as we might like, and by suggesting they are, we risk setting up a false binary that serves only to alienate students of faith.

The difficulty that we have reconciling faith-based appeals with our academic expectations may also shed some light on the way we currently construct "the academic audience," and on our own articles of faith, particularly notions of the "multicultural academy" which inform our definitions of academic discourse communities and our pedagogy. I want to suggest that faith-based reasoning and religious rhetoric test the limits of multiculturalism as a rhetorical framework for thinking about audience and may prompt us to reconsider our tendencies to define the academic audience exclusively in terms of shared values and beliefs.

In this chapter, I draw from my experiences teaching at a regional state university located in an evangelical community in order to complicate current discussions about teaching audience as a response to our students' faith-based reasoning and religious rhetoric. It is my argument that framing students' religious appeals in their academic writing exclusively as a problem of audience awareness underestimates the sophistication of many of our students and fails to address the epistemological differences between faith-based reasoning and academic arguments. Moreover, when we employ a narrowly constructed definition of audience, one defined by appeals to beliefs and values, we risk mischaracterizing academic audiences as both unified in their beliefs and in their hostility toward people of faith, or we risk accepting specious arguments because they appeal to our fundamental desire to be inclusive. I advocate for a broader conception of audience, one that takes into account Lunsford and Ede's critiques of constructions of audience and accounts for our students' purposes when they write for us in an academic setting.

Local Context

In 2004, I moved from California, where I had been teaching college writing at UC Berkeley, to Colorado Springs and a regional campus of the University of Colorado (UCCS). Berkeley, of course, is known for its liberal political culture and its diverse population. Although the writing courses I was teaching at Berkeley were not designated for English Language Learners, many of my students had come from other countries, or their parents had immigrated to the United States shortly before they were born. In my classes the majority of students were bilingual, several students were biracial, and most had received some education in the California public school system. These students knew that, with so many different people from different backgrounds living in close proximity in their communities, they were always on the verge of conflict that could erupt into violence. The wisdom of tolerance, the value of multiculturalism, the sheer beauty of diversity were ideas they accepted because they were aware of how such notions protected the delicate ecology of their daily existence. Respect for individual differences and tolerance toward others functioned as their first principles, which remained largely unchallenged when they entered the university.

When I first moved to Colorado Springs, I experienced a kind of ideological vertigo. In contrast to my students at Berkeley, most of my students at UCCS were raised and educated locally. Colorado Springs is predominantly white, middle class, and politically conservative, with a strong military presence, and a significant population of evangelical Christians. Colorado Springs boasts one of the largest and most prosperous mega-churches in the country and is the home of hundreds of Christian nonprofits, including Young Life, the Navigators, Compassion International, and James Dobson's Focus on the Family. Despite the different missions of evangelical organizations located in Colorado Springs, there is surprisingly little diversity among them in terms of religious views. Most grant the inerrancy of the Bible, emphasize a personal relationship with God, believe in a natural intersection among Christianity, free market capitalism, and a conservative ideology, and consider witnessing and proselytizing to be imperatives of their faith. Whether or not my students are religious, they understand religion, and a narrowly circumscribed version of religion, to be an informing principle in their lives. Among those students who are religious, many have been homeschooled or educated in one of a number of Christian academies in town, which means they are unlikely to have had educational experiences that challenge or complicate their faith commitments.

In addition to teaching rhetoric and writing courses at UCCS, I served as a writing program assistant and was charged with the task of reading students' exit portfolios, which consisted of two papers that students had written for classes while studying at the university. While reading portfolios, I came across the following paper, which was originally submitted for a course in meteorology and addressed the topic of cloud seeding. My reaction to this paper and to the papers I have received in my advanced writing courses have shaped my thinking about the struggle that evangelical students face when they write for an academic audience and the challenge that such students ultimately pose for writing professors who are committed to teaching our students the conventions of academic discourse in a diverse intellectual environment. The student begins her essay with the following paragraph:

I believe that God and only God can control the earth and everything on it; this includes the weather. Although I do not believe that we should try to control the weather, I do believe that some weather modification could be helpful if approached in the right manner. Many factors concerning global weather modification should be analyzed and assessed to make the best decisions regarding the positive outcomes that may arise from such weather modification. Among these factors would be cost, accuracy, ethics, legal issues, and technology. To better recognize weather and its predictability, more knowledge and accurate technology are absolutely necessary.

Although I had read a number of religious papers—philosophy papers about abortion that quoted extensively from the Bible and literature papers that moralized and catalogued a protagonist's sins—this paper struck me as somehow different. While this student is clearly asserting a statement of faith—she claims that "God and only God can control the earth and everything on it"—her statement is not only inappropriate for a scientific paper, but it also stands to undermine the rest of her argument about weather modification and the practical and ethical issues that such technologies raise. Her paper is grounded in competing and contrary premises: If only God controls the weather, how can humans also control it?

At first when I read this essay, I assumed that this student lacked rhetorical sophistication. The claims in her introduction, as well as the claims throughout her paper, were cast primarily in the agree/disagree mode, and she failed to demonstrate any deep or nuanced understanding of weather manipulation techniques or the practical and ethical considerations involved in implementing these techniques. Given the simplicity of her argument, it seemed likely that this student lacked the skills necessary for recognizing logical contradictions in her own writing.

I also considered that this student may have been struggling to begin this essay and that her statement about God's omnipotence represented an instance of perfunctory throat clearing, a religious version of "since the beginning of time." Like such throat-clearing statements, this student's testimony did not close off discussion of the topic, nor did it preclude a larger argument that assumed our ability to modify the weather. At the same time, her statement seemed so deliberate that I found it difficult to believe that she was unaware of its force or the way that it might undermine her argument.

Another explanation I considered was that this student neglected to include transitional text that would enable the reader to follow some implicit logic linking this statement about God to the rest of her argument. Perhaps she assumed that if human beings can do something like modify the weather, it must be God's will. Evangelical Christianity is predicated on a personal relationship with a God who monitors one's actions and whose will directly affects aspects of one's daily life. It is not uncommon to hear people in Colorado Springs talking in casual conversation about God's will for them. To credit God for the weather and our ability to manipulate it might not actually be a contradiction if one assumes that the hand of God can be witnessed everywhere[1].

While I puzzled through the logic of this introduction, trying to reconcile its contradictions, I could not escape the feeling that I was missing some larger point that would have made this student's testimony make sense. Although each of the possibilities I outlined seemed to offer a reasonable explanation for this student's introduction, each also presumed that the student was somehow deficient in her reasoning and her awareness of her audience. Either she was inconsistent in her logic, or she was unable to distinguish between filler and necessary text in her writing, or she was missing significant information in her discussion that would allow an audience to understand her. If I assumed that her problems were related to logic or her understanding of her audience, I could easily dismiss her as naïve, unsophisticated, or shallow.

I began to see this essay in a different light, however, when I began wondering what it might mean to see this student's testimony as deliberate, to understand this rhetorical move as an act of religious witnessing. To witness as a Christian involves testifying to one's beliefs to an audience of nonbelievers. As Rand notes, "Witnessing talk is the kind of faith-centered discourse about which writing professors complain most frequently" (359). Witnessing language is problematic for writing professors for a variety of reasons. As Anderson observes, the witness speaks from a position of authority that is inconsistent with the real rhetorical situations in which students writing for their professors find themselves. In order to be successful writers for academic audiences, as David Bartholomae argues, students need to employ our ways of knowing, of "selecting, evaluating reporting, concluding and arguing" before they actually possess the knowledge of the subject and its conventions (623). In the absence of the authority that a scholarly identity may provide, student writers may fall back on other authoritarian postures, those which they have access to through their teachers and preachers. They may address us as if they were authorities, rather than our scholarly peers, and may frame their arguments as "lessons on life" or "academic homilies" (Bartholomae 626).

While writing professors might be bothered by such authoritative postures, what troubles us more, according to Anderson, is not that such postures are foolish, but that they represent "foolishness that is unaware of itself, superficiality that is either/or, dogmatic and unexamined." Religious rhetoric is problematic for academic audiences because it is full of pre-articulated commonplaces that we as academics find it our job to question. Such statements as "God controls the earth" are not up for debate; they are assertions of immutable truth, not to be reconsidered in light of new or contradictory evidence. Even when such statements do not undermine the logic of our students' papers, as in the case in the meteorology essay, they strike us as unexamined, presumably because no one who scrutinizes his or her religious commitments could reach the same conclusions as our religious students.

Not only does religious rhetoric strike us as dogmatic, but it can also be alienating to nonbelievers. As Juanita Smart notes, for many people, witnessing language can seem intolerant and exclusionary (15). She writes that students do not understand "that much of the religious discourse [they invoke] is verbal code that can be estranging to an audience not conversant in that code, or whose identification with it is something 'other' than what the writer values" (18). She argues that the language of witnessing itself may not be immediately accessible to non-Christian readers, or worse, that such language is likely to offend academic readers who privilege diversity and tolerance. Smart's comment is revealing, however, because if academic discourse privileges diversity and tolerance toward different points of view, then we have no obvious grounds for excluding religious discourse.

Witnessing language clearly challenges the standards of authority, reasoning, and beliefs that we contemporary academics privilege. At the same time, our explanations for such language are limited when we presume that our students use such language naïvely. Perhaps the author of the meteorology paper was not confused at all. Perhaps she was concerned about the salvation of a reader whom she perceived to be godless. While, as a reader, I might find it patronizing that a student might presume that because I am an academic, I cannot also have religious commitments, it is no more patronizing than my assumption that this student is naïve, unsophisticated, or foolish. In fact, within students' religious rhetoric, should we look closely and differently, we might find implicit arguments for accepting other authorities, other kinds of evidence, other ways of knowing that are not as contrary to our beliefs and values as our responses to their rhetoric indicate.

Reflections on Constructions of Audience

In response to students' faith-based reasoning and religious rhetoric, composition scholars frequently invoke the concept of audience; however, the strategies that we use when we approach students who employ faith-based reasoning and religious rhetoric reveal our narrow definitions of this term. In part, we are still relying on the very constructions of audience that Ede and Lunsford sought to complicate in "Audience Addressed/ Audience Invoked," responding to what they perceived to be limited notions of audience circulating in the rhetoric and composition community. Ede and Lunsford criticize theories that focus on "the audience addressed" because such theories afford the audience the sole power of evaluating writing, the success of which "will be judged by the audience's reaction: 'good' translates into 'effective,' 'bad' into 'ineffective'" (158). Yet theories of "the audience invoked" overemphasize the power of the writer and do not adequately acknowledge the constraints placed on a writer by a rhetorical situation or the needs and interests of

readers (165). Both theories, they argued, "failed to recognize
. . . the fluid, dynamic, character of rhetorical situations and
. . . the integrated, interdependent nature of reading and writing" (156). When professors of writing write about employing
the concept of audience to respond to students' religious appeals,
we frequently limit our discussions to "the audience addressed."
In our attempts to define for our students who their academic
audiences are and what we value, we often generalize from our
own beliefs and experiences to make arguments about what all
academics privilege. In so doing, we define academics as a group
of people who possess consistent values and assumptions—or at
least who are united in our opposition to religious students and
faith-based claims. Such discussions of audience do not acknowledge individual differences of opinion or the complicated and
even competing systems of belief, standards of knowledge, and
linguistic conventions that characterize academic discourse both
within and across disciplines. Moreover, when we define academic
audiences in opposition to audiences who accept faith-based
reasoning and religious rhetoric, we fail to account for the many
academics who possess strong faith commitments and who are
able to reconcile their commitments with their intellectual work.

Ede and Lunsford note the ethical complications that can
result when writing is overdetermined by the needs and values of
an audience. In its most extreme form, this concept of audience
reduces writing to "pandering to the crowd" and excuses writers from the responsibility of arriving at good reasons for their
conclusions (159). If students simply appeal to our values, they
need not present us with sound arguments. When we reduce lessons about audience awareness to conversations about audiences'
values and beliefs, we miss an opportunity to discuss the ways
that academic discourse can function as a medium through which
diverse values and ideological commitments can be negotiated.
While this is not to say that academic discourse is value neutral,
as James Berlin notes, academic discourse does allow room for
self-criticism and self-reflection (732).

Framing discussions with students in terms of audience also
ignores the position that students have asked us to assume in
relation to their writing, the audience as it is "invoked" in their
texts. Students who begin papers with religious testimony place

themselves in a particular relation to their audiences, and while many audiences will find this position objectionable, we should not assume that such rhetorical positioning on the parts of our students is unintentional.

In their model of audience, Ede and Lunsford try to account for the writer's aims and suggest that it is the responsibility of a writer to "establish the range of potential roles an audience may play" (166). While Ede and Lunsford acknowledge that readers can reject the roles in which writers cast them, they ultimately fault the writer who is not able to convince a reader to take up these roles, for "writers who wish to be read must often adapt their discourse to meet the needs and expectations of an addressed audience" (166).

Ede and Lunsford ultimately privilege the power of the audience to determine a text's success or failure. If students' papers do not meet their professors' expectations, Ede and Lunsford conclude, students must have failed to conjure their academic audiences or they have been unable to draw from their past experiences or they have been prevented by "unconscious psychological resistance, incomplete understanding, or inadequately developed ability" from pleasing us (166-167). Because Lunsford and Ede presume that all student writers ultimately aim to please their professors, they must conclude that students whose papers do not match their professors' expectations have failed in their efforts.

When Lunsford and Ede revisit this argument in "Representing Audience: 'Successful' Discourse and Disciplinary Critique," they recognize that their earlier discussion of audience assumes that all students aim to succeed as scholars on our terms. They write that in their earlier essay they did not consider "that a student might find herself full of contradiction and conflict, might find the choices available to her as a writer confusing and even crippling—might in fact find it difficult, even undesirable, to claim the identity of 'writer'" (171). While many students do fail to communicate effectively with their academic audiences, others might not yet be persuaded to accept the conventions of academic writing on our terms. When we use arguments about academic discourse that are grounded in our beliefs and values, we are not likely to convince such students. And, for many of our students, meeting our expectations may not be their primary obligation.

The Limits of Current Constructions of the Academic Audience

I have found that my religious students are increasingly aware of how academic audiences might respond to their religious appeals. With such students, it becomes complicated and reductive to frame discussions of audience in terms of academic readers' values, working from the assumption that if students understood what beliefs we privilege, they would comfortably and willingly appeal to them. If we looked at the issue of faith-based reasoning and religious rhetoric with a more complex understanding of audience, one that acknowledges the "obligations, resources, needs, and constraints embodied in a writer's concept of audience" ("Representing" 165), we might find that our students deploy religious rhetoric intentionally, as a means for resisting our values or what they perceive are our values.

I worked recently with a student who showed me the limitations of simply asking writers to consider their audience's beliefs and values, particularly when the audience is an academic one. My experiences in an advanced composition course at UCCS have helped me to think through the limitations of framing discussions with students who employ religious rhetoric exclusively in terms of audience. The first assignment in my class is an argument for personal aims: I ask students to draw from their personal experiences to make an argument that might have resonance for a larger audience. One student wrote an essay drawn from her experience as a student at a prestigious Christian college. While enrolled in a first-year humanities course, she had written a paper and argued that her Christian faith was superior to reasoning as a way of knowing. Because of her argument, her professor told her that she did not belong at the institution and that she should consider attending a Bible college. This student wanted to write an essay to a general academic audience arguing that secular academics should accept faith-based reasoning in the classroom. Her argument was definitional in nature: she claimed that Christians were a subculture, and if academics truly valued multiculturalism, they would accept a Christian perspective as a valid one.

The problem with this essay was precisely that *I* was the audience. To frame the concept of audience in terms of beliefs with this student would likely have only confirmed her premise that religious perspectives were devalued in academic communities[2]. In many ways her position was a brilliant one to take. She had appealed to what she had accurately assumed were my commitments to diversity and attempted to frame her argument in terms I accept. At the same time that I acknowledged the rhetorical sophistication of her argument, my first response to her essay was one of anger because she was co-opting the language of multiculturalism to make this argument. Although attuned to the values of her audience, her argument struck me as logically flawed and fundamentally unethical.

When I read her essay, I thought immediately about my students at Berkeley. For them race, ethnicity, gender, sexuality, socioeconomic status—the facets that generally comprise discussions of diversity—were influential factors in determining their identities in the abstract, but they were also tangible forces in their lives that affected their access to opportunities. My students lived in two-bedroom apartments with their extended families. Their parents worked three jobs to feed and clothe them. Students were followed by security guards in department stores and were pulled over by the police while driving through nice neighborhoods. They were punished in school for speaking Spanish or Cantonese. They watched their parents receive substandard medical care when they spoke broken and accented English to physicians. The rhetoric of multiculturalism enabled my students at Berkeley to name their experiences, to theorize them, and to combat the real social forces that worked to disempower them and their families. It also provided them with access to the very sources of power—found in education—from which they had been traditionally excluded.

Issues of cultural identity for my students at Berkeley were intimately related to their access to power. In contrast, by identifying as evangelical, the student who wrote this essay assumed a privileged position within American society. Although evangelicals may represent a minority of Americans, they have considerable political power and dominate discourse conventions in the public sphere. This student seemed to be employing the rhetoric of victimhood in order to secure her privilege and to avoid making a more complex argument about the merits of a Christian perspective that would consider logical grounds for its inclusion in an academic discussion.

This student's argument was also particularly ironic given the history of the evangelical movement in the United States. The rhetoric of multiculturalism, which she invoked in her essay, was a product of the social movements of the sixties and seventies— civil rights, women's rights, GLBT rights. Such movements, after considerable struggle with the academic establishment, gave rise to departments like ethnic studies, women's studies, and gender studies. The irony is that the forces that radically transformed the landscape of the liberal arts helped to unify evangelical Christians and galvanize them as a movement in opposition to the very ideals of secular liberalism and multiculturalism that we in the academy embraced.

This student had very clearly appealed to what she assumed were the beliefs and values of her audience. She had done so, however, without fully examining her ethos and the problems inherent in portraying herself and all evangelical Christians as oppressed minorities. Moreover, she did not support her claims that evangelical Christians were a subculture and that their perspectives were not valued in the university, and she had failed to interrogate the history of multiculturalism as a movement in the academy or consider how evangelicals might be positioned in relation to this movement.

When I met with this student, I tried to frame my discussion with her not in terms of audience, but rather in terms of stasis theory. Rather than at the level of definition, I suggested, her real argument needed to be made at the stasis of conjecture. It is a commonplace that religious perspectives are excluded from academic discussions. I wanted her to interrogate this commonplace. Were religious perspectives actually excluded from the academy, and if so, what were the causes of this exclusion? Through such explorations, I hoped that this student would be able to identify some of the reasons why her religious perspective might not fare well in a "marketplace of ideas" in which the Bible was just a text among others and truth claims needed to be justified by widely supported premises and empirical evidence. I wanted her to explore her two ways of knowing—through faith and through reason—not to suggest that one was superior to the other, but rather to see if she could find some common ground.

Ultimately this student did not abandon her original argument. Perhaps it seemed like too much work to reframe her essay in the way I suggested. Perhaps the questions I posed to her were too hard for her to ask. In the end, she turned in a hastily executed, half-hearted revision of her paper and received a mediocre grade. I suspect that she walked away from this assignment feeling that my resistance to her argument was the result of my personal bias against Christians and that my assessment of her paper was evidence that such perspectives are devalued in an academic environment.

Although my experience with this student was discouraging, it taught me that it is not only the responsibility of religious students who attend secular universities to find common ground between their religious beliefs and the knowledge that they acquire in the university; it is also our responsibility as their professors to do so. And this may require us to reflect more deeply on how we construct academic audiences. When we banish religious topics from our classes or insist that no academic audience will be persuaded by claims of faith, we miss an opportunity to explore the way such topics and claims do challenge the very epistemologies that we privilege, and our students miss an opportunity to see faith-based premises as grounds for discovery rather than dogma.

As Stanley Fish has argued, the risk of suggesting that religious faith has a place in academic discussions means seeing religion not only as an object of study, but also as a serious "candidate for the truth." In many ways this seems antithetical to the liberal mission of the university that assigns "truth-value" for hypotheses that can hold up under scrutiny and revises its premises when new information becomes available. This is not to say, however, that faith and reason have no common ground. And it is incumbent upon us as academics to find such common ground with our students. It is not likely that they will seek it with us. And if forced to choose between the faith that they have known all their lives and what we are offering, it is clear which one they will select.

Reflections

As I was drafting this chapter, I spoke with one of my students who identifies as evangelical about what the author of the meteorology paper might have meant by her testament of faith at the beginning of the essay on weather manipulation. My student, who is both wise and self-reflective, posited that the author of this paper might just have been "covering her bases." The author of the meteorology paper may have understood that humans can actually manipulate the weather, but she sensed that taking such a position might offend God. Perhaps, my student speculated, she was just trying to please both of her masters.

Writing professors need to understand that for students of faith "the complex series of obligations, resources, needs, and constraints embodied in the writer's concept of audience" ("Representing Audience," 165) includes not only us but also communities of belief. When we position ourselves as an academic audience in opposition to the kind of audience that is persuaded by religious rhetoric and faith-based appeals, we force our students to compromise either their religious commitments or their success as students.

Moreover, when we read students' papers that employ faith-based reasoning and religious rhetoric as evidence of their failure to understand the conventions of academic inquiry, we miss what might be the basis for a compelling critique. Postmodern theory has taught us that there are valid arguments to make against what we as academics traditionally have privileged in reasoning and writing. In many disciplines, it is no longer the case that we view facts independently from ideology, value reason over experience, or ignore the contingency of our own positions. This of course does not mean that all arguments are equally valid or fundamentally ethical.

We do not want to discourage students from pursuing religious topics that have clear meaning for them, but we need to show them how to do so responsibly, not by appealing to our values, or what they perceive to be our values, but by understanding how appeals to audience are also dependent on the writer's ethos, the logic of the argument, and the historical and cultural contexts in which an argument takes place. We need to communicate that academic audiences are not merely ideological constructs but are comprised of competing epistemologies, discourse norms, and disciplinary conventions. Working from their first principles, students of faith have considerable room to enter into academic conversations and, as their audiences, we can attempt to show them how their beliefs might not be compromised when they engage in academic debate.

Putting It into Practice

The strategies we might employ when working with students who employ faith-based reasoning and religious rhetoric may also be applicable when working with student populations that inhabit increasingly atomized online communities. To help students negotiate the demand of their academic audiences, I want to suggest, first, that writing professors can teach the concept of audience in relation to the other rhetorical appeals. Rather than defining audience exclusively in terms of a reader's beliefs and values, we can show students how the persona of the writer and the writer's claims, reasoning, evidence, and assumptions are also implicated in the concept of audience. Second, writing professors can enable students to gain a better sense of the "obligations, resources, needs, and constraints" of their academic audiences ("Representing Audience" 165). We can ask students to analyze articles in their disciplines rhetorically. In so doing, we can help students discover how academic writers position themselves in their writing, how they make arguments, and what they assume without qualification. Third, writing professors can provide students with opportunities to negotiate their own values and beliefs within an academic community. We can host class blogs and provide opportunities for online chatting. Such technologies demand that students communicate in writing with their peers and model for students how to work through their ideas with those who have common concerns but may not share their particular perspectives. Finally, writing professors can acknowledge that students might see appealing to academic audiences as only one of the multiple obligations they face as writers. This will enable us to interpret students who resist our discourse norms and habits of mind in a more complex way.

Notes

1. As Sharon Crowley observes, this kind of reasoning is characteristic of fundamentalist discourse. For fundamentalist Christians, facts, like our ability to modify the weather, are not "proof of the existence of some human or neutral reality. . . . They are, rather signs of God's will. Their relation to divine premises must be interpreted" (159).

2. A number of studies have been conducted in recent years that challenge the assumptions that the professoriate is hostile to faith and persons of faith. For research on this topic, see *The Religious Engagements of American Undergraduates*, Social Science Research Council, June 22, 2007 < http://religion.ssrc.org/reforum/>.

Works Cited

Anderson, Chris. "The Description of an Embarrassment: When Students Write about Religion." *ADE Bulletin 94* (Winter 1998): 12–15. <http://www.adfl.org/ade/bulletin/N094/094012.htm>.

Bartholomae, David. "Inventing the University." *Cross-Talk in Comp Theory: A Reader*. 2nd ed. Ed Victor Villanueva, Jr. Urbana, IL: NCTE, 1997. 623–654. Rpt. in "Inventing the University." *Literacy: A Critical Sourcebook*. Ed. Ellen Cushman, Eugene R. Kintgen, Barry M. Kroll, and Mike Rose. Boston: Bedford, 2001. 511–524.

Berlin, James. "Rhetoric and Ideology in the Writing Class." *Cross-Talk in Comp Theory: A Reader*. 2nd ed. Ed. Victor Villanueva, Jr. Urbana, IL: NCTE, 1997. 717–738.

Crowley, Sharon. *Toward a Civil Discourse: Rhetoric and Fundamentalism*. U of Pittsburgh P, 2006.

Downs, Douglas. "True Believers, Real Scholars, and Real True Believing Scholars: Discourse of Inquiry and Affirmation in the Composition Classroom." *Negotiating Religious Faith in the Composition Classroom*. Ed. Elizabeth Vander Lei and Bonnie Lenore Kyburz. Portsmouth, NH: Boyton/Cook Heinemann, 2005. 39–58.

Ede, Lisa, and Andrea Lunsford. "Audience Addressed/Audience Invoked: The Role of Audience in Composition Theory and Pedagogy." *CCC* 35 (1984): 155–171. Fish, Stanley. "One University, Under God?" *The Chronicle of Higher Education* 7 January 2005.

Hairston, Maxine. "Diversity, Ideology, and Teaching Writing." *Cross-Talk in Comp Theory: A Reader*. 2nd ed. Ed. Victor Villanueva, Jr. Urbana, IL: NCTE, 1997. 697–713.

Hansen, Kristine. "Religious Freedom in the Public Square and the Composition Classroom." *Negotiating Religious Faith in the Composition Classroom*. Ed. Elizabeth Vander Lei and Bonnie Lenore Kyburz. Portsmouth, NH: Boyton/Cook Heinemann, 2005. 24–38.

Lunsford, Andrea, and Lisa Ede. "Representing Audience: 'Successful' Discourse and Disciplinary Critique." *CCC* 47:2. (May, 1996): 167–179.

Porter, James, E. *Audience and Rhetoric*. Englewood Cliffs, NJ: Prentice Hall, 1992.

Rand, Lizabeth, A. "Enacting Faith: Evangelical Discourse and the Discipline of Composition Studies." *CCC* 52.3 (February 2001): 349–367.

Sharlet, Jeff. "Soldiers of Christ." *Harpers Magazine* (May 2005): 41–54.

Smart, Juanita M. "'Frankenstein or Jesus Christ?' When the Voice of Faith Creates a Monster for the Composition Teacher." *Negotiating Religious Faith in the Composition Classroom*. Ed. Elizabeth Vander Lei and Bonnie Lenore Kyburz. Portsmouth, NH: Boyton/Cook Heinemann, 2005. 11–23.

Swearingen, Jan. "The Hermeneutics of Suspicion and Other Doubting Games: Clearing the Way for Simple Leaps of Faith." *The Academy and the Possibility of Belief: Essays on Intellectual and Spiritual Life*. Ed. Mary Louise Buley-Meissner, Mary McCaslin Thompson, and Elizabeth Bachrach Tan. Creskill, NJ: Hampton Press, Inc., 2000.

Vander Lei, Elisabeth, and Kyburz, Bonnie Lenore, eds. *Negotiating Religious Faith in the Composition Classroom*. Portsmouth, NH: Boyton/Cook Heinemann, 2005.

Williams, Bronwyn. T. "Taken on Faith: Religion and Identity in Writing Classes." *Journal of Adolescent Literacy* 48.6 (March 2005): 514–518.

———. "The Book and the Truth: Faith Rhetoric, and Cross Cultural Communication." *Negotiating Religious Faith in the Com-*

position Classroom. Portsmouth, NH: Boynton/Cook Heinemann, 2005.105–120.

Worth, Jan. "Hot-Spots and Holiness: Faith-Based Topics in Freshman Composition." *Conference on College Composition and Communication*. 21 (March 2002). ERIC.

CHAPTER FOURTEEN

Theorizing Audience in Web-Based Self-Presentation

ERIN KARPER

Niagara University

A teenager appears on NPR to protest that her mother read her friends-only LiveJournal posts; her mother, who also has a MySpace page, appears to provide a rebuttal (Lauritano-Werner). An aspiring student videographer posts video clips of underage drunken debauchery on his professional portfolio. Thousands of college students protest the September 2006 changes to the then-student-only social networking site Facebook after its interface is altered to automatically display information that was previously more concealed (Calore), and again when Facebook allows a larger audience access to the site. The mass media provide countless stories about the potentially dangerous details that children and young adults supply in their online activities as well as cautionary tales of individuals fired for the information they present about themselves on blogs or social networking sites. Meanwhile, *Time* named the "you" who participates in the various genres and media previously described (often called "the social Web" or Web 2.0) as the 2006 Person of the Year, demonstrating the growing significance of this engagement outside a strictly online culture. In and out of the classroom, people grapple with issues of who their audience really is and what is "appropriate" for an audience in Web writing situations, especially in situations in which they engage in Web-based self-presentation such as blogging, journaling online, participating on social networking sites such as Facebook or MySpace, or creating home pages and professional websites.

A common view of the audience awareness of people who engage in Web-based self-presentation is that those people simply do not understand or are naïvely unaware of audience when they write, and thus do not realize the problems that may occur in certain types of self-presentation. Lunsford and Ede both confirm and complicate this perspective in "Among the Audience" when they say "many students easily forget that when they post something on the Web they may encounter unwanted audiences" and later that "student[s] experience the Internet and many of its sites as fairly private, when the reality is that audiences are there all the time, browsing, searching, engaging, responding, sometimes accusing" ("Among" 56). While this view is not without merit, I argue for a more nuanced view of why and how people, especially "digital natives," view audience on the Web when creating self-presentations. People build assumptions about audience based on faulty data about how the Web works, and the quest for technological mastery or a need to demonstrate digital literacy when creating Web-based self-presentations may temporarily override all other rhetorical considerations, including audience. However, trust-filtering tools, which allow for access control on most Web sites, let people both address and invoke a specific audience, while audiences are becoming more interactive, due to technological and social changes in which "digital natives draw on the experience and advice of online communities to shape their interests and boundaries" (Woods)—that is, audiences now contribute to the creation of individual self-presentations. Finally, I consider how instructors might use these perceptions and new genres to help students learn how to critically consider audience and make appropriate choices for writing on the Web in personal or professional situations.

Addressing, Invoking, Involving, and Identifying: Perspectives on Audience and Web-Based Self-Presentation

While some have criticized the addressed/invoked dichotomy and synthesis of perspectives originally characterized by Lunsford and Ede ("AA/AI"; "Representing Audience") for not adequately conveying the complexities of audience or for placing too much of an emphasis on audience (Elbow, Reif), they nevertheless provide a useful way of considering individual perceptions of audience in Web-based self-presentation. Lunsford and Ede themselves question the audience addressed/audience invoked binary efficacy as applied to new media, saying that "these kinds of participatory communications challenge conventional understandings of both authorship and audience, even as they provide an opportunity for anyone and everyone to become both author and audience, writer and reader" ("Among" 53). However, they ultimately conclude that "the kinds of participatory communication that we have just described can, we believe, be encompassed within these two categories [of audience addressed/audience invoked]" and "that the categories of invoked and addressed audiences still inform the much more complex online communicating we do today" ("Among" 53). Many of the seemingly inappropriate choices that people make when creating Web-based self-presentations resolve when viewed as either invoking or addressing a specific audience—or in some cases, as attempting to collapse the dichotomy entirely and synthesize a perspective similar to the encompassing view of Ede and Lunsford at the end of "Audience Addressed/ Audience Invoked" (167).

Another perspective on audience I rely upon here is Kenneth Burke's notion of identification, which he calls the central aim of rhetoric, a real or imagined alignment of interests or linguistic assertion of identity between two things or people:

> In being identified with B, A is "substantially one" with a person other than himself. Yet at the same time he remains unique, an individual locus of motives. Thus he is both joined and separate, at once a distinct substance and consubstantial with another . . . . Similarly, two persons may be identified in terms of some principle they share in common, an "identification" that does not deny their distinctness. (21)

People shape (or do not shape) their Web-based self-presentations based on their perceptions of audience, and they invite or permit their audience to participate in the construction of their Web-based self-presentations. In "Among the Audience," Lunsford and Ede make reference to Henry Jenkins's notion of the "interactive audience," which can be seen as similar to Robert Johnson's "involved audience," both of which posit audience in an active role. When people model their Web-based self-presentations on the self-presentations of their audience, they can be seen to be engaging in Burkean identification.

One of Web 2.0's primary features is the ability to facilitate social interaction through different forms of media and to create a "collective intelligence" that differs from mere information provision: "a Web 2.0 service is one that provides the platform or service and turns it over to its users, who then create and maintain the content of that service. That content is then shown to others, who consume and extend the content. LiveJournal gives you things to read; del.icio.us gives you organized things to remember; Wikipedia gives you things to know" (Synecdocic). Web 2.0 sites allow people to engage in social networking (Facebook or Classmates) and in the creation of social media (LiveJournal or Wikipedia). Sometimes social media sites may have social networking features, and vice versa; all of them are examples of what Jenkins refers to as "media convergence," which is the "flow of content across multiple media platforms, the cooperation between multiple media industries, and the migratory behavior of media audiences who will go almost anywhere in search of the kinds of entertainment experiences they want" (2). Media convergence is a place where "consumption assumes a more public and collective dimension" (Jenkins 22) and key questions emerge about the shifting roles of author and audience: "What is an author, a composer, a communicator? How does a technologically rich media convergence shift or alter our own understanding of authoring, composing, communicating—and thus of building connections and creating meaning with one another and with ourselves as reflecting, reflective beings?" (Alexander 6). Clearly the technological, social, and rhetorical possibilities articulated by Web 2.0 (which is itself an articulation of these forces) are reshaping what is possible for both "author" and "audience."

While the Web as a medium is ever-changing and still in its infancy compared to other forms of discourse, some research has been done on Web-based self-presentation and about audience, especially with the generation of "digital natives" that is now entering adolescence and young adulthood. Lenhart's 2005 thesis focused on self-perception and audience in a small ethnography of bloggers; McLellan's 2006 thesis also surveyed users of LiveJournal and reported in part on their self-perception; and danah boyd's work on the users of MySpace discusses the role of identification and writing (including audience awareness) in social networking sites where users engage in Web-based self-presentation. A 2008 special issue of *Computers and Composition* that focused on media convergence offers many intriguing studies about Web-based self-presentation and its use in composition classrooms (Alexander; Reid; Williams; Anderson).

In one of those articles, Stephanie Vie offers an excellent study of "Generation M" students and their relationship with social networking sites such as MySpace and Facebook as well as implications for classroom use. Vie cautions that while the current generation of students are mostly comfortable with and fluent in the use of technologies, "Generation M students' comfort with technology does not imply . . . that they can understand and critique technology's societal effects" (10). The current generation of students (or at least those whose socioeconomic status has allowed them access to the technologies necessary for being a part of Web 2.0) may be technologically fluent, but not technologically literate. Theorists such as Selber, Hawisher and Selfe, Gurak, and Kress all concur that today's generation of students desperately need to become critically and rhetorically literate about and with technologies in order to navigate a world based on an "economy of attention" that demands the ability to do symbolic-analytic information work. Similarly, a lack of technological literacy and/or critical and rhetorical awareness about how technologies are used may be one of the key factors that causes users to make decisions perceived as being "unaware" of audience.

"Faulty Wiring": Misperceptions of the Web Leading to Audience-Inappropriate Choices

Some Web users may be or seem indifferent to audience perception of their self-presentations. For example, according to the 2006 report on bloggers issued by the Pew Internet and American Life Project (hereafter Pew Project), 52 percent of bloggers "say they blog mostly for themselves, not for an audience." What causes people to believe that a blog is a private endeavor that is not meant for an audience when it is inherently a public act? Much of this can be tied to a misunderstanding of the Web.

Many beginning Web users are unaware that their content will be indexed by search engines, especially if they do not link to other websites or if other users do not link to them. However, the increasingly sophisticated nature of search engines means that most forms of Web-based self-presentation are captured by search engines and available to all. Since search engines store local copies of content (a process called caching), this also means that even if a person removes their content from the Web, it may still be available in the archives of a search engine. While some bloggers are aware that they are "writing for Google," many others are unaware that "Google and its ilk enable a readership vastly larger than what the author envisioned" (Lenhart 81).

Web composers may also believe that they are protected through pseudonymity or anonymity offered by the Web. This is especially true with those who engage in blogging and online journaling, in which "a bit more than half of bloggers (55 percent) surveyed say they blog under a pseudonym or made-up name," in order to "avoid the problem of colliding life spheres and to protect personal privacy" (Pew Project, "Bloggers"). An excellent example is the number of academic bloggers who work under pseudonyms such as "CheekyProf," "Bitch, Ph.D.," or "The Invisible Adjunct." The content and tone of pseudonymous academic blogs is often different from that of academic bloggers who choose to use their actual names and provide identifying information about their affiliations. Pseudonymous bloggers believe that not revealing certain identifying details to their audience will keep them safe from possible consequences; therefore, they may decide to disclose information that they would not without pseudonymity in place. According to Lenhart,

> many bloggers feel relatively confident in their online anonymity, reasoning that connecting their offline selves to their online selves would be a more difficult process than the average person would undertake, and that the large number of other weblogs and personal websites makes it unlikely that theirs will be found by people they hope do not see it. (82)

However, pseudonymity does not ensure that an unwanted audience will be kept out while a desired audience will be attracted. Lenhart found that while some bloggers did promote their blogs to friends, family, and coworkers, "other bloggers took an opposite approach, and told almost no one in their offline lives of their blog's existence, hoping to keep their blog a highly personal and private space" and "many bloggers do not want co-workers to know about their blog, particularly not supervisors or others in positions of power over them" (79–80). In 2002, Heather Armstrong was fired from her job because she wrote about it on her blog, using her real name and the actual name of her company. Ms. Armstrong, like many other people who engage in Web-based self-presentation, assumed that the vast and sprawling nature of the Web meant that her words would not be readily available to her employers, and also that her employers would either not be technically proficient enough nor be interested in searching the Web for mentions of their company or their employees. Now a blogging "celebrity," her advice to other bloggers is "BE YE NOT SO STUPID. Never write about work on the Internet unless your boss knows and sanctions the fact that YOU ARE WRITING ABOUT WORK ON THE INTERNET" (Armstrong, emphasis hers).

Many who engage in Web-based self-presentation seem to engage with audience by invoking a specific set of interested and responsive parties to whom they address their content while simultaneously mentally excluding any members of an audience who might complicate, challenge, or provide consequences for the writer's self-presentation, such as family members, friends, employers, or co-workers. This audience is "disinvoked" through claims of their presumed lack of interest in using the Web or a lack of technological literacy on their parts. For example, 49 percent of bloggers surveyed by the Pew Project "believe that their blog readership is mostly made up of people they personally know" even though this may or may not actually be true. A person engaged in Web-based self-presentation may choose to focus on the desired audience they have invoked rather than the actual audience being addressed—an audience that could be composed of anyone with Internet access. As people become more aware that simply "disinvoking" an audience mentally does not prevent them from actually being addressed, they turn to tools such as trust-filtering.

"Trust-Filtering" and "Friends Only": Addressing and Invoking a Specific Audience

"Trust-filtering," "friends-locking," or "friends-only" involves restricting the visibility of and access to material posted on a blog, journal, or social networking site. In this situation, the audience may be defined and controlled by password-protecting certain posts, or by using tools provided by blogging, journaling, and social networking sites that allow people to control access to material by restricting it to other users who are logged into the site. Trust-filtering allows the writer to *both* invoke and address a very specific audience—through trust-filtering, "the audience called up or imagined by the writer" *can be exactly equivalent to* "those actual or real-life people who read a discourse" ("AA/AI," 156)—or, at the very least, the writer can assume that the two are equivalent. With trust-filtering tools, "knowledge of this audience's attitudes, beliefs, and expectations is not only possible . . . but essential" (156). In many ways, trust-filtering truly demonstrates the "synthesis of perspectives" described by Ede and Lunsford (167). Trust-filtering comes "naturally" to most digital natives, who tend to see Web-based self-presentation and the consumption of others' Web-based self-presentations as part of creating and maintaining previously existing relationships, or what the Pew Project calls the "intertwining of blogging, community, and relationship-building among teens" in their report on "Teen Content Creators and Consumers."

For example, LiveJournal, a popular online journaling site, allows users to define a "friends list" of other journals on the site as well as subsidiary "groups" of journals from the main list. While the "friends list" and "friends groups" are used to aggregate journals on a single page for reading, they are also used for access control. When making a post to a journal, users can choose the following access options from a drop-down list: "Show this entry to: Everyone (public), Friends, Just me (Private), Custom . . . " Choosing the "Just Me" option means that only the user can see the journal entry and must be logged in to do so; "Friends" restricts access to the journals defined by the user on their "friends list," meaning that only people who are logged in to those specific journals can see the entry; "Custom" allows a user to give viewing permission to specific subgroups of journals from their main "friends list." Similar access control options, often explicitly labeled as "privacy control," are available on sites such as MySpace and Facebook, and also on sites that focus on images, video, and visual media, such as Flickr and YouTube. Users of these tools often refer to this type of access control as "filtering," since they are sifting out a large audience and leaving behind a very small one. It is generally considered good online etiquette to indicate when one is using a filter by providing textual cues to accompany the technological ones so that other users are aware of the audience being addressed and invoked.

Trust-filtering causes people to believe that they can control exactly who has access to specific material by merging the addressed audience with the invoked one. This belief often leads writers to tailor material for the specific audience that they believe they are addressing and to invoke a specific role for the reader through the textual or technological cues which explain that the information is filtered (AA/AI 167). This belief could lead to some of the candid self-disclosure that has become a hallmark of most people's perception of Web-based self-presentations. According to a 2007 study from the Pew Project, 66 percent of teens who have created profiles on social networking sites limit access to their profiles.

Trust-filtering, then, by creating the illusion that one can both invoke and address a specific audience that has access to material, has an extraordinary influence on the rhetorical choices made in Web-based self-presentation. When they use trust-filtering, users are actually demonstrating a keen sense of audience awareness rather than a lack thereof: instead of the writer's audience being a fiction, as Ong once said, trust-filtering allows users to in fact create a specific and well-defined audience for a specific message, as well as shaping how the message is presented.

However, trust-filtering can fail for both technical and personal reasons, causing the writer to be addressing a larger audience than they are invoking. A user may forget to set permissions correctly and thus make something public that was meant to be filtered or private, the site may malfunction and reset the permissions on content, or the site management may allow a larger number of users to access the site. For example, companies and other types of employers have gained access to Facebook, an extraordinarily popular social networking site aimed primarily at high school and college students, which means that material that users had assumed was restricted only to an audience of their peers (and the occasional professor) is now available to a completely different—and often disapproving—audience. The "general public" has also gained access to Facebook. In late 2006, Facebook users were distressed when the site changed to allow the still-restricted audience more immediate access to information: upon logging in, users were given a news feed of information about their "friends" as defined on the site, such as when people had been added to or removed from a person's grouping of friends, or when someone's "status" as a boyfriend or girlfriend had changed. While Facebook had not compromised the information provided by users, users still felt that their information was being "overshared"—they wanted their audience to have to pull that information themselves rather than having it pushed to them when they entered the site. This led to online petitions and the creation of an entire site called "Save Facebook" to regain the privacy controls that users perceived as having lost (Calore; see also "Save Facebook").

Other people may also become an unintended audience by accessing the user's account or computer. For example, in the NPR story mentioned in the introduction, the mother read the daughter's access-controlled LiveJournal entries, some of which were about arguments between the two of them, by sitting down at her daughter's computer when she was logged in to LiveJournal. The daughter believed that she had controlled access and thus excluded her mother from her audience by restricting her journals to a specific group of LiveJournal users, but she had forgotten about the physical presence of her parent in the house (Lauritano-Werner). Trust-filtering can also fail if the person posting or any of the users in the specified audience have their accounts compromised by someone else, or simply if people in the audience choose to disclose the filtered content to others.

"Audience Override": When the Technical Overrides the Rhetorical

The audience problem for digital natives is not necessarily a lack of awareness; instead, it is the technical and human failures that allow for the unexpected presence of a larger unwanted audience. One example might be called "audience override," when the need to achieve control over or "play" with the technologies of Web composition overrides other rhetorical considerations, including audience, in the thoughts and actions of the composer. In research on beginning Web composers conducted in 2003 and 2006, I found that while beginning Web composers engaged with both rhetorical and technical issues during the processes of composition for the Web, there were moments when engagement with the technical process of composition overwhelmed rhetorical awareness. This would happen either when a composer was frustrated with "making it work" or when they were "just playing" to see what a specific program, technology, or command would allow them to create. Rhetorical awareness did not disappear entirely; however, many of the seemingly inappropriate or bizarre choices made by Web composers (such as background and text colors that made pages unreadable, or seemingly random embedded images, video, or music clips) can be explained by technical concerns temporarily overriding rhetorical concerns.

Beginning composers often choose to leave these rhetorically inappropriate choices either to demonstrate their technical mastery or because they do not want to spend time undoing their work; in either case, they will publish the work on the Web but dismiss it as "just play" when asked about the rhetorical implications. While my research was confined to composers creating static pages for self-presentation, I think that the "audience override" and/or "just play" perspectives can be extrapolated to explain some of the audience-inappropriate choices of people using dynamic systems for Web-based self-presentation, such as blogging or online journaling software and social networking sites.

The limits of Web composers' technical knowledge, skills, or resources may also lead them to make audience-inappropriate choices simply because they see no other viable options for completing a project. For example, in one of my writing for the Web classes, a student who was an aspiring videographer wanted to include a video clip of pictures set to music in an online portfolio assignment. The only pictures he had readily available that were his own work were pictures of his friends from a drunken party. The student's desire to show technical mastery ("I can create video clips with music") overrode the rhetorical consideration of audience ("Is showing pictures of people doing a keg stand set to a Green Day song going to make a favorable impression on the primary audience of my instructor and the secondary audience of employers who might see this portfolio?"). A similar incident happened in one of my first-year composition classes, where a student who was eager to use pictures on a home page but who was mindful of discussions of fair use and copyright decided to include pictures of himself posing with a giant inflatable phallus right under the paragraph where he discussed how much he wanted to be a physical education teacher and work with young children. While there were certainly other factors that influenced these students' choices, I would argue that their desire to use and show mastery of the technologies for Web composition combined with limited resource availability were significant factors in their decision to not critically consider audience and to make audience-inappropriate choices.

Building "Wikiality": Identification and the Involved Audience

A final perspective on the perception of audience in Web-based self-presentation is the idea of "wikiality," or "reality defined by consensus," which was first made popular on the satirical television show *The Colbert Report* and often used as a term when disparaging the collaborative construction of knowledge that takes place on the Web. However, the idea of wikiality is also a useful perspective for describing the behavior of "digital natives" when they engage in Web-based self-presentation, especially on social networking sites, in which, according to the 2007 Pew Project study, more than 55 percent of online teens participate. As McLellan explains, "In electronic media, physical locale no longer constrains us or fences in different social groups, creating a rhetorical space that is defined socially" (12). Johnson's model of "audience involved," while developed primarily in response to technical communication situations, is especially useful here in describing the ways in which audience is involved in the shaping of certain Web-based self-presentations: "In contrast to the addressed or invoked models of audience, the involved audience is an actual participant in the writing process who creates knowledge and determines much of the content of the discourse. . . . [T]he *involved* audience brings the audience literally into the open, making the intended audience a visible, physical, collaborative presence" (363).

Lunsford and Ede, in "Among the Audience," say that "interactive or participatory audiences fall somewhere along a continuum, from those who consume media and content on the Web in fairly traditional ways to the full shared agency characteristic of many online communities" (54). The concepts of "interactive" and "involved" audiences are quite similar, since they both describe how participation of the audience is an important part of social networking and social media on the Web. There are two major ways that an audience contributes to and helps to shape a person's Web-based self-presentation, most commonly on what are called "profile pages" on social networking sites. The first are expressions of approval, disapproval, or description, often called "woos," "snaps," rankings, or sometimes just "testimonials" and commenting systems, including "The Wall" on Facebook and the comment systems in place on sites such as Blogger, LiveJournal, and MySpace. These actions are the norm for users: the 2007 Pew Project study claims that "more than 4 in 5 social network users (84 percent) have posted messages to a friend's profile or page." The act of "friending"—adding a person to one's network on a site, for the purposes of trust-filtering, post aggregation, or simply as acknowledgment of a relationship—and the subsequent display of "friends lists" or other indications of the networks one belongs to on a specific site in Web-based self-presentations are also rhetorical gestures that reflect existing relationships, especially for teens, for whom "blogs are much more about the maintenance and extension of personal relationships" and for whom "blogs are often authored with select audiences in mind" (Pew Project, "Teen Content Creators and Consumers").

The presence of comments and feedback from an audience makes them visibly present and involved. For example, on a user's MySpace profile, a significant portion of the page is devoted to "Friend Space," where pictures, names, and links to a person's defined contacts are listed. Directly below that is "Friend Comments," where other site users leave comments that can range from testimonials about the user to more personal or conversational comments. The amount of page real estate devoted to the display of an explicitly addressed audience and comments from said audience is larger than the amount of space devoted to the person's writings—to see blog entries or additional writing from the person, one must navigate to a separate page. The audience is also given the option to "rank a user," which becomes part of the person's self-presentation. OKCupid, another social networking/dating site, allows users to add comments about another person, which become part of that user's profile, as well as to "woo" a user by adding a positive comment. In addition to displaying on a user's profile their friends as well as any site-related groups they have joined, Facebook also allows users to add to the discourse available on a person's Web-based self-presentation through "The Wall," which is a commenting system built into each user's profile page. Facebook users can also see the changing relationships between users through the "feeds" available for display on profile pages or from the "home page" that users see when they log in. These feeds inform them when people have "become friends" or "entered into a relationship." One might argue that blogrolls (lists of links to blogs that a blogger wishes to indicate affiliation with that are displayed in the sidebars of a person's blog) serve the same function for blogs and other forms of social media as friend displays or feeds do for social-networking sites.

As people seek to have an audience involved in their Web-based self-presentations, another strategy can be seen at work in their attempts to attract an audience who will become involved: identification, in which "belonging in this sense is rhetorical" (Burke 27–28) and "a speaker persuades an audience by the use of stylistic identifications; his act of persuasion may be for the purpose of causing the audience to identify itself with the speaker's interests; and the speaker draws on identification of interests to establish rapport between himself and his audience" (Burke 46).

For example, in my research on beginning Web designers who were building Web pages to assist their searches for an academic job, I discovered that they used identification strategies in order to indicate that they belonged to a particular profession and to a particular discourse community or set of discourse communities within that profession. They engaged in this identification by locating the pages of mentors, colleagues, or friends who were in similar positions and then creating pages that formed identifications with them through the use of similar rhetorical strategies (which can be seen in the visual rhetoric of the pages as well as in the designers' talk about them) in order to persuade an audience of their standing in that community. Similarly, people constructing profile pages on social networking sites will often base their self-descriptions, interests, or other identifying information on those of their friends, as well as using the display of "friends lists," group memberships, and other site-based connections as a form of identification with others. The manifestation of the "involved audience" and identification-focused practices demonstrate a much more nuanced and sophisticated view of audience than is typically assumed of people engaged in Web-based self-presentation. I believe that many of those so engaged are aware of audience to the point of involving them in the construction of discourse as well as practicing identification, albeit not always on a conscious or reflective level.

The shaping of self-presentation through audience involvement and engagement in identification strategies in order to achieve a specific purpose by conforming to the needs and desires of a specific audience is perceived as normal for most digital natives. Richard Woods, in a commentary on the divide between digital natives and digital immigrants, says that "parameters are increasingly set by 'wiki-thinking,' peer groups exchanging ideas through digital networks. . . . A telling symptom is blogging. Where once schoolchildren and students confided only in their diaries, now they write blogs or entries on MySpace.com—where anyone can see and comment on them." As Hawisher and Selfe describe in *Literate Lives in the Information Age*, young people "depend on the help of their peers and on their own efforts to figure out the skills they needed in the coming years" (205). In her research on LiveJournal users, most of whom would be classified as digital natives, McLellan found that "traditional assumptions of the dangers of the Internet to obscure identity affected the respondents little, if any; instead they seemed to prioritize the promise of relationships with other users that mimed traditional off-line friendships" (2). We can see all of these attitudes made manifest when people engage in identification and allow their audiences to shape their self-presentations online.

Putting It into Practice

While not every rhetorical act in which students engage is immediately applicable to the writing classroom, many of the ideas regarding the audience awareness skills of "Generation Next" or "Generation M" raise questions that could be applied there: How could we translate some students' more honed rhetorical perceptions from the Web to the writing classroom? Can we take advantage of the audience awareness built by trust-filtering to help users understand more general concepts of audience? How do we teach students to critically consider audience and make appropriate choices for writing on the Web in personal or professional situations? How does the co-opting of "native" Web genres such as blogs, home pages, online portfolios, and wikis into educational settings change ideas about audience and audience appropriateness in the minds of students? What do professors need to know about audience when they use these genres? Although this chapter cannot answer all of those questions and so much good writing pedagogy is dependent upon the rhetorical situation(s) in which the course is situated, I can offer three general pieces of advice.

First, open up discussions of audience and genre to include examples of Web-based self-presentation, even in classes that are not focused on the Web. Since writing teachers are often charged with "making audience real" for students, why not use a situation with which many students are familiar and with which they do see a real and genuine audience? For example, as part of an in-class activity on analyzing different genres and rhetorical situations, I include Facebook pages, blog entries, online portfolios, and other Web-based genres along with other more traditional print-based genres for students to analyze. Students are often intrigued by

the novelty of analyzing a "non-school" genre, and the resulting analyses often provide a fruitful way of helping students to
understand why certain types of writing can be acceptable in one
rhetorical situation and not in another. For example, students in
my visual rhetoric class analyzed the different genres of MySpace
profile pictures and discussed how they engage the viewer's gaze.
Similar assignments might ask students to classify or even to
parody the "generic" constructions of social networking and/or
social media sites.

Also, since rhetoric and composition courses, especially first-
year composition courses, are most often tasked with "making
audience real" for students, using rhetorical situations with
"audience involved" may be useful in helping students to build
better concepts of audience. For example, students in one of my
visual rhetoric courses analyzed some of the cards available in
the PostSecret project (a collaborative art project that is situated
both online and offline and that also contains an online community) and then created their own postcards that were submitted
to the project. Even though the audience was "the anonymous
Internet," the idea of making secrets public that the PostSecret
project exemplifies provided a useful and fruitful situation in
which to discuss audience, especially concepts of the involved
audience and the unintended audience. (See Vie, Williams, and
Anderson's articles for additional examples of how to include
social media in the classroom and relate it to audience.)

Second, before using Web genres such as online journaling,
blogging, or social networking tools in a class, critically consider
students' previous experiences with these genres and how the
educational use of this type of genre may be very different from
their existing experiences as well as how the classroom setting
influences their production. If students are already voluntarily
engaging in Web-based self-presentation for personal reasons,
they may find being obligated to do it for academic reasons to be
artificial and inappropriate, and disengage from the experience.
However, if students can come to an understanding of how this
type of work will help them to learn as well as how this type of
participation is similar to and different from their existing online
participation, they may be more apt to engage fully. (For more on
the mixed successes of blogs and social networking tools in the

classroom, see Krause 2004). It is also important to consider (as numerous theorists and practitioners have cautioned) that while students may (or may not, depending on their levels of access) be comfortable using social media/social networking/Web 2.0 technologies, they most likely do not possess the critical, rhetorical, and technological literacies necessary for a full and complete understanding of how and why they work. By providing them with access to both theoretical and practical knowledge, we give them access to these literate practices. For example, in my writing for the Web courses, I ask students to read sources about audience analysis, "wikiality," media convergence, and the attention economy, and to discuss how they see and situate themselves as participants through in-class discussion, online discussion, and the creation of Web-based technology literacy narratives and webtextual analyses of social media and social networking sites.

Finally, encourage reflection and discussion of audience when doing Web-based projects, especially Web-based self-presentation such as online portfolios, journals, or blogs. Engage in audience analysis activities: in a Web writing or Web design course, encouraging students to adopt a user-centered design perspective leads naturally into audience analysis and consideration. Students can also be provided with or relate their own "cautionary tales" about Web-based self-presentation via news stories or created scenarios. For example, students in my writing for the Web and first-year composition classes are often eager to talk about changes to Facebook's news feeds or whether or not universities should block access for student-athletes. While this does not guarantee that students will make appropriate choices (as my own experiences cited earlier can demonstrate), it does help them to become more critical consumers and producers of Web content and to develop the functional, critical, and rhetorical literacies necessary for engagement with the twenty-first century (Selber). It is also important, as Vie cautions in her study of using social-networking technologies in the classroom, to "look at the deepening divide between students and instructors—not only in terms of the skills and abilities that preclude a digital divide but also the participatory democracy encapsulated in each classroom" (23), and to critically consider our uses of social networking and social media in the classroom lest they replicate problematic power dynamics.

Works Cited

Armstrong, Heather. "About This Site." *Dooce*. (2007). 22 Jan. 2007 <http://www.dooce.com/about.html>.

boyd, danah. "A Blogger's Blog: Exploring the Definition of a Medium." *Reconstruction* 6.4 (2006). 22 Jan. 2007 <http://reconstruction. eserver.org/064/boyd.shtml>.

———. "Friendster and Publicly Articulated Social Networks." 2004. 22 Jan. 2007 <http://www.danah.org/papers/CHI2004 Friendster.pdf>.

———. "Friends, Friendsters, and Myspace Top 8: Writing Community into Being on Social Network Sites." *First Monday* 11.12 (2006). 22 Jan. 2007 <http://www.firstmonday.org/issues/issue11_12/boyd/ index.html>.

Burke, Kenneth. *A Rhetoric of Motives*. Berkeley: U of California P, 1969.

Calore, Michael. "Privacy Fears Shock Facebook." *Wired News*. 6 Sept. 2006. 22 Jan. 2007 <http://www.wired.com/news/technology/ 0,71739-0.html>.

Ede, Lisa, and Andrea Lunsford. "Audience Addressed/Audience Invoked: The Role of Audience in Composition Theory and Pedagogy." *CCC* 35 (1984): 155–171.

Elbow, Peter. "Closing My Eyes as I Speak: An Argument for Ignoring Audience." *Everyone Can Write*. Oxford: Oxford UP, 2000. 93–112.

Hawisher, Gail, and Cynthia Selfe. *Literate Lives in the Information Age: Narratives of Literacy from the United States*. Mahwah, NJ: Lawrence Erlbaum, 2004.

Johnson, Robert R. "Audience Involved: Toward a Participatory Model of Writing." *Computers and Composition* 14.3 (1997): 361–376.

Karper, Erin. "Ordinary People Do This: Rhetorical Examinations of Novice Web Design." Diss. Purdue University, 2004.

Krause, Stephen. "When Blogging Goes Bad: A Cautionary Tale about Blogs, Emailing Lists, Discussion, and Interaction." *Kairos* 9.1 (2004). 24 Jan. 2007 <http://english.ttu.edu/kairos/9.1/binder. html?praxis/krause/index.html>.

Lauritano-Werner, Bly. "The Effort to Keep an Online Diary Private." *National Public Radio*. 24 July 2006. 22 Jan. 2007 <http://www. npr.org/templates/story/story.php?storyId=5579002>.

Lenhart, Amanda B. *Unstable Texts: An Ethnographic Look at How Bloggers and Their Audience Negotiate Self-Presentation, Authenticity, and Norm Formation*. Thesis. Georgetown University, 2005. 22 Jan. 2007 <http://lenhart.flashesofpanic.com/Lenhart_thesis.pdf>.

Lunsford, Andrea A., and Lisa Ede. "Among the Audience: On Audience in an Age of New Literacies." *Engaging Audience: Writing in an Age of New Literacies*. Ed. Elizabeth Weiser, Brian Fehler, and Angela González. Urbana, IL: NCTE, 2009. 42–69.

Lunsford, Andrea, and Lisa Ede. "Representing Audience: 'Successful' Discourse and Disciplinary Critique." *CCC* 47:2. (May, 1996): 167–179.

Mason, Jean. *From Gutenberg's Galaxy to Cyberspace: The Transforming Power of Electronic Hypertext*. Toronto: CITD Press, 2001.

McLellan, Kathryn. *"LiveJournal is a Conversation with the World": An Examination of the Effects of Interpersonal Communication on Personal Blogging*. Thesis. University of Chicago, 2006.

Pew Internet and American Life Project. "Bloggers." 19 July 2006. 22 Jan. 2007 <http://www.pewinternet.org/pdfs/PIP%20Bloggers% 20Report%20July%2019%202006. pdf>.

———. "Social Networking Websites and Teens: An Overview." Jan. 2007. 22 Jan. 2007 <http://www.pewinternet.org/pdfs/PIP_SNS_ Data_Memo_Jan_2007.pdf>.

———. "Teen Content Creators and Consumers." 2005. 22 Jan. 2007 <http://www.pewinternet.org/pdfs/PIP_Teens_Content_Creation. pdf>.

Reiff, Mary Jo. "Rereading Invoked and Addressed Readers through a Social Lens: Toward a Recognition of Multiple Audiences." *JAC* 16.3 (1997): 407–424.

"Save Facebook." 8 Sept. 2006. 25 Jan. 2007 <http://www.savefacebook. com/>.

Selber, Stuart A. *Multiliteracies for a Digital Age*. Carbondale, IL: Southern Illinois UP, 2004.

Woods, Richard. "Report: The Next Step in Brain Evolution." *The Sunday Times* (UK) 9 July 2006. 22 Jan. 2007 <http://www.times online.co.uk/article/0,2101-2256968,00.html>.

CHAPTER FIFTEEN

Reading Audiences

DAN KELLER
The Ohio State University

David said he was bad at reading. When asked to explain what he meant by "bad," he talked about vocabulary and retention and the fact that he does not read very often. When I visited David a few months before he started college, he was browsing three different Internet sites while watching TV, and he had various genres and media within his reach—novels, comic books, magazines, newspapers, text messages, email, televised news, etc. Throughout the interview, David engaged with and talked about the various media in the room. It was difficult to reconcile the "bad reader" image of David with his casual willingness to surround himself with such a literate environment. What does it mean to be a "bad reader" in this scene?[1] It is filled with interesting subjects: multitasking, information overload, the competition of media for our attention and time, and the role of education in consumer society, to name a few. The issue of audience is also strong here: David assumes various audience roles to effectively make meaning from these experiences. As he reads and writes in such an environment, he shifts genres and media as rapidly as he moves from the role of audience to author. Within a span of a few minutes, he reads an eBay page, composes a text message to a friend, receives a text message, reads online news, and composes an email to a school advisor. These literacy events are also happening in front of someone who is a researcher and a teacher—another audience layer.

According to recent studies, David's multimedia environment is fairly typical of middle-class teens (Roberts and Foehr). The proliferation of communication technologies has changed how we produce, receive, and perceive texts. Henry Jenkins's examination of media convergence explains how media are being consolidated in technology, how content flows across media, how media reshape each other, and how they provide deep levels of participation for users. Media convergence blurs lines between author and audience, producer and consumer. Such changes have caused Andrea Lunsford and Lisa Ede to revisit their understanding of audience, raising questions about authorship, participation, and ethics. An important point for them is the kind of oscillation David does between author and audience in this multimedia environment; they note how the "roles of writers and audiences often conflate, merge, and shift" ("Among" 48). As Lunsford and Ede state, the "deeply participatory nature of electronic forms of communication provides for writerly agency," resulting in "diverse forms of multiple authorship and . . . the kind of mass authorship that characterizes sites such as Wikipedia and Google News" ("Among" 48).

Media convergence also provides new opportunities for us to revisit "readerly agency" and multiple audience roles, concepts I will pursue in this chapter. In "Audience Addressed/Audience Invoked," Ede and Lunsford write that audience "refers not just to the intended, actual, or eventual readers of a discourse, but to *all* those whose image, ideas, or actions influence a writer during the process of composition" (168). One of those readers, of course, is the writer herself: she occupies different audience roles for other texts, and those different roles affect her when she takes on the author role. While many factors affect the construction and reception of audiences, in this chapter I will focus on how our students' conception of audience is influenced by their experiences as readers of different genres and media. I will show how students' various reading experiences—particularly with multiple genres and media—converge and conflict with reading in educational settings; I will also suggest how we can respond pedagogically to help students think about the audience roles they play.

First, though, we need to examine how we perceive students as readers, audiences of the various texts in their lives. These perceptions affect how we approach pedagogies of reading, audience, and technology. As students create new media texts outside of school, and as we ask students to create them in school, we will need reading pedagogies that help students comprehend, interpret, and make use of a broad range of texts.

Perceptions of Students as Readers

We have vast theoretical and pedagogical resources to help students become better writers. As we occasionally lament the abilities or willingness of some students, we at least feel supported by this system of scholarship and training. However, the situation is different when it comes to reading, which, for college, is largely seen as a remedial issue. Most of the scholarship on reading is found in the field of education, which gives the impression that reading is something to be taught and learned by high school. A major sponsor of reading research, the International Reading Association is, as Marguerite Helmers observes, "an organization to which most college professors do not belong" (4). This lack of a focus on reading can only hinder our attempts to teach writing for audience, especially as we redefine the boundaries of educational texts with blogs, wikis, and multimodal videos.[2]

Taking responsibility for reading pedagogy means reevaluating how we perceive our students as audience. Talking with colleagues in hallways, at meetings, and at conferences, we recognize and even repeat the tropes: Students don't read enough; they spend too much time on cell phones and Facebook. While it's difficult to disagree with these statements, it's even harder to let them go uncontested. A number of scholars have weighed in with some cynical views of students, their reading failures, and the fault of consumer culture and digital media (Bauerlein; Birkerts; Edmundson); however, the National Endowment for the Arts' (NEA) report "To Read or Not To Read: A Question of National Consequence" has gained the most attention. The NEA notes yet another significant decline in voluntary reading among teens and young adults; while it does not blame new media, it makes the implication as it states, "Whatever the benefits of newer electronic media, they provide no measurable substitute for the intellectual and personal development initiated and sustained by frequent reading" (6).

There are two problems with the NEA portrayal of reading.

First, while the latest NEA report includes data for online reading, it often does not delineate the kinds of reading being done; blogs, instant messages, news websites, online magazines, and online books may as well be the same. Second, the report reinforces the notion that "accumulated literacy" is sound pedagogy; such pedagogy results in a curriculum of coverage and shallow reading practices. The view of reading here is a simple one: it is an act of correctly decoding symbols. With "reading" being equivalent to literary reading, the students I interviewed—much like the NEA—did not consider their time on the Internet to be "reading." Yet many of the sites they listed reading regularly were online versions of print magazines; somehow, reading *Time* or *Cosmopolitan* online did not qualify as either "reading" or "time on the Internet."

The dismissal of online reading and the simplification of traditional reading promote misunderstanding of our students and the audience roles they take on. In a time of media convergence, it should be no surprise that many people—especially traditional students—turn to the Internet for their reading. When I began my study on students' reading practices with various media, I assumed that they would spend hours browsing the Internet, getting lost in endless chains of hyperlinks—that they would be a "captive" audience. But what students repeatedly said about their time on the Internet was that it was "fast and convenient," and that they were simply using it to get what they needed. In the interviews and observations, I was surprised by the agency and purpose they had as readers, as audiences.

In her senior year of high school, Diana juggled a part-time job, two sports, and three advanced classes: "I work at Old Navy eight to fifteen hours a week, I run track, and I play field hockey for school, and I have two AP classes and college English, and I'm working on scholarships, so I'm busy with school a lot." With that kind of a schedule, she laughed when I asked about her time on the Internet, saying, "No, I don't really spend too long on there. I might search for some news I heard on the radio or TV for more info, but I don't linger." Diana noted that she had even gotten into the habit of following news stories across media, piecing together information from a radio blurb, another brief mention on TV, a brief article in *Time* magazine, and then more information from a variety of websites. She valued discovery, and she appreciated the challenge of magazine articles and websites that were "beyond my knowledge range." Even though these authors did not address her, she tried to take on different audience roles to make sense of the texts and to get the information she wanted.

David did not have Diana's schedule, and he did spend a lot of time on the Internet, but it was with a few dedicated sites. "I don't wander around much. I go to eBay, some [video] gaming sites for tips and codes, and to some news websites. It's just fast and it's all right there." Although David did not follow stories across media the way Diana did, he seemed more comfortable managing multiple online tasks than she did. While waiting for an eBay update, he would have other windows open for ESPN.com, for gaming sites, and for an online game that could be played within the span of a few minutes; all of them could be abandoned at any moment if eBay needed more attention. David rarely strayed from these sites, and when he came upon a gaming or a comic book site that was more scholarly than expected, he quickly clicked away. Unlike Diana, he focused on sites that he felt addressed him as an audience.

Instead of the typical image we have of media holding students captive, we can see media convergence as a solution for how students can take some control over the abundance of information. Media convergence makes it convenient for students to read online; they can access information from newspapers and TV and perform other tasks at the same time. While it's easy to tag such convenience as "lazy," it's also important to keep in mind some other factors that complicate how we see their online reading. In the interviews I conducted, students expressed feeling inundated by the speed of our culture and the amount of information in their daily lives—from school assignments, from twenty-four-hour television with its hundreds of channels, from text messages and cell phones, and from the Internet; they were somewhat aware of how these situations and media both complicated and made their lives easier. The situation they described was one of living in an "Attention Economy," with an overabundance of information and a scarcity of attention (Lanham; Lankshear and Knobel, *New*); in such an economy, the need for improved technological filters and critical, transmedia reading becomes paramount. Using the Internet allowed them to find sites and information that met their needs as an audience, filtering out the "TV news and the [magazine] stories and the advertisements that have nothing to do with me," as Tim put it.

As we ask students to take on multiple authorship roles, we need to keep in mind the multiple audience roles they have outside of school. Some students will be like Diana, seeking out audience roles with content and genres that are unfamiliar and challenging. Others will be like David and Tim, who seek out familiar texts and take on fewer audience roles than Diana. Of course, this range of reading experiences is nothing new. Also, merely exposing students to different audience roles will not necessarily improve their writing for different audiences. Yet when so many more audiences are available to students through the Internet, we should work to improve their audience awareness by encouraging reading practices similar to Diana's. Indeed, my students who read in similar ways tend to be more adept at writing for different audiences and using different genres and media. (In the "Putting It into Practice" section, I provide some strategies for teaching flexible audience perspectives.)

The second misperception promoted by the NEA involves the simplification of reading. At the heart of this is the mistaken belief that any reading will result in "better" reading. Although experienced prose readers might have more confidence and patience, such attributes do not necessarily lead to the kinds of reading we want, which are often critical and rhetorical. The act of reading novels and newspapers does not translate into being able to read Socrates, Renaissance poetry, or even Mark Twain. In these instances, when we say, "Students don't know how to read," we are often ignoring the roles of audience, genre, and prior knowledge—issues I will attend to more in the next section. This oversimplification of reading also occurs with new media. Just as we sometimes unfairly blame students for problems with reading traditional texts, we also sometimes overestimate their expertise with digital texts because they seem so comfortable with new technologies. Thus, we are surprised when students have trouble navigating and discussing blogs and wikis. Part of the problem is often the educational context, but it can also come from how genre and medium influence audience.

In many educational contexts, the texts assigned to students have neither invoked nor addressed them; the responsibility is ours to help students make sense of that audience gap. With traditional print reading, that gap usually involves specialized vocabulary and references—or "jargon," as students put it. Audience difficulties can multiply with digital texts. In a digital media class that focused on literacy, students read scholarly print articles with relative ease. However, they had trouble reading literacy blogs, which conflicted with their expectations of blogs and scholarly arguments. With a blog, students expected brevity, opinion, and informality; on the scholarship side, they wanted the traditional discourse moves. Instead, they found a strange combination of those expectations, stumbling through blog posts that alternated between personal and the scholarly; that linked short posts together to (nearly) complete the argument; that included links to other bloggers' arguments and a larger perspective than they had anticipated. I expected the blog reading to be easier, but I spent more time helping students read them. When we regard reading as less of a complicated act than writing, as something students should have already learned, we cut off a vital part of how we can help them become more thoughtful, audience-aware readers and writers.

In making this defense of how students read, I do not intend to fully absolve students from these complications. Students regularly admit to shirking assignments, and they regularly admit to spending too much time on Facebook. To help explain this and to understand our students better, we should look at the literacy "mindsets" mentioned by Lunsford and Ede via Colin Lankshear and Michele Knobel. The audience roles students seek out are certainly affected by growing up and spending years interacting with new media. As a result, students may have "very different kinds of values and priorities and sensibilities than the literacies we are familiar with" (Lankshear and Knobel, "Sampling" 7). New media literacies contribute to a "cyberspatial-postindustrial mindset" that sees knowledge and information in terms of participation, collaboration, and distribution, as opposed to the "physical-industrial mindset," which values authors, experts, and a traditional sense of ownership (9–11). To put these mindsets into more concrete terms, the collective intelligence of wikis and blogs is contrasted with the traditional book written by an expert author.

The former is more likely to be valued by the "cyberspatial-postindustrial mindset" in large part because of how it offers "relatedness through participation" (Lankshear and Knobel, "Sampling" 13). Michael Schrage observes that the Internet is more accurately a "relationship revolution"; to depict the Internet as a web of information "is a bit like saying that 'cooking' is about oven temperatures, it's technically accurate but fundamentally untrue" (qtd. in Lankshear and Knobel, "Sampling" 12). Much of the technology students have grown up with has been aimed at not just communicating, but *connecting* with others. Students may value wikis, blogs, Facebook, text messages, and YouTube more than traditional forms of reading because of how they get to connect to other people, alternating as authors and audiences. In that oscillation, they become audiences not merely responding privately to an author's words, but audiences who are able to respond textually and visually to others. They are audiences who not only seek out authors and spaces who have addressed them, but they also change those spaces and have some measure of control over how they are addressed. For instance, Tim tended to skim video game magazines, but he more actively read gaming blogs because of the potential dialogue. As Tim said, "The magazines are good for quick skimming, looking for certain info or whatever. But I like the blogs better. They're informative, too, but I spend longer on them because I want to figure out what to say." With magazines, he read for information; with blogs, he often read as a potential writer.

As much as this may help us understand why students are drawn to certain texts and media, we should not depict this attraction to "relatedness" as limited to the young. Having an "insider" audience status has spread through much of our culture. We pay extra money for the special features on DVDs that take us behind the scenes. The Thursday Next series of novels—aimed at a well-read audience—included an Internet address to access "deleted scenes" and "bloopers" from the books. Many people follow the "viral marketing" campaigns of TV shows and movies, some of which are participatory games; read, listen, and respond to the podcasts and weblogs from musicians, writers, actors; write fan fiction of their favorite novels; and remix songs by musicians. Clearly, many of us have become accustomed to this level of audience participation.

While the "cyberspatial-postindustrial" and the "physical-industrial" mindsets are a useful binary, we should not privilege one over the other or see them as absolute, rigid categories. Nor should we see such binaries as a progress narrative—or an apocalyptic one—in which the "cyberspatial" will completely replace the "physical." Because of the wealth and overload of information, we still need the "physical-industrial" mindset, with individuals and institutions that have the time and expertise to provide accurate information. While some bloggers break news stories and even correct professional news organizations, people still tend to respect and seek the knowledge of experts and professional journalists. Indeed, as a lurker on various Internet forums over the past decade, I've seen people cite Wikipedia and shady websites without much critical reflection, but I've also seen a surprising number of teenagers disparage the use of Wikipedia and blogs as worthy sources in debates; even as these teenagers criticize an element of the "cyberspatial mindset," they are clearly embracing the sharing and distributing of knowledge.

Shaking free of some of the misperceptions about how students approach reading and new media is required before exploring issues of audience with them in a respectful, effective manner. In this section, I pointed to the complexity of reading and the factors influencing how students choose audience roles. In the next section, I point to the conflicts that can arise from students' multiple audience roles and previous reading experiences with various genres and media.

Convergence and Conflict: Genres, Media, and Prior Knowledge

At the end of their latest essay, Lunsford and Ede, with a nod to Cindy Selfe, recommend that we "help our students to learn to conceive and produce a repertoire of texts" ("Among" 59). When they later describe how students at Stanford translate a "research-based argument" into "various genres and media" (59), it sounds similar to Kathleen Blake Yancey's call for teaching the "circulation of texts"; in this paradigm, we should teach writing as a technology, emphasizing how texts change (for different genres, media, audiences) and how delivery affects other rhetorical elements such as invention, style, and arrangement. Thankfully, the authors recognize the difficulties involved with such a curriculum and state that they cannot "draw absolute conclusions about what writing teachers should do in this age of new literacies" (60). Part of this curriculum's difficulty stems from the multiple, interdependent factors involved with how texts function; rules of thumb are hard to establish when rhetorical situations insist on being unique. In traditional classrooms, creating a sense of audience for written essays that end up being read only by the teacher is difficult enough. The bar is raised even higher when creating texts that mix various genres and media, trying to determine how they work rhetorically, generically, and technically.

We can decrease the difficulty of such a task by having students read for audience in sophisticated and flexible ways. If we ask students to compose an essay and then transfer that essay to a wiki or a blog, we need to help students read those different genres and media, studying not only how blogs and wikis and essays function as texts, but how they function as social practices as well (Devitt). That is no small task. The emphasis on social practice is important because of how we can take multiple audience positions—often contradictory—with the same text. For instance, a student's political and religious roles may conflict with how she is expected to perform in a classroom when responding to a controversial text. Beyond issues of content and controversy, the mere performative aspect of the student's role changes reading drastically. Reading a blog in school will be a different literacy event from reading that blog at home, and students will bring different strategies and purposes and beliefs to those different events. They become different audiences.

Literacy and genre theorists have emphasized the importance of roles people play in reading and writing:

> Part of what all readers and writers recognize when they recognize genres are the roles they are to play, the roles being played by other people, what they can gain from the discourse,

and what the discourses are about. Picking up a text, readers not only classify it and expect a certain form, but also make assumptions about the text's purposes, its subject matter, its writer, and its expected reader. (Devitt 12)

How students conceive of the "expected reader" is connected to—among other things—their previous reading experiences. How were they addressed before, or rejected, or ignored? What was the social context? How did genre and medium affect their audience role? Statements by literacy and media theorists about the cultural ecology of texts have been underscored by genre theory (Devitt), schema theory (McCormick), and rhetorical theory (Brent): we only make sense of a genre or of a particular reading when we place it in comparison to other genres and readings, by recognizing what something is and what it is not. That is, people draw on their previous reading experiences and their previous audience roles to make sense of current situations. As readers encounter texts in different contexts, the relationship between audience and text changes.

We can see some of this play out in an example from a class I taught on "Reading Popular Culture." At the beginning of the satire and irony section of the course, I handed out an article from *The Onion*, a satirical news website that reproduces the news genre beautifully. Without knowing its source, they read "Freshman Term Paper Discovers Something Totally New About *Silas Marner*" as a straight piece of news. Many students expressed surprise that a freshman had managed to find something—an obvious piece of symbolism—that had eluded scholars. The many humorous cues in the piece eluded students until I pointed them out. The point is not that my students should have gotten it, but that the role they played in that reading situation was unfamiliar. No prior reading experience prepared them for an ironic text in the classroom, and they did not expect to discuss humor with their teacher in the classroom. When they recognized the news genre—the dull, objective tone that signals something real—they adopted the expected audience response. The medium was also a factor: when teachers hand out paper, the goal is usually a studious, serious undertaking. If a student were to come across the same article on the website, with an adult sitting next to her in an Internet café rather than standing over her in a classroom, then the roles involved would change drastically.

Genre, medium, prior knowledge, and the social context contributed to my audience taking on a particular role and response to the text. To illustrate the point further, I draw on my work and the work of Ellen Evans and Jeanne Po; these studies involve reading, the issue of audience expectations, and how those expectations were shaped by previous experiences with various genres and media. These examples should give us different ways in which to think about some of the obstacles preventing students from adopting productive roles.

When the students in my study made the transition from high school to college, their reading experiences had not prepared them for college expectations. David, for instance, had conflicting ideas about his role in his English class. Although the teacher gave students resources for analyzing ads and websites, David struggled with the assignments because of his own experiences with such texts. The analytical resources helped him read ads and websites in a technical way, but they ignored other contexts that influenced David as a reader. When I asked David about these assignments, he talked about how the assignments made him adopt a critical, almost negative stance in his writing. David said, "I understand how the ads should be criticized, but I also like parts of them. I didn't know how to say that, or if I could say that. I ended up writing about things that went against my main point." He took pleasure in ads outside of class, and he had trouble thinking about websites in limited, technical ways. David's website analysis slipped into how websites copied other sites' designs and how their links were significant—things he regularly paid attention to as he visited sites, but were irrelevant to the assignment. As a reader with conflicting roles, he could not become the right audience. As a result, his analysis and his writing went off topic and seemed contradictory.

Diana struggled in a different way in her history class. An above-average student and a confident writer, she placed out of English but could not figure out what her history teacher wanted in the essay assignment. Her previous experiences with history textbooks had been easy because reading for tests was, as she said, "nearly an innate skill." The essay asked her to critically examine two historical moments and to make connections between them. Not satisfied with the textbook's assistance, she turned to the Internet, even though her teacher discouraged online research. She felt more comfortable tracing ideas across websites that were more interactive than the history textbook. Along with the help of a friend on an Instant Messenger program, she found seven websites and forums that discussed the historical moments, and some of them disagreed with each other and the textbook. She didn't know what to make of these discrepancies: "Shouldn't history be more fact and less ambiguity?" Frustrated, she abandoned the Internet, turned back to the textbook, and wrote the essay, "winging it the whole way. It was awful."

In this situation, Diana's school-endorsed literacy—reading the textbook—was being supplemented and complicated by the non-endorsed reading of various websites: university webpages on history, history forum threads, and historian bloggers. She pieced together information from various sources, getting help from her friend and wrestling with epistemological issues she didn't know could exist. Diana's employment of the distribution of knowledge and collective intelligence reflects the "cyberspatial-postindustrial" mindset to a degree. However, the opposing mindsets, the different relationship to the text, and her uncertain role in the class prevented this moment—rich with learning potential—from going anywhere. With an assignment that matched the learning task she had set for herself, Diana could have advanced her understanding of history, of how knowledge is constructed, and how historians write differently for different audiences.

David struggled with a different audience role for familiar texts; Diana felt limited by her situation and tried to incorporate digital texts. Evans and Po's students are in a different situation, feeling frustrated by digital reading that they want to be more like traditional reading. As Evans and Po state, because students are surrounded with digital texts, "they are attributed with a willingness to embrace new electronically based forms of reading and writing, something they have been accustomed to in lives circumscribed by technology"; however, digital texts in the classroom "elicited a surprising amount of frustration and anxiety from our students" (57). Their study complicates some of the assumptions we make about students as users of digital media.

Evans and Po examined students' reactions to reading hyper-text fiction, which created significant obstacles in terms of genre and medium. The authors explain some of the significant changes of reading on a screen: "We lose the visual cues—the length of a page, the boundaries, even the ability to flip the page over—that enable us to get a sense of what we are reading." We also lose "indentations, margins, and page numbers to help us figure out where we are on a page" (58). The combination of the medium and the genre posed problems for expected narrative conventions: hypertext fiction often prevents readers from predicting where the story will go, from picking up important cues and story elements, and from having a sense of closure. The students expected and felt frustrated by the absence of these print text conventions.

In addition, the students associated certain behaviors with reading fiction that were different from reading on a computer, and they felt frustrated by the combination of the two. Even though the students felt comfortable with technology, their regular behaviors with the computer were at odds with their regular behaviors of reading a fictional narrative. When students approached reading fiction on a screen, they wanted the experiences they associated with reading fictional narratives: curling up with a book, flipping through pages, being relaxed (62). Reading a narrative on the screen was too drastic a change. The reading they associated with the computer—reading for information and communication—was at odds with the aesthetic reading expected from the hypertext fiction (63).

Although Evans and Po provide a valid, convincing explanation of the students' experience through Louise Rosenblatt's transactional theory, I want to emphasize the importance of medium and genre in the conditioning of students' reading behaviors. The previous reading experiences the students had with a particular genre created an expectation not just of how the genre should later function, but in what form the genre would be delivered; also the reading behaviors they associated with the computer and the Internet conditioned the genres and the audience positions they expected to encounter. In many ways, they took on audience positions they found uncomfortable. As Evans and Po suggest, this should make us reconsider how quickly and easily we attach comfort and mastery of digital texts to students; they also note how we have to make more of a pedagogical effort in these situations. This study should also make us pay more attention to how genre, medium, and prior reading experiences work together on students as audiences.

Putting It into Practice

Throughout this chapter, I've argued that reading pedagogy is an integral part of teaching audience. We expect students to be able to shift freely and easily between genres and media because they seem at ease with such moves in their daily lives. However, such shifts become more difficult in educational contexts. As we sometimes overestimate students' expertise with new media, we underestimate how much assistance they need with reading different genres and media. We need to help students foster an awareness of how audience functions in various genres and media, particularly when they relate to reading and writing situations in school. As we bring different genres and media into class, we should ask students to discuss and write about their experiences outside of school. How do they read these different texts? What expectations do they have? What do they think will be different about reading these texts in school? Student need to engage in reading as a metacognitive act, being aware and in control of what they are doing as they read. Some of the following activities will address this metacognition as they address the topic of audience.

Flexible Reading

In his examination of media convergence, Jenkins characterizes the literacy practices associated with new media as playful and experimental. That playfulness should also characterize exercises aimed at helping students with audience awareness. When reading any kind of text—an essay, a blog, a wiki, a personal or institutional webpage—have students imagine alternatives regarding the layout (font, space, color); the choice of images and words; genre and medium; and any other feature that could affect how audiences are addressed. How might a different image—and be specific—invoke a different audience? What if certain words were replaced to make the tone harsher or softer? How would that affect the addressed audience? The very act of slowing down to pay attention to such features is likely to not only improve general comprehension, but also help students see the myriad factors that invoke various audiences. This low-stakes exercise also has been successful for class participation because of how its playfulness mitigates against fears of "dumb answers."

Taking the previous exercise to the next step involves reimagining and repurposing a text for a different audience. This can be a brief in-class assignment, a group effort, or an extended essay/digital text. In doing this, the students must first identify some possible invoked and addressed audiences by observing specific features and being able to articulate how they affect audience. Next, they have to attempt a consistent refashioning of the text so that it works for a different set of audiences. How would it be different for a nonacademic audience? How would it change for a more formal audience? The point of this exercise is not to create a perfect product but to test how audience can function. When I've assigned something like this, students attached a brief cover letter explaining their choices.

Reading Audience in Images

A more focused look at the influence of visuals is worthwhile as images and video continue to spread as significant parts of communication. Despite the prominence of images, they tend to be invisible; they add color to websites, magazine covers, and TV news, but viewers rarely stop to examine how those images affect them and their relationship to the text. Given how images can frame a news story, represent an event, and contribute to a MySpace/Facebook identity (Stephens; Williams), students should not have a hard time understanding their importance and power. Using Photoshop, simple paint programs, and web editing tools, students can experiment with audience through visuals.

One way to do this is to have students select a website—a university or governmental webpage, MySpace profile, a news site, etc.—and read it carefully for how the images interact with the text. Because images tend to be what our eyes are drawn to, students should record their initial thoughts as the audience of the images: How do they create a sense of purpose and tone or tell a story? How do specific elements of the images create these effects? Then students should look at the text and its relationship to the images, which should give them a clearer sense of the intentions behind the visuals. How are these images designed to affect audiences? Students can then find images that present a slightly different message or a wildly different one. By saving the webpage and editing it, students can test the results of their changes with other students. For instance, one group of students edited a university webpage to include different versions of student and teacher diversity through the images; other students then read the edited page, recorded their reactions, and discussed how various audiences might respond to the changes. As Ede and Lunsford stated in "AA/AI," audience is "an overdetermined or unusually rich concept, one which may perhaps be best specified through the analysis of precise, concrete situations" (168). With these exercises, students cannot pin down "audience" in any definite way, but they gain a lot of experience thinking about audience in critical and creative ways.

Conclusion

Teaching audience to students is an important but difficult goal. A prominent obstacle is how often we misunderstand or negatively characterize the choices students make as audiences. These misunderstandings can lead to pedagogical decisions that ignore their complex reading lives. As we incorporate new media into our teaching, we will need more studies of how students approach various genres and media in their reading and writing. In line with the participatory nature of new media, we should develop reading pedagogies that can help students see texts as mutable objects, taking them apart to see how they work and changing them to see the effects of those changes. Embracing some of the values of new literacy mindsets and making connections with traditional reading could help students like David, Tim, and Diana find more productive roles in the classroom.

Notes

1. David and the other case study participants have been given pseud-onyms. During the final months of high school and their first semester of college, I interviewed nine students about and observed their reading practices with various media at home and at school; I was primarily interested in how students' in- and out-of-school literacy practices conflicted and converged. The students' family members and teachers enriched my interpretations of the interviews and observations. The study was approved by the IRB.

2. Many composition textbooks include sections on reading strategies; the Council of Writing Program Administrators includes "critical read-ing" in its Outcomes Statement for First-Year Composition. However, reading theory/pedagogy has been largely absent in composition's major journals, books on composition pedagogy, and the Conference on Col-lege Composition and Communication. I see little evidence that reading pedagogy is a vital part of composition theory and practice.

Works Cited

Bauerlein, Mark. *The Dumbest Generation: How the Digital Age Stupe-fies Young Americans and Jeopardizes Our Future (Or, Don't Trust Anyone Under 30).* Penguin: New York, 2008.

Birkerts, Sven. *Gutenberg Elegies: The Fate of Reading in an Electronic Age.* New York: Fawcett Columbine, 1994.

Brent, Doug. *Reading as Rhetorical Invention: Knowledge, Persuasion, and the Teaching of Research-Based Writing.* Urbana, IL: NCTE. 1992.

Devitt, Amy. *Writing Genres.* Carbondale, IL: Southern Illinois UP, 2004.

Ede, Lisa, and Andrea Lunsford. "Audience Addressed/Audience Invoked: The Role of Audience in Composition Theory and Peda-gogy." *CCC* 35 (1984): 155–171.

Edmundson, Mark. *Why Read?* New York: Bloomsbury Publishing, 2004.

"Freshman Term Paper Discovers Something Totally New About *Silas Marner*." *The Onion.* 23 Sept.1997. 15 Feb. 2007 <http://www.theonion.com/content/node/39205>.

Helmers, Marguerite. "Introduction: Representing Reading." *Intertexts: Reading Pedagogy in College Writing Classrooms*. Ed. Marguerite Helmers. Mahwah, NJ: Lawrence Erlbaum, 2003. 3–26.

Jenkins, Henry. *Convergence Culture: Where Old and New Media Collide*. New York: New York UP, 2006.

Lanham, Richard. *The Economics of Attention: Style and Substance in the Age of Information*. Chicago: U of Chicago P, 2006.

Lankshear, Colin, and Michele Knobel. *New Literacies: Changing Knowledge and Classroom Learning*. Buckingham, UK: Open UP, 2003.

———. "Sampling 'the New' in New Literacies." *A New Literacies Sampler*. Ed. Michele Knobel and Colin Lankshear. New York: Peter Lang, 2007. 1–24.

Lunsford, Andrea A., and Lisa Ede. "Among the Audience: On Audience in an Age of New Literacies." *Engaging Audience: Writing in an Age of New Literacies*. Ed. Elizabeth Weiser, Brian Fehler, and Angela González. Urbana, IL: NCTE, 2009. 42–69.

National Endowment for the Arts. "To Read or Not To Read: A Question of National Consequence." 19 Nov. 2007. 10 Feb. 2008 <http://www.nea.gov/research/ToRead.pdf>.

Reiff, Mary Jo. "Rereading Invoked and Addressed Readers through a Social Lens: Toward a Recognition of Multiple Audiences." *JAC* 16.3 (1997): 407–424.

Roberts, Donald, and Ulla Foehr. *Kids & Media in America*. Cambridge, UK: Cambridge UP, 2004.

Salvatori, Mariolina. "Conversations with Texts: Reading in the Teaching of Composition." *College English* 58 (1996): 440–454.

Stephens, Mitchell. *The Rise of the Image, the Fall of the Word*. Oxford, UK: Oxford UP, 1998.

Williams, Bronwyn. "'What South Park Character Are You?': Popular Culture, Literacy, and Online Performances of Identity." *Computers and Composition* 25.1 (2008): 24–39.

Yancey, Kathleen Blake. "Made Not Only in Words: Composition in a New Key." *CCC* 56.2 (2004): 297–328.

CHAPTER SIXTEEN

Writing Assessment as New Literacy

LEE NICKOSON-MASSEY
Bowling Green State University

Lisa Ede and Andrea Lunsford's influential 1984 article "Audience Addressed/Audience Invoked" remains the touchstone for audience-oriented theorists and practitioners. It is difficult for compositionists to conceive of writing and, by extension, writing pedagogy, as something removed from a sustained inquiry into audience. Arguments for service learning and many other pedagogies of engagement in the composition classroom, for example, are understood as efforts largely grounded in attempts to create for students the kinds of complex audiences Ede and Lunsford identify. The influence of AA/AI is present in nearly all work on composing on a sort of subterranean level—it has become so deeply ingrained that it is simply a part of an implicitly shared knowledge of how we conceive of audience.

Naturally, however, scholarship on audience has not stood still in the last twenty-five years. Lunsford and Ede themselves, revisiting their work twelve years after AA/AI and now again two and one-half decades later, have revisited many of their original insights in new ways, reflecting changes in how we understand the writing process and, of course, in the writing technologies that are now a part of our students' and our own classrooms and lives. Such is the case with similarly influential early work on teacher response. Also published in the early 1980s, Lil Brannon and C. H. Knoblauch's "On Students' Right to Their Own Texts" (1982) and Nancy Sommers's "Responding to Student Writing" (1982) quickly became guidelines for how we conceived of instructor response commentary, benchmarks that remain at the center of composition and writing assessment scholarship today. And, while changes in how we theorize and understand audience and writing assessment have not occurred in a vacuum, they have, perhaps inevitably, run parallel to each other and to those of other subfields of rhetoric and composition that with more direct crossover will continue to enrich our understanding of audience even further. In particular, contemporary conversations in writing assessment attend to the deeply rhetorical, theoretically sophisticated, and context-dependent nature of composing—of writing, reading, and responding.[1]

In this chapter, then, I propose that a deeper understanding of the issues we face both when we assess others' writing as well as when we teach others to become astute readers and assessors of writing can enrich our understanding of audience in important ways. Namely, to assess writing is to be an active, engaged, and inquisitive audience for someone else, and even for oneself. And, by extension, to *teach* assessment—to focus on its terminologies, problematics, and possibilities—in our writing classes is to teach audience *not* as a disembodied other, or even as a concrete, embodied other, but as a community in which one is oneself a participant. Such an approach encourages us to become co-investigators with our students in extended examinations of the fluid dynamism of rhetorical situations, of reading and writing (and, I'd add, responding) as interconnected acts that Ede and Lunsford first espouse in AA/AI. As a way to illustrate my point, I turn to a discussion of a situated, classroom-based study of a composition pedagogy in which writing assessment was treated as an integral component of instruction in the development of writing.

My Study

I served as the teacher/researcher for a classroom-based study of a second-semester writing class at a large Midwestern university with the goal of investigating student and teacher experiences with a composition pedagogy that featured explicit, sustained attention to writing assessment.[2] I examined what happened when I practiced a social, feminist, and process-based pedagogy that included studying the vocabulary and practices of writing assessment as an integral and explicit component of process-based writing pedagogy.

I began our initial class meeting by asking students to reflect on and openly discuss their working definitions of "good" writing, writing key terms and ideas on the board: "it has to flow;" "good writing includes supporting details." Such statements were common. Not long into the brainstorming session, students began to comment that, though they may use the same terms—terms like "flow," "support," and "detail"—to talk about writing, they often used them in different ways and to signify different things. A result of our early conversation was that the students became aware of the assumptions they shared—and those they did not—about academic writing. This reflective attitude about response and assessment, moreover, carried over into every other aspect of the class. In short, we made response—self, peer, and instructor—our shared language. In addition to discussions about our understandings of what constitutes good writing, which we revisited throughout the semester (and which revealed students' progressively more sophisticated understandings about response and assessment), we included attention—written and verbal—to discussions of writerly/readerly expectations in each class meeting through various informal and formal activities. These activities included developing guiding questions for informal peer work with sample published pieces of writing; drafting informal writers' memos used to introduce drafts to peer and instructor readers; discussing student assessments (and student self-assessments) of peer, self, and instructor responses; discussing my strategies and methods for response; and hearing from guest speakers (the director and the assistant director of the writing program and other instructors of the same course) about their approaches to writing, reading, and responding. All of these activities led to a formal, collaborative assessment of peer portfolios.

I was careful to structure every class meeting to include some form of group work, most often including some example of peer response in order to promote writing as a socially bound, reflective practice. Group work served an important additional function as well by providing us regular opportunities to both collaboratively develop and simultaneously problematize our class-based assessment lexicon. The data indicate that the students found the sustained, collaborative, and public process of developing expertise with the strategies and vocabulary necessary to effectively function as careful readers of others' texts and authors of constructive, generative response commentary the most challenging component of the class. One student described her experience as "daunting:" "I knew it was important work, and I wanted to write comments that were really helpful and honest. Responding to writing is hard work!" What the students and I discovered together over the course of the semester was that developing an expertise as successful, rhetorically effective respondents (and eventually assessors) of each others' work is at least as challenging as generating strong drafts.[3]

The students grew accustomed to working together in groups of two or three as they were regularly challenged to question, complicate, articulate, and ultimately make public to the class positions on the many topics addressed throughout the course of the fifteen-week semester. Regular participation in a small group of two or three of their peers promoted a sense of community among the students, and many of them later described these groups in anonymous surveys and course evaluations as establishing a much-welcomed sense of familiarity and trust that the other members respected what they had to say. The commonly held understanding students came to hold of peer response work was that it was "all about helping each other out." Peer response groups established an immediacy of audience that, as the semester progressed, was complemented by a sense of familiarity, safety, even intimacy—and trust. At the same time, the basis of this familiarity was a shared and increasingly complex sense of both the purpose of responding and the ways to approach response work effectively. In other words, the students became more comfortable with themselves and with each other as writers/readers and as responders of multiple texts, even as the whole of the class moved closer to developing a site-specific lexicon of response. Mike, a soft-spoken junior majoring in industrial technology, described his experiences with response in the class:

> I think the peer response we're getting is suggestive. You know,
> they help you out. I think the more people you give [the draft] to

the more you get, too, so that's helped me quite a bit. It seems like when we go to do our peer response it gets really quiet really quickly. Everybody just goes and gets started reading and then really, really trying to help each other out with their comments and suggestions, which is good.

Like many of his peers, Mike previously had reported finding peer response unhelpful, adding that, though he was sure it was important, he "really wasn't sure how to do it" and so it was "kind of a waste of time." Like most of his classmates, Mike couldn't recall ever receiving explicit instruction on peer response.

The comments students supplied on an in-class survey I distributed the first day of class provided some surprising and instructive insights into how the students identified themselves as writers, as audiences for response commentary, and as recipients of formal assessments of their writing. Interestingly, fewer than half (seven of the seventeen students) reported having a clear understanding of the function of instructor commentary, some describing it as a narrative version of a letter grade, others suggesting teacher response comments were to demonstrate an ideal text against which the student draft was read. Fewer still—four students— reported identifying a relationship between peer response and instructor commentary. Comments that Carl, a second-semester senior leisure studies major, shared during a midterm interview suggest a link between students' perceptions of their ability to effectively engage and translate response commentary in future attempts at writing and their perceptions of their skills at producing effective response commentary themselves. He observes, "Not too many people can break down a paper and say, move this here and move this there. They just read the paper and say, 'um, intro was a little short,' 'I think you need a comma there,' 'add a little more here,' and 'your conclusion looks good.'" Carl's comments speak to an absence of agency. Reading and responding to others' written work are complex rhetorical and intellectual tasks that he views as extremely difficult for most students to even engage, let alone develop. Carl's final remarks on response are insightful, provocative, and commonsensical: "Maybe you don't get too much information from peer critiques for the simple reason that we don't really know what we are looking for." In order to effectively engage in response (i.e., perform as readers and writers of assessments who are confident in their understanding of response as a complex rhetorical moment), then, students must be provided with careful, explicit instruction in writing assessment as the language, too, of response. This instruction can take many forms.

When viewed in conjunction with the class's earlier discussions of student experience with peer and teacher response, this attention to the terminology commonly used to communicate such evaluations and experiences brings into focus the full range of audiences as Ede and Lunsford conceive of them in AA/AI: "audience refers not just to the intended, actual, or eventual readers of a discourse—but to *all* whose image, ideas, or actions influence a writer during the process of composition" (168). In any given previous peer response experience, the exigencies of the present moment (drafting *this* paper for *this* class) and the perceived exigencies of some future moment of academic or professional writing (delivering a professional report to a senior colleague) coalesce into the complex unity of audience addressed and invoked. But it is not only in the blur of inhabiting the spaces between audiences real and imagined, but also in the manner in which the roles of writer and respondent inform each other that we find the complexities of author and audience as Lunsford and Ede describe in "Among the Audience." The reciprocal nature of the relationship between writer and reader is evident in such moments as when a second-year business major, who is himself drafting an argument on the effects of the current national economic environment on local small businesses, simultaneously plays the role of active reader as he begins the first lines of his peer's draft for the same assignment, positioning himself as a fellow student of psychology. Writer and respondent are joined in a common cause—identifying and enacting strategies for producing an effective written argument.

One of the most immediate and powerful insights I gleaned from the study was that I could not fully appreciate student experiences with writing assessment, and with the challenges of developing the analytical skills of writing and reading in academic settings, without also attending to their experiences with and subsequent perceptions of peer response activities. It was in the context of peer response activities that they most commonly—and most visibly—used the language of assessment. Moreover, when responding to and receiving responses from their peers, students are able to experience the immediacy and the reality of "audience" in ways not possible even when writing for teachers, whom they may know well but who likely take essays home, read them on their own time, and return them (in most cases) with written commentary but little or no face-to-face discussion. It is in those moments, then, when students read *and evaluate* comments made in response to their work—as well as the response commentary they draft through peer (and self-assessment) commentary—that they practice the kind of sophisticated theory of audience Ede and Lunsford describe in AA/AI:

> The addressed audience, the actual or intended readers of a discourse, exists outside of the text. Writers may analyze these readers' needs, anticipate their biases, even defer to their wishes. But it is only through the text, through language, that writers embody or give life to their conception of the reader. In so doing, they do not so much create a role for the reader—a phrase which implies that the writer somehow creates a mold to which the reader adapts—as to invoke it. Rather than relying on incantations, however, writers conjure their vision—a vision which they hope readers will actively come to share as they read the text—by using all the resources of language available to them to establish a broad, and ideally coherent, range of cues for the reader. (169)

As I prepared to teach the class represented here, I imagined that the students would grow comfortable in the role of respondent and envisioned them becoming such capable assessors of academic writing that they would be able and willing to participate in the actual grading of each other's writing at the end of the semester. The data gathered that semester demonstrate that the students were indeed capable of producing extended, nuanced assessments of writing. By the twelfth week of class, during which students submitted their fourth essay project with all earlier drafts on which their peers had provided commentary attached, nearly every one of the seventeen students produced rhetorically persuasive responses to their peers' drafts, in many cases expertly wielding the language of writing assessment to formulate both formative commentary and authoritative, summative evaluations of others' writing. But they resisted strongly assuming any responsibility for one another's portfolio grades. Though they had graded each other's work, they were extremely resistant to those grades determining any portion of their peers' grades for the course. In what I refer to as the "revolt," the students collectively, through numerous well-reasoned and well-articulated statements of rationale, refused to assign a grade to each other's writing. Instead, they just as persuasively argued for an alternative approach in which they'd submit the collaborative assessment narratives each assessment triad had produced in response to three peer writing portfolios. In short, they called on me to assess their assessments of each other's writing, which I agreed to do. This turn of events is startling in the clarity of its implications: the students' refusal to assume any responsibility for other students' portfolio grades serves as a powerful reminder that, no matter how much one might try to displace traditional notions of institutional power, a writing classroom that operates within the current prevailing university structure can never be truly decentered.

Similarly, irrespective of how formative we make our comments on students' writing, they will still carry the full weight of institutional authority, which can be neither abdicated nor even, it seems, shared, though writing assessment—the language that represents institutional authority in the space of the writing classroom—can function as a meaningful form of communicating and making knowledge. I found I could not dismiss the institutional, power-laden connotations of the word *assessment* in a class that I strove to recast as student-centered and democratic, if for no other reason than because my students will not, or cannot, let it go. It was naïve of me to think that a one-semester composition course could somehow relocate or displace years of student history with instructor response and assessment.

Introducing response and assessment as meaningful activities, I learned, requires sustained inquiry into the complexities of audience as "dynamic and fluid," as Ede and Lunsford describe it. This inquiry situates the writer's peers as an immediate, but not the ultimate, audience for several of the assigned writing projects, in this case a series of essays drafted for others who share the writer's particular academic and career interests. My students taught me that they must first understand audience as a social, context-dependent rhetorical concept before they can be expected to appropriate any meaningful vocabulary of assessment. Students self-identified as members of a shared academic experience—as fellow (student) writers and readers of academic arguments *who were aware that they were each also in the process of learning expectations of field-specific audiences and conventions just as they were learning those of our particular writing class.* The same can be said of the demands placed on the students not as writers but as respondents: they were challenged to read as an immediate (or addressed) audience when asked to provide peer response commentary while at the same time they faced the challenge of imagining themselves as members of a discipline-specific discourse community to which they did not belong (an audience invoked).

Roles and Responsibilities

Lunsford and Ede write and compellingly model in each of their essays on audience the need for us to remain vigilant about the responsibilities involved in any rhetorical moment. Perhaps the most significant insight I took from the study, then, was the important distinction students made between the roles of student- and teacher-respondent. It is not the activity of assessing writing itself that proved untenable for the students. Response and assessment can be meaningful, thought-provoking student activities or they can be instructor activities. However, because of institutional power structures, a student's self- or peer-response comments—in essence her assessments of her own work or that of her peers'—can never "equal" that of the instructor.

Interestingly, it is also possible to make this point from the opposite direction: just as assessment that looks like formative response still carries the air of institutional authority, peer response that does not carry the weight of official expertise and authority nevertheless involves complex acts of evaluation (both by the responder and, with regard to the comments, by the person being responded to). All seven of the students who volunteered for midterm interviews in my study, for example, described the peer response commentary they themselves drafted as "assessment."

For example, Susan sees her peers' comments as assessing her writing at the same time that she assesses the relative helpfulness of those comments:

> The peer comments I get back are usually really helpful. I can always count on getting advice on how to rewrite my conclusions. . . . My peer critiques usually say the same thing: "this is the weakest paragraph of the paper, you should spend time getting the reader to see your overall argument," or "you want readers to leave your paper knowing why you wanted them to consider your argument."

Here we find Susan assessing the ability of the response comments she has received to effectively support her effort to improve the draft. But these comments also have a distinctly summative, evaluative character—"this is the weakest paragraph of the paper"—even as they are designed to be generative, to facilitate effective revision. Susan assesses her peers' comments, just as she sees their responses as assessments of her work. Read this way, assessment becomes a dynamic that is, as Huot tells us, inherent in acts of reading and response. The concept of assessment as intricately connected to response, as reflected in Susan's and her peers' comments, goes against our traditional understandings of assessment as monologic and final.

In this respect, assessment and response are, at their best, collaborative and mutually informing acts that grow from context-specific understandings of writing, response, and assessment as complex rhetorical acts. Any assessment of student writing ideally resembles formative response rather than summative evaluation, and response practices ostensibly involve assessment of the given text. Writing assessment thus becomes the most important and visible point of contact between writers, readers, and institutional discourses. Far from being the sole province of the teacher, the vocabulary of assessment actually forms the basic language, or conduit, we ask students to access when we assign any task involving response.

Understood in this way, response commentary becomes a second form of academic literacy that students functioning as peer respondents are challenged to take on, another discourse they are asked to master. As authors of the writing projects we assign them, students practice developing written arguments appropriate to specific academic communities, and as authors of response comments, students practice developing written forms appropriate to those situations and those communities. Just as it is important to "establish a broad, and ideally coherent, range of cues for the reader" ("AA/AI" 167) of an academic paper, so too is it important for them to establish such intersubjective rhetorical space with their reader based on common assumptions about what response comments are supposed to do and look like.

How do they establish that shared sense? In the same way they do when learning to write more conventional academic genres. Just as students have long been encouraged to read examples of what represents "good" writing before they begin the work of drafting what it is they have to say, so too do they look to exemplary texts when negotiating the rhetorical complexities of response commentary and assessment. What serves as a better—and more relevant and accessible to students—model of response than the instructor commentary we provide students in the margins and at the close of the drafts they submit to us?

Instructor response becomes all the more significant, then, when we consider that students look to our assessments of writing—to the content and the format of our responses—as the primary representation of target response commentary. In their article, ""Moving beyond the Written Comment: Narrowing the Gap between Response Practice and Research," Jane Mathison Fife and Peggy O'Neill argue that instructor response comments, whether formal or informal, written or oral, represent complex pedagogical practice; the questions and suggestions we craft in response to student writing are the result of our careful consideration of audience and purpose—what it is we believe students need to be made aware of and attend to in order to further develop their abilities as writers. We (believe we) know what is missing from the text, what needs to be there but isn't, or what is there and shouldn't be, and thus we design feedback that, when read (we hope), will (we hope) supply the student with the prompts needed for new insight and understanding into how best to communicate effectively within the rhetorical situation at hand. In doing so, however, we also provide models students may use as resources when developing their own literacy skills as readers of and responders to various forms of writing. They become in this way the audience they invoke, thereby closing the gap between themselves and the audience(s) for whom they write.

When we consider that our assessments may very often provide the script by which students practice the roles of academic writers and readers, we must ask ourselves if our response commentary—the assessments of writing we provide students—is as effective a teaching tool as it might be. If, as Richard Straub suggests, response comments are only as good as the thinking and response—and, now, the written response to others—they elicit, what do we, or might we, use our written assessments of student writing to communicate, to model? Recognizing that response comments amount to an expression of the reading norms of academic audiences, and calling on Ede and Lunsford's continued theorizing of audience as a rich, multifaceted and fluid rhetorical concept, it seems we are responsible for providing students with response comments that then model an understanding of that rhetorical complexity. By assigning comments specific to the particular student draft, we signal an interest in the argument—in the student and what she has to say. This in turn, as Sommers and others have recently argued, presents response as an invitation for the student to join a larger discussion in ways that she finds meaningful. In this respect, students would ideally conceive of the instructor as one of many readers, but someone who is genuinely interested in learning from the (student) writer rather than as someone whose responds by listing what she has "done wrong" (Sommers, "Across the Drafts" 255). Knoblauch and Brannon similarly revisit work in teacher response in a recent reflective piece that they frame as a discussion of the teacher-student relationship. They attend to writer and reader dynamics (teacher as author of commentary and student as reader of it) as well as the relationship between teacher as reader of drafts and student as author of those drafts. Knoblauch and Brannon remind us that response to student writing offers us "a chance to dramatize the presence of a reader whose needs and expectations can and should influence writing" (Introduction, "The Emperor" 15). In addition to addressing the student-as-writer directly, teacher response serves an additional function, representing revision as a student/writer-based activity, thus invoking a student reader who engages thoughtful assessment commentary and is invested in meaningful revision.[4]

Assessment and Audience

The subtitle of Lunsford and Ede's recent revisiting of AA/AI, "On Audience in an Age of New Literacies," signals the evolution of the discipline and, as a result, our work as compositionists. Much has changed over the last twenty-five years. The context is indeed much different. Early twenty-first-century notions of such key terms as *author*, *text*, *audience*, and *meaning* reflect a social and cultural paradigm that is in many ways quite distinct from that in which we operated several decades ago. Lunsford and Ede note that the emphasis is much less on the individual—the author, the text, the audience—and much more on the collaborative, "participatory," with an emphasis on meaning-making as socially mediated and specific to a particular context. In "Among the Audience," Lunsford and Ede attend to what, for the purposes of this discussion, is the most impactful of these developments; that it is not only *what* we write and teach but also *how* we make knowledge and in fact understand and interact with the world that provides us new dynamic sites of inquiry. Lunsford and Ede ground their discussion in exploring the theoretical and pedagogical implications of a continued migration from alphabetic to new literacies in order to explore the possibilities such a monumental shift might bring to how we understand and practice audience as a rhetorical concept:

> [W]e are particularly interested in the role that new literacies are playing in expanding the possibilities of agency, while at the same time challenging older notions of both authorship and audience. In addition, observations of and talks with students—as well as changes in our own reading, writing, and researching practices—have alerted us to new understandings and enactments of textual production and ownership. ("Among the Audience" 43)

As the preceding discussion suggests, writing assessment theory can function as one such new literacy. Explicit attention to writing assessment as a socially and contextually dependent literacy provides us the rhetorical scaffolding necessary to arrive at new understandings and practices such as Lunsford and Ede suggest. As such, writing assessment functions as a sort of participatory rhetoric—as a means of locating, analyzing, and communicating response to a given text. Careful, collaborative inquiry into context-specific vocabularies and methods of writing assessment can serve as a classroom literacy we engage in with our students in order to study not only acts of composing but also the attendant processes involved in reading and responding as rhetorical happenings.[5]

Lunsford and Ede powerfully advocate that compositionists place ourselves in the position of co-learner in order to explore the various meanings *audience* has (and might have) not only for students' writing but their lives as well. "Such explorations," they write, "might well begin with unpacking the problematics of viewing the teacher as the audience for student writing. . . . [T]he teacher remains *an* audience for student texts, but by no means the only audience" ("Among" 57). Understanding writing assessment as literacy provides a new form of inquiry for collaborative study of numerous complex rhetorical concepts, such as *audience* as experienced in particular, localized settings (like the composition classroom) and as experienced through the multiple roles we ask our students to inhabit in such spaces: readers, writers, and writers/readers.

How to teach students the skills and experiences needed to develop the literacies involved with various forms of classroom writing assessment practices has long remained at the center of our work as compositionists, even as we struggle to remain "current" ourselves. And how to best understand and use response commentary as a pedagogical tool remains the central focus of much work in writing assessment. Sonya C. Borton and Brian Huot issue a call for us to practice composition pedagogy and writing assessment as rhetorical acts even as we revise the scope of our instruction to include attention to multiple, new literacies. They write:

> The instructional process associated with *all* composing tasks, including multimodal projects, should be informed both broadly and deeply by a *rhetorical understanding of composition*. Within this context, all multimodal assignments, all instruction in the use of digital and nondigital composing tools, and all assessment of multimodal compositions, should be tailored to teaching students how to use rhetorical principles appropriately and effectively. Similarly, all multimodal composing tasks should be aimed at producing effective texts appropriate for a specific purpose and audience. ("Responding and Assessing" 99)

Borton and Huot's call for us to engage writing, and the assessment of writing, as rich rhetorical acts reflects nicely much of the recent writing assessment scholarship.[6] "Writers develop by being *read*." This first sentence of Chris Anson's article "Reflective Reading: Developing Thoughtful Ways to Respond to Students' Writing" (302) reflects the impact social theories of writing, teaching, and learning have. We've come to hold that writers and readers both develop by engaging in conversations about thoughtful, formative evaluations of all kinds of written texts. Viewed in the context of classroom practices, socially and context-based assessment efforts most often take some form of student self-assessment narratives and peer or group response commentary. Contemporary writing assessment theory thus positions assessment as dialogic and as a site of inquiry.[7] We've come to view classroom writing assessment as very much grounded in the belief that writers create readers and readers create writers in powerful ways, as Ede and Lunsford first claimed in AA/AI, and yet the newly created readers, writers, texts, and realities may go unexamined. If it is in an examination of the negotiation of writer, audience, medium, and context that new understanding is possible; and if we acknowledge the fluidity of the relationships between the various elements of the rhetorical situation as Lunsford and Ede depict it in "Among the Audience," a collaboratively theorized and practiced classroom writing assessment provides a language of writing, reading, and responding that makes examinations of such connections possible.

Conclusion

In "Among the Audience," Lunsford and Ede challenge writing teachers to attend to the responsibilities inherent in teaching composition in an age of new literacies, stating that it is "essential for teachers and students to consider the multiple reciprocal responsibilities entailed in writer-audience relationships" (62). While writing assessment is not a "new" literacy, it can be recast in new and exciting ways as an explicit site of inquiry and thus function as a powerful pedagogical tool. When conceived as a locally grown and situated language of response, writing assessment can, as my research indicates, provide an opportunity for students to explore with their teachers the many writerly and readerly expectations, motivations, and responsibilities that are involved in any act of written communication, especially when communication is understood as a socially and contextually based concept. Indeed, Lunsford and Ede themselves argue that we can learn much from paying explicit attention to the complexities involved with writing and reading as deeply rhetorical acts in our writing classes. "Among the Audience" forwards collaborative projects as a means for approaching such work, though with the caution that we do more "than *assign* collaborative projects," that we must also be careful to provide a "theorized rationale" for our approach (58). Reimagining the role writing assessment plays in the writing class invites us to recast ourselves as well from *the* distanced expert responder/assessor to that of *a* member of multiple and participatory audiences. Thus, our responsibilities as teachers of writing do not end with the completion of the final comment on a student draft; rather, our response commentary marks the beginning of a new series of conversations where we engage our students as fellow writers, readers, and respondents of texts. "There are no guarantees that either the process or the outcome [of writing, reading, speaking, or listening] will be ethical," Lunsford and Ede remind us: "This is an understanding that we can—and should—bring with us when we enter our classrooms, especially first-year classrooms" (64). Conversations that place writing assessment at the center of our work as teachers of writing require us to remain self-reflective—of our own practices, subject positions (social, political, institutional, and so on), and purposes. Such conversations demand much: time, energy, commitment, and even risk as they call on us not only to rethink classroom pedagogy but also our roles as writing teachers. The rewards of such a commitment, however, can be great.

Notes

1. I want to take a moment to address a terminological issue, because terminological clarity is important to the success of my argument. Writing assessment scholars have recently sought to problematize the distinction between "response" and "assessment." Huot comments on murkiness of assessment terminology and warns that referencing grading and testing as synonymous with assessment results in "uncritical and unexamined discourse" ("Toward a New Discourse" 163). He furthers his warning in a subsequent argument: "The result of [the] strong connections among grading, testing, and assessing writing is that any possible connection between the teaching and the evaluation of student writing is seldom questioned or discussed. This has led us as a profession to believe that assessing student writing somehow interferes with our ability to teach it" (*(Re)Articulating Writing Assessment for Teaching and Learning* 3–4).

2. Prior to its implementation, this study received approval by Illinois State University's Institutional Review Board, among whose official duties is to ensure that studies involving human subjects are conducted legally, ethically, and humanely.

3. The class arrived at rather specific understandings of successful, rhetorically effective writing over the course of the semester. "Good" writing addressed the assignment directives but also demonstrated the author's "presence in the text," which meant the reader perceived the author to have effectively balanced her argument with existing discussions on the same topic. Good writing included details and "challenged the reader to see the topic from the author's point-of-view." Good response commentary represented close reading, was written in direct response to the author's response prompts, and contained both examples from the text and specific solutions or possibilities for revision. To be *good* (i.e., rhetorically effective) was to demonstrate agency.

4. Engaging in meaningful revision, after all, is the objective of process-based pedagogies. But, as White reminds us, our students tend to remain uninformed on revision as a rhetorical practice, attempting instead to decode the messages transmitted through instructor response so that

they can provide us in subsequent drafts what it is they think we want. White calls for a pedagogy that includes instruction in self-assessment as a rhetorical concept, adding that we cannot expect our students to participate in "genuine revision" if they "lack the ability to assess what they have written" ("The Changing Face of Writing Assessment" 11). Though I do not include attention to student self-assessment here, I consider it in many ways the counterpart or complement to peer response.

5. The CCCC *Position Statement on Teaching, Learning, and Assessing Writing in Digital Environments* (2004), the NCTE-CCCC *Writing Assessment Position Statement* (2006), and NCTE-WPA *White Paper on Writing Assessment in Colleges and Universities* (2008), for example, are each grounded in conceptions of learning, teaching, writing, and assessing writing as social acts.

6. Perhaps most powerful is Huot's argument that we must teach our students how to assess writing for themselves if we are to provide them "with the authority inherent in assessment." He adds that failure to teach assessment results in the "continued disjuncture" students experience in their roles as students and *writers* ("Toward a New Discourse" 169). Broad builds on the notion of assessment as an interpretive, rhetorical act by arguing that we assess writing in the context in which it was produced, as an attempt at rhetorical effectiveness rather than as read against "a fixed, predetermined outside standard," in which stakeholders make public individual criteria each brings to their assessment of writing.

8. Asao Inoue's 2005 article, "Community-Based Assessment Pedagogy," and Deb Martin and Diane Penrod's, "Coming to Know Criteria: The Value of an Evaluating Writing Course for Undergraduates" both report findings from classroom-based research projects in which the authors/researchers introduced assessment as a subject of inquiry.

Works Cited

Anson, Chris. "Reflective Reading: Developing Thoughtful Ways to Respond to Students' Writing." *Evaluating Writing: The Role of Teachers' Knowledge about Text, Learning, and Culture.* Ed. Charles R. Cooper and Lee Odell. Urbana, IL: NCTE, 1999. (302–324).

Brannon, L., and C. H. Knoblauch. "On Students' Right to Their Own Texts: A Model of Teacher Response." CCC 33 (1982): 157–166.

Broad, Bob. *What We Really Value: Beyond Rubrics in Teaching and Assessing Writing.* Logan, UT: Utah State UP, 2003.

Ede, Lisa, and Andrea Lunsford. "Audience Addressed/Audience Invoked: The Role of Audience in Composition Theory and Pedagogy." *CCC* 35 (1984): 155–171.

Fife, Jane Mathison, and Peggy O'Neill. "Moving beyond the Written Comment: Narrowing the Gap between Response Practice and Research." *CCC* 53.2 (Dec. 2001): 300–321.

Huot, Brian. *(Re)Articulating Writing Assessment for Teaching and Learning.* Logan, UT: Utah State UP, 2002.

————. "Toward a New Discourse of Assessment for the College Writing Classroom." *College English* 65 (2002): 163–180.

Inoue, Asao B. "Community-Based Assessment Pedagogy." *Assessing Writing* 9 (2005): 208–238.

Knoblauch, Cy, and Lil Brannon. "Introduction: The Emperor (Still) Has No Clothes." *Key Works on Teacher Response: An Anthology.* Ed. Richard Straub. Portsmouth, NH: Boynton/Cook. 2006. 1–15.

Lunsford, Andrea A., and Lisa Ede. "Among the Audience: On Audience in an Age of New Literacies." *Engaging Audience: Writing in an Age of New Literacies.* Ed. Elizabeth Weiser, Brian Fehler, and Angela González. Urbana, IL: NCTE, 2009. 42–69.

Lunsford, Andrea, and Lisa Ede. "Representing Audience: 'Successful' Discourse and Disciplinary Critique." *CCC* 47:2. (May, 1996): 167–179. Martin, Deb, and Diane Penrod, "Coming to Know Criteria: The Value of an Evaluating Writing Course for Undergraduates." *Assessing Writing* 11 (2006): 66–73.

Sommers, Nancy. "Across the Drafts." *CCC* 58:2 (December 2006). 248–257.

————. "Responding to Student Writing." *CCC* 33.2 (1982): 148–156.

Straub, Richard. "Response Rethought." *CCC* 48.2 (May 1997): 277–183.

White, Edward M. *Assigning, Responding, Evaluating: A Writing Teacher's Guide.* 4th ed. Boston: Bedford/St. Martin's, 2007.

————. "The Changing Face of Writing Assessment." *Composition Studies* 32:1 (2004): 109–117.

INDEX

wikiality and, 277–81
Sellers, P., 138
Service-learning projects, 135
Shaughnessy, M., 32
Shirky, C., 45
Simon, S., 245
Simons, H. W., 11, 24
Sirc, G., 58
Slash fiction, 101
Smart, J., 174, 253
Smit, D. W., 190
Soap operas, 99
Social networking sites, 46
  collective intelligence created
    by, 269
  ethical issues of, 62
  privacy issues of, 56–57,
    273–75
  public relations writing and,
    136–40
  self-presentation on, 266–83
Sociologese, 8
Sommers, N., 305, 316
Speech, writing versus, 11–12
Spinuzzi, C., 171, 173, 176
Stanford Study of Writing
  (SSW), 50–51
Star Trek, 99–100, 101
Steehouder, M., 120
Stevens, S. M., xiii, 231
Strangers, as audience, 214–17,
  221–23
Straub, R., 316
Street Sense, 211, 213
Stroupe, C., 92
Student learning, assignments
  for monitoring, 180–82
Students
  agency and identity of,
    30–31
  authority of, 77
  as authors, 77
  as digital natives, 187, 267
  first-year, 147–64
  perceptions of, 288–94
  as readers, 288–94

as teachers, 192–93
views on intellectual property, 50
Sunstein, C. R., 58, 63
Swales, J. M., 193
Swearingen, J., 248

Tannen, D., 93
Tapscott, D., 58
Taylor, M., 3, 4, 6–9, 16, 22, 23,
  29, 79
Teachers
  as audience, 57, 80, 175–76
  students as, 192–93
  in writing-for-publication
    courses, 192–97
Technical writing, 19, 96, 113, 114
  audience theory in, 120–21
  personas and scenarios in, 115–16
Technology, new literacies and, 43
Tedlock, D., 23
Television characters, audience
  relationship with, 95–96
Television viewing, interactive
  nature of, 98–99
Textsites, 189, 200–202
Theorizing, 15
Thomas, A., 55–56, 66
Transactionality, 186
Translation
  in author-reader relations, 231
  cultural harm from, 233
  potential for change, 235–40
  power differences and, 232–35
  shifting subjectivity, 235
Trust-filtering, 273–75
Twitter, 61–62
  ethical issues of, 62

Unilever, YouTube marketing campaign of, 138–39

Vander Lei, E., 248
Venn, C., 233, 234

Venuti, L., 233, 244
Verplank, B., 117, 118
Video, reading audience in, 301–2
Video games, authorship in, 65
Vie, S., 270
Villanueva, V., 231, 240, 241
Voice
  defined, 94
  research on, 94–96

Wall, M., 98
Wall, S., 7, 23
Wardle, E., 171
Warner, M., 46, 209, 214, 224
Washington Parks and People
  (WPP), 216–17, 218
Watson, K., 93
Weaver, J. B., 93
Web 2.0, 45, 46, 48, 64–65, 136,
  137, 219, 269. *See also*
  Social networking sites
  collective intelligence created by,
  269
Wenger, E., 199
White, E. M., 321
Wicks, R. H., 96
Wikiality, 277–81
Wikipedia, 269
Williams, B. T., 247, 248
Williams, D., 58
Wishful identification, 96
Witnessing, in faith-based reason-
  ing, 252
Wodtke, C., 120
Wood, S. D., 120
Woods, R., 267, 280
Worsham, L., 36
Worth, J., 247
Worthington, D., 93

WPP. *See* Washington Parks
  and People
Writers. *See* Authors
Writing
  genre theory and, 168–72
  Mitchell and Taylor view of,
  6–9
  versus oral speech, 11
  in specific settings, 177–80
  success in, 34–35, 36, 37–39
Writing-for-publication
  courses, 186–89
  activity theory and, 191–92
  description of, 189–91
  feedback/iteration differences in, 197–99
  guest speakers in, 199
  instructor and editors for,
  192–97
  objective category, 199–200
  textsites and, 200–202
  writing in profession and,
  200–202
Writing instruction, in adjunct
  courses, 3
Wysocki, A., 58

Yancey, K. B., 295
Young, R. E., 23
YouTube
  marketing campaigns on,138–
  39
  privacy controls on, 274

Zappala, J. M., 142
Zhu, W., 243
Zimmerman, T., x

EDITORS

M. Elizabeth Weiser completed her PhD in rhetoric and composition at Texas Christian University. An associate professor of English at The Ohio State University, she teaches courses in discourse analysis, style, rhetorical theory, and publication. Her book *Burke, War, Words: Rhetoricizing Dramatism* was published in 2008, and she has a number of articles on Burkean theory, historiography, narrative and psychology, and style. She is currently coediting a feminist historiography collection and working on a monograph on museums and identification. She was a Fulbright Fellow in Turkey, has won various awards, and was named the nation's Emerging Burke Scholar in 2008.

Brian M. Fehler teaches undergraduate and graduate courses in composition, technical writing, and rhetorical history and theory at Tarleton State University in Stephenville, Texas. He is the author of *Calvinist Rhetoric in Nineteenth-Century America* as well as articles and book reviews that have appeared in *Rhetoric Review*, *Rhetoric Society Quarterly*, and *Christian Scholar's Review*. A regular presenter at national conferences such as Rhetoric Society of America and the Conference on College Composition and Communication, Fehler earned his PhD in rhetoric from Texas Christian University in 2005.

Angela M. González teaches composition and writing center theory and pedagogy, popular and cultural rhetoric, and Latina literature at Whitworth University. With a 2007 PhD in rhetoric and composition from Texas Christian University, she has presented and written on the graduate writing center and writing across the curriculum, and she is a member of the review board of *Composition Studies*.

CONTRIBUTORS

Bob Batchelor teaches in the School of Mass Communications at the University of South Florida. He is also a doctoral candidate in English at USF. Bob graduated from the University of Pittsburgh with bachelor degrees in history, philosophy, and political science. He received a master's degree in American History from Kent State University. A noted popular culture expert, Bob is the author or editor of ten books, including *The 2000s* (2008), *The 1980s* (2007), and the four-volume *American Pop: Popular Culture Decade by Decade* (2008). Visit him on the Web at www.bobbatchelor.com.

David Beard (PhD, rhetoric and STC, University of Minnesota, Twin Cities) is assistant professor of writing studies at the University of Minnesota, Duluth. While completing a monograph on modern rhetoric (and the tradition running from Frege through the semanticists to Berthoff, in both composition and communication), he also writes about audience and auditory culture. With Richard Enos, he coedited *Advances in the History of Rhetoric* (2007).

David Dayton holds a PhD in technical communication and rhetoric from Texas Tech University. In 2004–2005, he was named Teacher of the Year at Southern Polytechnic State University (Georgia). He is now an assistant professor in the English Department at Towson University in Baltimore County, Maryland, where he primarily teaches workplace writing and information design. He won the 2002 Outstanding Dissertation in Technical Communication Award and the 2003 Award for Best Article Reporting Historical and Textual Studies in Technical or Scientific Communication—both from the National Council of Teachers of English. In 2008, he was elevated to the rank of associate fellow in the Society for Technical Communication.

Lisa Ede is professor of English and director of the Center for Writing and Learning at Oregon State University. **Andrea A. Lunsford** is professor of English and director of the Program in Writing and Rhetoric at Stanford University. Lunsford and Ede have been writing collaboratively for more than twenty-five years and have published a number of essays and book chapters. They have also coedited two collections of essays and coauthored a study of collaborative writing, *Singular Texts/Plural Authors: Perspectives on Collaborative Writing*. Their coauthored and coedited work has been recognized with the CCCC Braddock Award and the MLA Mina P. Shaughnessy Award.

Traci Freeman received her PhD in English from the University of Texas at Austin. She taught college writing at the University of California, Berkeley, for two years before joining the faculty of the writing program at the University of Colorado at Colorado Springs in 2004. She currently directs the writing center at UCCS and teaches courses in the writing program, including in advanced composition, women's rhetoric, and writing center theory and practice. Her research interests include women's autobiographical writing, writing center theory and administration, and teacher education.

Erin Karper completed her PhD in rhetoric and composition at Purdue University. She is an assistant professor of English at Niagara University, where she teaches courses in writing for the Web, social media, and visual rhetoric. She has written a number of articles on the rhetorical aspects of Web writing and design for *Computers and Composition, Business Communication Quarterly*, and several peer-reviewed anthologies.

Dan Keller completed his PhD in rhetoric and composition at the University of Louisville. He is an assistant professor of English at The Ohio State University, where he teaches courses in composition, popular culture, digital media, and history and theories of writing. He has been published in the *Writing Center Journal* and in several edited collections, including *Multimodal Composition: Resources for Teachers*.

Sharon McKenzie Stevens completed her PhD in rhetoric, composition, and the teaching of English at the University of Arizona. She is senior lecturer in English and media studies at Massey University (Aotearoa/New Zealand), where she teaches courses in academic and technical writing and trains other teachers. She is the author of *A Place for Dialogue: Language, Land Use, and Politics in Southern Arizona* (2007) and coeditor of *Active Voices: Composing a Rhetoric of Social Movements* (2009). Her other publications include chapters in collections and articles in *Rhetoric Review and Science, Technology, & Human Values*. She is the 2007 recipient of Massey University's Vice-Chancellor's Award for Excellence in First-Year Teaching.

Phyllis Mentzell Ryder, an associate professor of writing, helped to launch the new, independent writing program at The George Washington University. She teaches courses on the rhetorics of social protest, critical multiculturalism, and community organizing, and has published articles in *Rhetoric Review* and *JAC: Rhetoric, Writing, Culture, Politics*, among others. Her current project, a book titled *Public Writing and Writing Publics*, analyzes the cultural and political functions of public discourse and argues for a pedagogy of public writing that is rooted in community-based research. It has been accepted as part of the cultural studies/pedagogies/activism series at Lexington Books (a division of Rowan and Littlefield).

Lee Nickoson-Massey is assistant professor of English and member of the rhetoric and writing faculty at Bowling Green State University. Her scholarly interests include writing assessment, graduate student education, composition pedagogy, and feminist approaches to the study and teaching of writing. She is coeditor of *Feminism and Composition: A Critical Sourcebook* and has recently published a coauthored piece on graduate student education and professional development in *Computers and Composition*. Her current research includes projects on writing assessment, graduate student education, and research methods.

Tom Pace completed his PhD in composition and rhetoric at Miami University (Ohio). He is the coordinator of first-year writing at John Carroll University, where he teaches a variety of undergraduate and graduate courses, including first-year and advanced writing, composition theory and pedagogy, and introduction to film. His research interests revolve around the history and theory of teaching writing and rhetoric, especially stylistics. He is the coeditor of *Refiguring Prose Style: Possibilities in Writing Pedagogy* and is currently coediting a Jesuit rhetoric collection.

Marie C. Paretti is an assistant professor of engineering education at Virginia Tech, where she co-directs the Virginia Tech Engineering Communications Center. She also directs the Engineering Communications Program for materials science and engineering and engineering science and mechanics, a three-year communications-in-the-disciplines program. Her research focuses on engineering communication; interdisciplinary, global, and virtual communication and collaboration; and design education. She has published extensively on teaching and learning communication in the disciplines, and in 2008 coedited a special issue of *IEEE Transactions on Professional Communication* on communication in engineering curricula.

Alexandria Peary holds an MFA (poetry) from the University of Iowa and a second MFA (poetry) from the University of Massachusetts, Amherst. She is currently at the dissertation phase of her PhD in composition from the University of New Hampshire. She is the writing program director and an associate professor at Daniel Webster College. Her book, *Fall Foliage Called Bathers & Dancers,* was published in 2008, and other work has appeared in journals including *The Gettysburg Review, jubilat,* and *The Massachusetts Review.* Her article on poetic license in nineteenth-century composition textbooks is forthcoming in *College Composition and Communication.*

Traci A. Zimmerman completed her PhD in English at Case Western Reserve University. She is an associate professor in the School of Writing, Rhetoric, and Technical Communication at James Madison University, teaching courses in authorship, literacy, and rhetorical theory. Her research interests span several centuries: the fifteenth century and the beginnings of the print revolution; the seventeenth century and the birth of the reader; and the twenty-first century, where definitions of text, reader, audience, and author collude and collide. Her current research is inspired by her involvement with the CCCC-Intellectual Property Caucus and her interest in the ways in which authorship theory informs and interrogates current IP law.

This book was typeset in Sabon by Barbara Frazier.
The typefaces used on the cover are Formata Light and Formata Regular.
The book was printed on 50-lb. Williamsburg Offset paper
by Midland Information Resources.